School System Administration

HOW TO ORDER THIS BOOK

BY PHONE: 800-233-9936 or 717-291-5609, 8AM–5PM Eastern Time

BY FAX: 717-295-4538

BY MAIL: Order Department
Technomic Publishing Company, Inc.
851 New Holland Avenue, Box 3535
Lancaster, PA 17604, U.S.A.

BY CREDIT CARD: American Express, VISA, MasterCard

I. CARL CANDOLI, Ph.D.

School System Administration

A Strategic Plan for Site-Based Management

TECHNOMIC
PUBLISHING CO., INC.
LANCASTER · BASEL

School System Administration

a TECHNOMIC®publication

Published in the Western Hemisphere by
Technomic Publishing Company, Inc.
851 New Holland Avenue
Box 3535
Lancaster, Pennsylvania 17604 U.S.A.

Distributed in the Rest of the World by
Technomic Publishing AG

Printed in the United States of America
10 9 8 7 6 5 4 3 2 1

Main entry under title:
   School System Administration: A Strategic Plan for Site-Based Management

A Technomic Publishing Company book
Bibliography: p. 229
Includes index p. 231

Library of Congress Card No. 90-71213
ISBN No. 87762-728-2

Contents

Preface

This work is an amalgamation of a variety of influences, concepts, and notions that have been tested during the author's tour as a superintendent of large school districts during the 1970s and 1980s. It attempts to recognize the emerging realities of school administration and poses one view toward alleviating the myriad problems being faced by school systems.

Among the many persons who played a major role in the development of the site-based management concept were members of two boards of education that supported the testing of the model as presented and administrators and staff of those school systems who accepted and supported a dramatic departure from the status quo and make the site-based management concept work.

Special gratitude is due to Dr. Gary Wegenke, Superintendent of the Des Moines, Iowa School System for his coauthorship of the chapter on finance (Chapter 6). Dr. Wegenke is an honored and trusted colleague whose contributions are appreciated.

Personal thanks are also offered to Ms. Marilyn Finney and Ms. Mary Pacheco, who provided invaluable assistance in manuscript editing and production without which this book could not have been prepared.

Finally, the author's family, wife, Joan and children, Julie, Carol, and Louis, who have remained loyal, understanding, and supportive during a career filled with uncertainties and disruptions. They are appreciated more than ever and deserve better than they have received. Joan, particularly, has provided stability and consistency to the family and has never waivered in her support.

Introduction

This book is an effort to place the evolution of the American school system and its current status in a context that encourages the reader to think of the many opportunities available to the educational administrator for playing a role in the restructuring of the system to meet today's needs. For at least the past decade, the cry for restructuring the school system has become louder and more pronounced, yet the traditionalists among us have merely tinkered with the system while charges of ineffective systemic leadership grew and became almost indefensible. The traditional method of operation was fine and did the job of providing educational services for the past hundred years. Unfortunately, American society has changed and the previous values and methods are no longer appropriate.

Chapter 1 examines the evolution of the American school system and traces the evolution of American society to set the stage for the consideration of a restructured school system. The current state of our society should determine the way we organize to deliver educational services, and we must be alert to ongoing changes in our society in order to make corresponding changes in the school system.

Chapter 2 traces the development of the office of superintendent of schools and provides several models of school system organization for the reader to consider. These models range from the traditional to a variety of models to use in the restructuring process. This chapter also establishes the basic functions of any school system and suggests the appropriate way to organize to provide these functions. The functions are presented in the context of site-based management.

Chapters 3 through 9 are the presentation of the seven functions as they should be conceived for implementation of a site-based management approach. Each chapter is written for the school system that has made or is making the decision to embrace the site-based management model and is searching for the mechanism to enable initiation of the site-based approach.

Chapter 10 deals with the governance issues and explicates the role of the federal government, the state, and the local school board. It also suggests a building-level context for the reader's consideration.

It is hoped that this book will provide a blueprint for those districts opting for a site-based management approach to school system organization. The author firmly believes that his experience in two major school districts with site-based management and the results garnered from those experiences make the concept a most viable one.

CHAPTER 1

The American School System of Today

A. HISTORICAL CONTEXT

The chronology of the development of the American educational system is well-known and need not be reviewed in detail. However, it is important to recognize that the evolution of American society from agrarian to industrial to technological has given birth to comparable developments in the educational sector. The problem faced by most school systems today is that they have yet to move from the industrial to the technological stage in their development.

Education has played and continues to play an important role in American society. The efforts of the early American settlers to provide educational opportunities for their children, even while they lacked the conveniences of the homes and towns from which they came, is best exemplified by the establishment of the Boston Latin Grammar School as the first secondary school in America in 1635 and the founding of Harvard University in 1636. Education was recognized early on as the basic building block of American society.

Formal recognition and legitimization of the educational system began in the United States with the Massachusetts laws of 1642 and 1647 requiring the establishment of common schools. The Massachusetts law of 1642 was the beginning of compulsory education in America. While the law did not require that children attend a school, it did place pressure on a town to see that parents provided for instruction in the home. The 1647 law ordered

(1) That every town having fifty householders should at once appoint a teacher of reading and writing and provide for wages in such manner as the town might determine

(2) That every town having 100 householders must provide a grammar school to fit youths for the university, under a penalty of five pounds (afterward increased to twenty pounds) for failure to do so (Cubberly, 1920, 363)

These laws pioneered the common-school concept in America.

Although New England led in the establishment of the American public schools, other regions of the emerging country provided support for the establishment of the many and varied parochial/church schools in the United States. In the middle colonies, New York, Pennsylvania, and Maryland, where Baptists, Catholics, Lutherans, Mennonites, Moravians, Presbyterians, Quakers, and other religious denominations were represented, the concept of the parochial school was developed. Instruction was carried out in the home under the direction of the clergy. Private schools that were developed in the larger centers of population were church schools supported by church funds and by the tuition paid by families who could afford it. Even today, these schools are recognized as essential elements of our total educational system.

To students of American education it is quite apparent that, by the time the colonies were ready to declare their independence, two patterns of education had emerged: public schools, having their beginnings in Massachusetts and the other New England colonies, and private schools, still largely under the direction of church groups. The courts have generally agreed that the interest of the state in an education for all children can be served in both public and private schools. This was interpreted by the Supreme Court in decisions rendered in *Pierce v. Society of Sisters of the Holy Name of Jesus and Mary* and *Farrington v. Tokushige* and *Stainback v. MoHock Lok Po* that established the rights of parents to send their children to private schools.

EDUCATION AS A STATE RESPONSIBILITY

Because no provision was made in the Constitution for the federal support or control of education, that right was given to the various states with the passage of the Bill of Rights in 1789 and ratified by the states in 1791. Article X of the Bill of Rights states that "the powers not delegated to the United States by the Constitution, nor prohibited by it to the States, are reserved to the States respectively, or to the people." This clause indicates that growth of state control of education was entirely acceptable to the founders of our federal government.

However, from time to time the federal government must intercede to protect the interests of citizens as in the *Brown v. Board of Education of Topeka* cases and the many related cases dealing with the right of students to be guaranteed equity in the provision of educational services by the state. Increasingly, the federal courts are called upon to adjudicate equity concerns ranging from the right of each student to have access to adequate facilities to the right of students to have access to comparable resources for their education. While most of the equity decisions are rendered in the various state courts, the federal courts have been required to adjudicate those equity cases involving federal legal requirements such as the variety of desegregation cases that have been tried over the years since the original *Brown* case.

BASIC PRINCIPLES OF SCHOOL SYSTEM EVOLUTION

There are several basic principles about school system evolution in the United States. These include the following:

(1) Universal education is essential. The early settlers of the United States had great faith in education. Some of the founders of America expressed their belief that ignorance and freedom are incompatible. Thomas Jefferson expressed it best when he said, "If a nation expects to be ignorant and free, in a state of civilization, it expects what never was and never will be."

(2) Education should be free. A variety of court cases and decisions were involved in establishing this principle. In the 1800s, several actions by the various states provided the mechanism for the school systems to levy taxes for the support of public education. Included in the more famous cases was the *Stuart v. School District No. 1 of Village of Kalamazoo* that gave the local school district the right to levy taxes for the support of secondary schools. Previously the power to tax for the support of public education was for the support of elementary schools.

(3) The state has the responsibility. The Constitution, by not mentioning education, left the regulation and control of education to the states. Towns, cities, villages, and rural areas were formed into school districts and were asked to meet the state requirements in providing schools.

(4) Local districts operate the schools. Although the state is the responsible party as far as education is concerned, the development of the public school systems in the United States has never been a top-down development. State governments accepted the responsibility to regu-

late the formation, support, and standards of the school program so as to equalize the educational opportunity. For purposes of operation, the state delegates most of its own powers to the local district.

(5) Federal participation is desirable. Starting with the land grant for the support of the establishment of public schools and colleges, the federal government has had a long history of involvement in education. Along with direct support for the public schools in Washington, D.C. and the various military dependent schools around the world, the federal government has provided support in the form of various programs like the Civilian Conservation Corps, the National Youth Administration, the Works Progress Administration, aid to impacted school districts, assistance to veterans for advanced schooling, the National Defense Education Act support for education, the Vocational Education Acts, the Elementary and Secondary Education Acts, and other direct expressions of support for public education.

(6) The school system should be extended. While common schools were among the first to be established by law, the extension of education to the higher grades and to the universities was the result of the unyielding demand for educational services by the citizens of the country. This thirst for knowledge has permitted the development of a first-rate community college system throughout the nation and a fine system of state colleges and universities in every state.

(7) The separation of church and state must be maintained. While religion played an important part in the development of American schools, the principle of separation of church and state has been reinforced time after time through the courts. Cubberly (1920, 692) points out two factors that he says served to bring about the secularization of the public schools. They were (a) the conviction that the life of the Republic demanded an educated and intelligent citizenship and, hence, the education of all in common schools controlled by the state and (b) the great diversity of religious beliefs among the people forced tolerance and religious freedom through a consideration of the rights of minorities.

(8) In a democracy, education is the avenue for upward mobility and equity. In American society, the one path available for achieving the personal goals and aspirations of its citizens is through the educational system. Historically, American education provided recent arrivals to our country the knowledge with which to achieve progress and to attain the personal goals that the United States represents. The landmark Supreme Court decisions in 1954 and 1957 in the *Brown* cases followed by the torrent of reinforcing decisions during the

1960s and 1970s ascertain that the vehicle of education is a most important one for the American public.

CHARACTERISTICS OF THE PUBLIC SCHOOL SYSTEM

As the effects of industrialization began to impact America and as the concept of mass production of goods became a reality, the development of a variety of cities and towns was mandated in order to provide the needed manpower for the emerging industrial society. Examples of early industrial developments include the many "mill towns" of New England and the several sea ports of our coastal states. Usually, the birth of a city is tied to the creation of a particular industry or related group of industries that, because of labor demands, attract large numbers of people. Thus, Chicago grew as the "hog butcher" of the world and as the transportation center of the midwest; Detroit became the automobile center of the country; New York the mercantile, commerce, and financial center; Minneapolis the grain center; Philadelphia the shipping center; and so on.

Likewise, smaller cities grew as a result of commercial and/or industrial development. Many textile centers developed in New England; automobiles became the focal point of several Michigan cities; steel production gave birth to the Gary, Hammond, East Chicago complex; and stockyards and food production stimulated several other cities.

The increased concentration of population in industrializing America led to the creation of larger, more comprehensive school systems. As the need for a more highly trained labor pool grew, the public school systems responded by creating expanded educational programs to meet vocational needs.

The evolution from one-room to multi-unit school systems paralleled the growth of industrial America. Consolidation of previously small, inadequate rural schools into large efficient school systems also proceeded to change the look of the American schools. Recognizing that a larger sized student body is needed to produce a diversity of program possibilities, today's public school system offers the student many diverse options.

Traditionally, schools in America were governed by the elected or appointed boards of education. The one-room schools were easily governed for they merely involved a single teacher, and the board accomplished the governance function as a matter of course during the school year. As the one-room school gave way to the multiroom school, the board of trustees also accomplished the governance function, but recognizing their shortcomings in instructional matters, they appointed a principal teacher or principal to direct the instructional affairs of the multi-unit school. The board continued to look after the financial affairs of the school but assigned the educational activities to the principal. As the country became more industrialized, the school systems grew into the multi-unit, multicampus school systems that we know today, and local boards began to recognize the need for a chief executive officer. The position of superintendent of schools was first established in Buffalo, New York, in 1837 and provided for the management of the school system under the leadership of a single person. The board of education continues to set policy and to establish the governance structure for the school system, but the day-to-day operation of the school system is delegated to the superintendent. Initially, the superintendent was the instructional leader of the school system, but as the demands upon the system grew more complex and as the shear size of the operation expanded, the total operation became part of the responsibility of the superintendent.

As the school districts grew, the governing staff of the district also grew. The office of business manager became an early addition to the cadre of specialists needed to facilitate the smooth operation of the school system. Also added were specialists of every type and description to accommodate the emerging and complex needs of the modern school system. (Chapter 2 will show several types of organizational schema that are prevalent across the country.) The important consideration here is that, as school organizations grew in complexity and size, the era of the specialist was born. School administrators became more and more specialized in their expertise with the superintendent and the principal emerging as the generalists of the school system. The dramatic growth of the American school system and the corresponding growth of the staff of specialists that were needed to support the teaching cadre of the school system have led to a bureaucratic development that is both huge and sometimes counterproductive.

UNIQUE CHARACTERISTICS OF THE AMERICAN SCHOOL SYSTEM

While the model for the American school system was taken from the European countries, the people have built a uniquely American system of education. There are certain characteristics that set the American system apart from every other system in the world and must be considered as one studies the American system of education. These include the following:

(1) The schools belong to the people. Nowhere in the world do the rank and file have as much to say about their schools as do the people of

the United States. While the state does have the responsibility for education, the people, through representative democracy, have the ultimate say in the operation of their schools. In addition, the people participate in their local school decisions by virtue of their participation in the local school board process. This is unique among nations of the world and is a most impressive element in American education.

(2) Public education is predicated on opportunity for all. While this goal is yet unachieved, American education is moving in that direction, and every effort is expended to make this goal a reality for all. The equity movement is permitting the realization of a considerable shifting in resources toward those districts that have been historically tax poor. In state after state, equalization plans are being drafted and implemented that provide comparable resources for all children.

(3) Programs are adjusted according to needs. As the American school system has developed, the purposes of education have broadened, the number of students have increased, and the range of abilities, interests, and needs of children have been extended.

(4) Pupils learn a democratic way of life. As public schools have developed, we have come to realize that responsible action, such as that required of every citizen in a democracy, with a minimum of compulsion from external authority, is something to be learned. Children must learn to be democratic and learn what it means to be responsible and what the consequences of irresponsible behavior are, just as they must learn the knowledge and skills necessary for the vocation they choose to follow.

(5) The school has a unique role. As the purposes of the school have encompassed the total development of the child, a greatly increased number of duties and responsibilities have been assigned to it. The curriculum has expanded to include the teaching of the many skills needed in a democratic society, and services have also increased in number and in kind. The major function of services to pupils has been to create those conditions under which learning best takes place.

B. EMERGING CONCERNS

One of the facts of the technological society that has impacted the educational sector is the reality that the historic opportunity to conveniently assign 40 to 50 percent of the clients to unskilled, agrarian, and manual labor vocations is no longer available. The demand for unskilled labor is quickly drying up and cannot be recalled. Our technological brilliance has served to eliminate most opportunity for earning a livelihood, marginal though it might be, by performing tasks requiring little or no schooling. The changing demands of the labor market have also mandated the acquisition of a certain number of skills as a prerequisite to gainful employment. The capacity of our society to absorb, either on the farm or in the city, millions of uneducated or undereducated persons is fast disappearing. Indeed, certain skills of cognition are needed to engage in manufacturing work and other types of activities required in the production and delivery of goods and services.

Additionally, the realities of modern technology demand far more sophistication on the part of workers than ever before. The rapid changes in our technological society have mandated a multiplicity of skills that are necessary for survival. As we have evolved from an agrarian, family-centered, gemeinschaft society to a contractual, diverse, urban, gesellschaft society, the requisites for participation have placed increasingly greater importance on the acquisition of educational skills and the capacity to articulate and communicate.

The number of variables impinging upon our society have multiplied. Dramatic breakthroughs have occurred in transportation with the jet age, in communications with television, in storage and retrieval of information with computers, in agriculture, in merchandizing, in housing, and in all areas of society where change is a constant. Yet educational systems have not responded to those massive changes except by continuing to project and protect the status quo. A time traveler could enter a classroom of 1948 and observe the same activities as in 1989. All of the tremendous and vast technological changes have had little impact on American schools. True, there have been add-ons here and there, but basic structural changes reflecting a new and emerging role have simply been nonexistent.

Public school systems have traditionally been reactive in nature. Crisis situations have forced responses; i.e., Sputnik forced the awareness of science and math needs, lack of skilled technicians forced major expansion of technical/occupational curricula, overproduction of college degrees forced growing career education attempts, and so on. New and refined curricula have always been made in response to pressures generated outside the educational system. It seems that the posture of being proactive had never been seriously contemplated, and, as a result, behavior patterns of reaction to crisis became the norm for school districts.

However, since society has become more complex and the pace has increased, there is a heightened awareness of inherent inadequacies.

With resource pools drying up and the growing educational needs of clients, the school system has little choice but to search for more efficient, effective ways of delivering educational services. The typical add-on mentality, reinforced in an expansionary climate, must be examined in the light of a cycle of decreasing enrollments, fewer resources, and greater educational needs.

School systems are caught in a tide of increasing expectations by clients on the one hand and decreasing resources with which to serve them on the other. Demands for services far outstrip the system's capacity to provide these services. Many youngsters must be supplied with a variety of nutritional, health, psychological, and social services in order to function in the educational setting. These services are important because, without them, many students cannot hope to attain educational success. They are, however, very expensive and severely drain available resources. As demands are increased, delivery systems become strained and often break down, and resultant educational problems are attributed to the educational system.

Additionally, the process of societal change has caused severe dislocations in school systems. As change has accelerated, pressures for systemic change have not been adequately addressed. As a result, school systems are often viewed as ineffective, obsolete bureaucratic organizations. The analogy of placing a Model T automobile on a modern super highway and expecting normal traffic patterns is an appropriate comparison.

The rise of the science of management has further served to complicate the existence of school systems. The typical system, bound to tradition, to internal promotion, and to the status quo, has not been able to engender acceptance and understanding of such concepts as management by objective, PERT charts, input–output measures, evaluation designs, performance expectations, product evaluations, planning activities, and the like. Historically, leadership positions have been the reward of longevity, of conformity, and of blind acceptance, rather than of creativity, of commitment, and of leadership ability. Therefore, the leader who dared to rock the boat was not long for the position. Those who questioned decisions were made to feel disloyal. The reward system reinforced protection of the status quo and did not emphasize the needs of the clients of the system.

It is small wonder that, as societal dislocation and evolution proceeded, pressure for change has grown in the educational sector. As the

1980s progressed, many systems were caught up in the need for basic systemic change, and several important dichotomies were being addressed.

C. DICHOTOMIES

A very long, exhaustive list of dichotomies can easily be generated when one thinks of the realities of school systems. It is the author's intent to discuss the major inconsistencies he perceived during years of active involvement in administering a large school district. These dichotomies are in no particular order and of varying consequence, but they are important to the school administrator.

THE DICHOTOMY OF EFFICIENCY VS. HUMANISM

Most educational leaders are committed to efficiency in the operation of public institutions. In fact, administrators have embraced the concepts of scientific management to the point where they become so highly structured and so conscious of procedural and systemic protocol that they become almost rigid in their responses. In the name of efficiency, administrators tend to treat every situation the same way, regardless of the varying symptoms. Educational administrators have become efficient, so much so that they are in danger of becoming sterile in their responses to educational needs. In their zealousness to become superefficient, they have tended to overspecialize so that, in the larger school systems, it is virtually impossible to get appropriate responses to requests and/or needs that deviate from standard practice.

Educational leaders really are concerned about the human nature of the educational enterprise. Educators are very aware of the heterogeneity of the student body and of the diverse needs of the students. An increasing number of school districts are trying to become more flexible and less mechanical in their approach to students. For example, guidance services react to individual needs of students and are becoming less paper oriented. Likewise, school systems are becoming more attuned to the need for bilingual services for certain students that come from a non-English speaking home. Care must be exercised not to routinize the response so that the pattern of rigidity is repeated and institutionalized.

Although it is important to administer the school system with high efficiency, it is equally important to think in terms of input–output relationships in order to assess the real efficiency of procedures. Perhaps far greater educational benefit can accrue from actions other than those dictated by the cult of efficiency. Maybe a different definition of efficiency is needed, recognizing that effective management sometimes dictates responses to situations that are not traditional and/or legitimized in procedural handbooks.

THE DICHOTOMY OF HOMOGENEITY VS. HETEROGENEITY

This dichotomy has been with us for several decades, especially since school systems have become large, diverse organizations. More recently, the legal implications of homogeneity have caused educators increased concern.

In American society, residential patterns have developed along homogeneous lines. This is particularly true in the suburban developments that have proliferated in the past three decades. Suburbs of every price range dot the countryside surrounding major cities, and each suburb is populated by families very much alike in income, interests, size, vocation, and background. Invariably, these suburbs have spawned school systems that reflect the particular bias of the area. Thus, we find highly academic New Triers, Evanstons, Scarsdales, and others in every urban area of the country. Less affluent areas have also developed relatively homogeneous systems to serve their clientele. Unfortunately, as these homogeneous areas developed, certain segments of the population were excluded. Among those excluded were racial minorities (income is too often related to color), the elderly, the uneducated, and the undereducated. The aforementioned have been forced to remain in the city where they too have congregated into relatively homogeneous groups. Thus, cities are being forced into more and more homogeneous conditions with one overriding variable as a criterion: poverty. Cities are increasingly inhabited by poor people. True, they may be white, black, brown, yellow, or red, but invariably growing numbers are poor.

But the American dream is based upon heterogeneity. The fact that anyone can participate in this society is an expression of the strength in diversity. Yet the reality is that it is more difficult for Americans to recognize heterogeneity, let alone appreciate the potential of a diverse citizenry. There is great danger to American society if it does not come to grips with the dissonance caused by the search for homogeneity and develop a tolerance for and recognize the strength in heterogeneity. As our demography changes and as we become more diverse and less alike, we must develop ways to incorporate more diversity into our total approach to problems and become more flexible as we interrelate with one another.

THE DICHOTOMY OF CENTRALIZATION
VS. DECENTRALIZATION

In the 1980s, this issue has been a recurring theme in most school systems of this country. Decentralization models have proliferated, with most major school districts attempting in one way or another to decentralize their administrative structure. New York, Chicago, Detroit, and other urban centers have tried to devise ways to effect a more responsive educational system as have Fairfax County, Jefferson County, and other large suburban schools. Educational theorists ranging from Levine to Argyris (1957) to Cunningham to Fatini (1974) have developed decentralization models for consideration.

Concerns over extreme centralization are well-founded and appropriate. Bigness leads to remoteness; remoteness leads to impersonal responses; and this *is* bad, especially in a people-oriented institution like a school.

The demand for a more appropriate response to educational needs became very loud during the 1970s, as a variety of decentralization proposals were made and tested by a number of the larger cities. Many theorists, including such persons as Cunningham, Levine, and Havighurst, published extensively in the area of decentralization. Invariably, each of these experts confirmed the need for decentralization. Campbell et al. (1970, 303) recommended a consolidation of small districts but also went on to say that "in districts of more than 40,000 pupils, size does become a potential variable in creating a bureaucracy also impenetrable by citizens and unyielding to professionals." The need for building-level participation on such issues as facilities, planning, curriculum, discipline, and personnel has been repeatedly expressed by citizen's committees and students. Levine and Havighurst (1977) identified a number of problems and imperatives associated with metropolitan development. These problems can be summed up by saying that

> . . . the organization of an independent society is charged with tasks it cannot do alone. The problems which are so severe in the modern metropolis are attributed not so much to lack of technical knowledge for coping with them, as to the underlying attitudes in the established political arrangements which prevent us from applying this knowledge to their solution (Campbell et al., 232).

Here, then, is a major challenge to the educational system.

It would appear, as one reviews the work of a number of experts in the field, that everyone has a definition of decentralization and that many of the efforts are doomed to failure because their potential results were not clearly thought out. However, it is not a question of decentralizing or centralizing: the issue is what activities should be more highly centralized and which ones are important to be decentralized to the level closest to the student. It appears that, in many instances, decentralization efforts were really attempts to respond to political pressures rather than attempts to effect meaningful educational change so that students of a particular school system could be better served. In city after city, decentralization became closely associated with community control, and the overarching basis of the demand for community control was political and not educational.

As one examines the bureaucratic structure of large school systems and before one can make any decisions regarding decentralization, the evolutionary beginnings and the development of a particular structure must be taken into consideration, and the original primary functions of each of the strata, as well as the present ones, must be assessed. In their attempts to decentralize their school systems, many of the larger districts have noted the fact that the decentralized units created are relatively homogeneous. These units tend to become advocates of a particular point of view or of a particular background. Very little attention is paid to the need for a diverse student body, to the urgency for addressing particular and unique educational needs, and to the requirement of making the school system more responsive to the students it serves.

To further complicate the issue, in all too many instances decentralization has been used as a vehicle to avoid compliance with civil rights laws, particularly in the area of student desegregation. It appears that many school districts have used the decentralization vehicle to avoid facing up to the Supreme Court requiring that students be provided with a viable racial mix.

Decentralization efforts have been resisted by central office administrators who have been reluctant to yield authority or to delegate responsibility partly because they want to keep the authority for themselves and partly because they are not confident in the capacity of lower level administrators to handle that responsibility.

Several crucial preliminary decisions must be addressed as school systems consider this dichotomy. First, the question should not be whether or not to decentralize but, rather, what to centralize and what to decentralize. Second, if the decision is made to decentralize, then a careful examination of routine and mechanized functions that could be relegated to a more highly centralized mode is in order, and those functions that directly impact the educational program should be carefully examined for decentralization to the buildings or even the classroom level.

For example, functions such as data processing, purchasing, routine maintenance, and other services that do not directly impact the educational program can be centralized even beyond the local school district level to regional or state levels, but such crucial functions as program priorities, program development, curriculum delivery systems, services to students, personnel selection, and allocation of funds must be decentralized to the building level.

This is a radical departure from the traditional method of having central office personnel determine the priorities and how they should be met on a systemwide basis. It's still appropriate and necessary for school districts to develop systemic goals and objectives that become the parameters for local units, but the delivery system and the program priorities for meeting those systemic goals must become the purview of the individual buildings and, in some cases, of teams of teachers and/or individual teachers. Individual buildings, working in concert with their particular communities, should make the final decision on the allocation of resources once the resource pool has been decentralized to the building level.

As these new administrative units become clearer and as people become more comfortable working with them, changes will occur and models will evolve that have not heretofore been offered for general consumption. Many central office administrators tend to be suspicious and, in fact, negative regarding the capacity of building principals and local administrators to make important decisions. This suspicion is inappropriate and counterproductive in addressing the needs of students. It seems to me that it is far more important to take risks in allowing local personnel to make final program determinations—or at least have local input into these decisions—rather than impose centrally determined priorities upon a wide and disparate group of students and professionals who did not participate in the development of these priorities. Although there will be occasions when local staffs blunder and do not meet any professional standards of performance, controlled decentralization is generally far better and will ultimately result in improved educational services to students.

In the final analysis, it is important to suggest that the resolution of this particular dichotomy will vary from school district to school district. What may be appropriate for Lansing, Michigan, may not be appropriate for Rochester, Minnesota, and even less appropriate for San Jose, California. However, given the unique realities existing in all of the major school systems, it is appropriate to develop decentralization strategies that will allow local variables to be considered, as plans are laid for effecting an improved delivery system to serve students in that particular locale.

THE DICHOTOMY OF INTEGRATION VS. SEGREGATION

There are few, if any, major school systems in America today that are not faced with the issue of *Brown v. Topeka*. The two *Brown* decisions in 1954 and 1955 laid the groundwork for a whole body of case law dealing with this particular dichotomy. The issue of segregation is one that is never far from the surface of any major school system and one that school administrators must face on a daily basis. This dichotomy permeates the other dichotomies because it impinges upon all major school systems. Most communities have enclaves of minorities. These concentrations are the result of many noneducational decisions made over time, decisions that include Federal Housing Authority (FHA) decisions on mortgage policy, the lack of consistent open housing policies until the recent past, covert and even overt racism throughout the majority of society, and the economic reality as it affects race in America.

The policies established by political bodies have certainly impacted and compounded the problems faced by school districts because they must deal with the educational needs of a diverse student body.

Starting in 1954 with *Brown I*, the courts have increasingly turned their attention to the denial of rights of minority children by virtue of segregated school systems. This has been the most emotional issue ever to surface in American education. The requirement to desegregate has caused severe dislocations in most of the major school systems of the country. The shifting demography of the nation is indicative of the trauma caused by the legal requirement to desegregate. While the courts have become less active during the 1980s, the requirement is still very much in order and must be taken up again in the near future. It is tragic to think that we have not yet been willing to face the need to obliterate the last vestiges of the dual school systems of the past.

THE DICHOTOMY OF RICH VS. POOR

This dichotomy is closely related to the preceding one and to the homogeneous and heterogeneous dichotomy as well. Increasingly, we have a system in our country that further punishes those unfortunate enough to be born to poor parents in a location that is devoid of a tax base, while others who are fortunate enough to be born to families of means in locales with an extensive tax base, are provided certain advantages that the poor child does not have. Legal battles have been fought over the issue of whether or not it is the state's responsibility to provide equal educational opportunity to all students in the state, regardless of one's station in life or location of birth or parentage. The first such case that burst upon the American scene was *Serrano v. Priest*. After many states addressed the implications of *Serrano*, *Rodriguez v. San Antonio* was carried to the federal Supreme Court where it was decided, unfortunately, that the right to an education is not a federally mandated right and that this right is the purview of the various states. This means that legislatures and state courts must determine whether the right to equal educational opportunities is provided for in their own particular state constitution. It is well-known to educators and most citizens that the location of business interests serves as a tremendous resource to certain school districts, while neighboring communities that may be the bedroom community serving those particular businesses are denied participation in the resources generated by them. This is inherently unequal and tends to provide differentiated resources for similar needs across the state and indeed across the country. Fortunately, in state after state, the legislative bodies are making the issue of equal financial resources a front-burner issue and are taking positive action.

THE DICHOTOMY OF COGNITIVE AND AFFECTIVE LEARNING

The final dichotomy to be mentioned is one that becomes more and more crucial to school systems. There are legitimate arguments on either side of this issue. On the one hand, people say, and rightfully so, that without cognitive development there is little hope for a particular student to survive in today's society. The argument runs that, if one does not have simple computational skills and is not able to read, articulate, or write, the likelihood of gainful employment and of earning a living during the course of one's life is very limited.

These arguments are well taken and certainly deserve serious consideration. On the other hand, there are those who, again rightfully so, suggest that cognitive development is not enough in a democratic society. If the student does not develop the capacity to make individual value judgements, to establish personal priorities, to recognize societal obligations, to deal with the mores of a particular society, all the cognitive growth in the world will not enable the person to achieve self-sufficiency in her/his lifetime. There is much to be said for each point of view, and they need not be mutually exclusive; in fact, they should not be. Critics point out that Hitler's Germany had, in fact, eradicated illiteracy. However, members of the same society also eliminated six million human beings. Other critics point out that the capacity to love oneself and one's neighbor is insufficient to earn a livelihood. Persons without cognitive skills, no matter how developed their feelings, will become burdens on society. The resolution of this dichotomy must rest on a judgement by school systems that both types of learning are important in American society and both must be addressed. Certainly, the development of cognitive skills is an obligation for all school systems, and, certainly, these skills must be guaranteed to every student that passes through a particular school system. Beyond the development of cognition, efforts must be extended to create a condition for mutual understanding, for mutual appreciation, for the establishment of values that are central to societal success, and for an understanding of differences that impinge upon all of the students in a school system. These developments are parallel and very important for success in today's society. It seems to me that one cannot be accomplished without strong attention to the other.

D. DEMOGRAPHIC REALITIES

As one examines what is happening in most urban areas of the country, it becomes clear that, since the close of World War II, the urban centers have had a great deal of population change. It can generally be said that the population of the metropolitan areas has dramatically shifted. Before the automobile provided the way for people to commute great distances to their work, people tended to live near their place of work in order to take advantage of the various mass transit opportunities. But since World War II, the mass transit systems of most metropolitan areas have become eroded to a point where they are inadequate to meet the needs of a mobile, metropolitan community. For example, most areas have completely done away with the street car, having changed mostly to bus transportation. However, in many areas, the bus system has become inadequate and almost inoperative because it lacks the necessary customers to support it. In larger cities, the subway or elevated train system has also become a limited operation because people have moved from that mode of transportation to the automobile. All of this, of course, has made it possible for people to live great distances from their place of work and to gather themselves in locations of their choice and means. This population shift continues with the reality that at least 20 percent of the American public changes residences every year so that, over a period of five years, the potential exists for a complete 100 percent turnover in any area.

Typically, the cities, because they are older, have the only available reservoir of moderate-cost, older housing. While the city does have older and less expensive housing available to persons, the suburbs have grown and also have the capacity to provide for a variety of housing needs ranging from low-cost apartment dwellings to expensive, exclusive country estates. Because of the mobility of the population, the availability of a wide range of housing in any metropolitan area, and the independence from the mass transit system with subsequent dependence on the auto, the capacity of citizens to live farther away from their workplaces has grown along with the increase in the diversity of available housing. People are no longer intimately and irrevocably tied to a particular city or mode of transportation in order to participate in whatever activities they choose and, more importantly, to find their way to work.

As the reality of an energy shortage dawned, changes in existing patterns accelerated. More energy efficient vehicles, car pools, alternative modes of transportation, and a return to housing more convenient to the employment location have all become important considerations.

The historical evolution is known to all. Over the past four or five decades with the general improvement in agricultural technology, there has been a mass exodus from the rural farm area to the metropolitan areas and/or cities. This is due to a variety of circumstances, but most importantly it is due to the fact that, as industrialization developed, opportunities for gainful employment became much more available in population centers. At the same time, mechanization arrived at the farm so that thousands of small marginal sharecropper farms were abandoned.

Working a small farm became so inefficient and unproductive when compared to the large mechanized farms that the owners simply had to give up their attempt at tilling the soil in order to survive. Modern agriculture requires far fewer workers to produce much more so that the rural population has declined dramatically.

This migrant farm population, mostly poor and considerably less able to cope with the vagaries of city life than their more urban brethren, was largely composed of both white and black poor people and, in more recent times, poor Spanish-speaking, migrant workers. As these former farm dwellers moved to the metropolitan areas, the only kind of housing available to them was the more inexpensive, older, and obsolete housing found in the central city. For reasons of survival, these people, as they moved to the city, formed homogeneous enclaves where they could not only protect one another from the uncertainty of urban life but where

they could also feel more comfortable knowing that they were sur-
rounded by a culture supporting similar tastes and ambitions.

These farm to city migrations were preceded by the wave of immigrants from Europe who were really the basis for the original pool of
labor power needed by industrializing America. The European immigrants came to this country because of the opportunity to gain productive
employment in the variety of manufacturing businesses being developed
in the United States, to participate in the development of the farms in the
open areas of the country, and to provide certain skilled trades that were
lacking in a developing America. The Europeans, largely by virtue of
cultural background and language barrier, settled in neighborhoods of
the urban centers so that it was not, and still is not, unusual in some cities
to find Polish neighborhoods, Italian enclaves, German settlements, and
so on. These people, particularly the first generation immigrants, worked
very hard at preserving their cultural heritage. It was not uncommon to
find local shopping areas, grocery stores, notions stores, clothing stores,
and so forth, where the native tongue was the primary language spoken
and where native holidays and church activities were all a reflection of
the traditions developed in the homeland. In addition, these people were
escaping severe poverty in Europe and were oriented to home ownership,
the development of community, and the primacy of the family so that
there was little movitation for them to participate in so-called melting pot
activities. They were self-sufficient and were able to insulate themselves
and their fellow countrymen from the broader society. Indeed, native
language Saturday schools were prevalent in many areas to pass the culture and language on to succeeding generations.

However, as their children matriculated in the public schools, they
began to question traditions, began to meet and enjoy the company of
young people of other cultures, and ultimately began to marry outside
their own culture so that a gradual diffusion of the strong traditional cultural ties became apparent. World War II led to further diffusion. Many
of the young people were in the military, and their elders had to accept
a rapidly changing society to enable the war effort to proceed. As the
World War II effort began to gain momentum, the need for defense-
related workers became clear, and the untapped pool for such workers
was the rural population that was barely surviving on the farm. A significant portion of this population was black, and the World War II era saw
a massive migration of poorly educated, black rural citizens from the
South to the large cities of the North where jobs were available in defense
related industries. It was a natural transition to move from the sharecropper role of the South to the ghetto of the North where people of like per-

suasion and color gathered. The rapid influx of new citizens to the cities created great demand for housing and led to the establishment of slum regions in most urban centers of the country.

Given the prosperity of postwar America and the tremendous boom in housing in concert with the restrictive housing policies of both federal and state governments, it is no wonder that, as housing became available, the American dream of the single family dwelling with a yard, play area, and so forth was translated into the development of millions of homesites in the rapidly exploding metropolitan areas of the country. Most cities became landlocked by mushrooming suburbs. Starting in the late 1940s and accelerating during the 1950s and 1960s, the outward movement continued in America. This movement led from the cities to the immediate environs of the suburbs. It led to the fulfillment of what for many people is the American dream: home ownership. It also led to the gigantic new towns with their mass-produced single family dwellings. Although these developments met the original goal of alleviating a serious housing shortage, they also provided mind-numbing dullness as houses began to look almost identical street after street. People moving to these areas suddenly discovered a lack of all of the amenities that had been available to them in the city.

With the growth of suburban areas, school systems developed to serve the educational needs of the increasing number of families with school-age children. Typically, the people who were most interested in suburban living were those who had been urban citizens, had married, and had participated in the baby boom following World War II. As families grew, the need for living space increased and suburban communities developed. FHA loan policies were most tempting, and these, combined with Veterans Administration loans, made it desirable for those qualifying for the loans to move to the suburbs. Many of these families had school-age children. They had a positive orientation towards education and a commitment to the development of a fine school system to serve their children. As these people moved to suburbia, the development of the fine (though homogeneous) school systems began.

Until the recent past, suburban school systems have had a very enviable record in terms of local support for education. Because of the importance of education, upwardly mobile citizens tend to be supportive of the educational system. Suburban areas exhibit a willingness to tax themselves far beyond usual expectations to support the local school system and provide the diversity of programs they feel are necessary for their children.

Examining the history of metropolitan development, one finds that, in the past two decades, cities are in a population decline. At the same time, the transition from rural America to urban America is complete. Over 80 percent of the American people live in what might be classified as standard metropolitan statistical areas (SMS). The suburbs are developed and are now feeling the same aging traumas the cities experienced three decades ago. The new suburbs, known as exurbs, now ring the cities and the original suburbs.

A change in national attitudes toward birth control and toward working wives has sharply reduced the birth rates so that the number of school-age children has stabilized and, in fact, may show some signs of a reduction during the 1990s. City and suburban school systems are entering a period of relative stability in terms of numbers of students to serve. This should allow a concerted effort toward the improvement of educational services to meet the needs of the students. As the tremendous expansion of the metropolitan areas of the country proceeded, an irony emerged. The city, which became anathema to those who flocked to the suburbs, still provides most of the cultural, recreational, and educational facilities of great importance to a metropolitan area. For example, most of the great museums, art centers, galleries, and opera houses are located in the central cities. These facilities are supported by the cities and by taxpayers who are far less affluent than their suburban neighbors. Ironically, these facilities are utilized by suburban clientele, who feel the need to participate in such cultural, recreational activities. Adding to the irony is the fact that the great cost of supporting these cultural centers falls upon the city to the exclusion of the suburbs, yet the greatest use of these facilities is made by people living in the suburban areas.

Of more recent concern is the move to the suburban areas by commerce, business, and industry. It is not surprising that this has happened because, as the more affluent and highly educated clientele move, businesses are forced to move where their clients live. Over the past fifteen or twenty years, huge shopping and commercial centers have been built near emerging population concentrations. Many of the fine stores that were located in the center city have developed branches in outlying areas so that they may be near the persons who can afford to buy their merchandise. Industry, too, has moved for a variety of reasons. Because of the technological expansion, American industry has become very sophisticated. Workers have had to be highly skilled and trained to provide the kinds of labor important to American industry. As the pool of trained labor moved farther and farther from the city, industry has moved to be near this source of trained, highly skilled manpower.

In addition, as the transition continues from an industrial to a technological economy, existing factories and production facilities prove to be inefficient and not easily adaptable to technological development. Therefore, these existing facilities finally reach a point of diminishing returns. As far as the industry is concerned, it is much easier to build a modern, production-oriented facility near a trained pool of manpower than it is to replace, repair, and/or update existing facilities that have been rendered obsolete.

Although the picture is bleak, there are some hopeful signs and activities that, if allowed to reach culmination, will provide new life and renewed hope for school systems. As renewal efforts are continued, cities and now suburbs are finding that people respond favorably to such efforts. The result is that, through renewal practices, many metropolitan areas have turned their particular situations around and have found that, as this process continues, the schools, the other agencies, and the municipal government will also make a real effort to change and become more responsive to the citizens. All of this, of course, places the responsibility squarely upon the school system to become a more responsive, flexible institution that is able to respond to the needs of its citizens by developing programs that reflect the current state of the education art.

E. EMERGING EDUCATIONAL NEEDS

The most important educational need is the capacity of the school system to provide educational programming for a diverse student body. This is much easier said than done. The student population includes the very affluent, traditional, old-line families of a particular school district, the blue-collar families, the black population in many systems, and the newly arrived Hispanic and Oriental citizens who must be accommodated by the instructional programs provided by the school district. Their needs are diverse and sometimes in opposition to one another.

A second need that is obvious in most school districts is to reorient the professional educator to the realities of modern day life. This has great implications for the allocation of resources in school systems. Most of the personnel have a level of experience that makes it more difficult to change ingrained habits. It is difficult for persons who are trained to deal with a rather homogeneous student population to suddenly be forced into a situation where they must provide diversity and flexibility, tolerance and understanding of young people—people who come to school with varying degrees of readiness and interest and yet are suddenly in a situation where they must be served. Massive retraining programs are needed in the immediate future to enable school systems to respond adequately to the needs of the diverse student population now enrolled. A greater capacity to deal with bilingualism and biculturalism is important, for the fact remains that, though there is strength in diversity, school systems have not yet learned to harness that strength into a constructive force.

A third and related need is restructuring of the school system so that it can deliver services to the multiplicity of clients. In subsequent chapters one concept of decentralization will be examined. The charge is that a process be developed that will allow—indeed encourage—school systems to provide flexible programming to meet locally identified and perceived needs so that students may be served.

A fourth need is the identification and procurement of resources with which to carry out the massive educational task. A statewide and/or national priority system of providing resources to meet identified educational needs should be developed. The *Serrano* and *Rodriguez* decisions indicate that there will be considerable activity towards equalizing educational resources in the future. Equity battles will be fought on a state-by-state basis. Indeed, the struggle for equity has been initiated in many of the fifty states and the results are promising for success in this arena.

A fifth need is the need for comprehensive, coordinated planning activities to proceed not only in the educational system, per se, but between and among the diverse agencies designed to serve a community. There must be better utilization of existing resources and less duplication of efforts between and among agencies in order that scarce resources can be efficiently utilized. Therefore, it becomes crucial for school systems to develop a total planning approach involving the educational system, the social services system, the municipal system, the police system, and other metropolitan systems so that the resources may be channeled to the highest priority and duplication can be eliminated.

Finally, there is a need for broader involvement in the concerns and problems of the educational system. A recognition of the interdependence of the total metropolitan area is slowly beginning to grow and must be expanded. The recognition of the need to strategically plan for the delivery of all services needed in a community and that all services are mutually supportive must be emphasized.

School systems must lead in the identification and resolution of the common problems faced by all of the agencies. The combined, coordinated planning effort should lead to a recognition of the most pressing needs and a corresponding allocation of resources toward meeting those high-priority needs. The concept of shared resources so that the diverse needs of a population can be addressed by drawing upon the combined efforts of a variety of agencies and systems throughout a metropolitan area is probably the last chance for the school system to meet their obligation to their students.

SUMMARY

This chapter provides a background and insight into the evolution of the American school system. From the historical perspective, the chapter moves on to the current status of the American school system, delving into the related concerns of an urbanizing country and those implications for the system of education.

The demographic realities of the country are also examined for implications for the operation of the schools. As is noted, demographic changes that have occurred over the past four decades have dramatically changed the kinds of needs that the school system must respond to.

Demographic change, urbanization, and technological innovations all impose the need for the system of education to manifest appropriate changes in order to keep it a viable one. The chapter attempts to delineate the specific societal changes that educational institutions must be aware of in order to do the job of educating current students for the world of the future.

CHAPTER 2

The Superintendency and Organizational Patterns

Among school systems of America, a wide variety of organizational patterns exist; some developed to meet unique needs of a particular school system, while others developed somewhat like the old fairy tale, Topsy, just growing and growing until they reached their present state. It appears that most school systems in the United States are very centralized organizations with decisions emanating from the central office and being transmitted to the various divisions and schools throughout the system. There are and have been many attempts at decentralization, particularly over the past twenty years. The success rate has been minimal, perhaps because the whole concept of centralization/decentralization has not been adequately explored prior to decentralization activities.

This chapter will attempt to briefly review the different concepts of organization and present one concept of a decentralized school system for examination by the reader.

The evolution of school systems referred to in Chapter 1 tends to reinforce the original concept of centralization. Actually, the move towards centralization began almost immediately as school systems developed under the direction of town selectmen or the school committee. In Massachusetts, prior to the passage of the Massachusetts School Laws of 1642, schools became mandatory and were supported by taxes. As school systems grew from one-room to two-, four- and eight-room schools to a multiple number of units in a city, the centralization movement became a very powerful one. The history of the development of the superintendency is a case in point.

There were actually two movements that appeared to have created the need for the superintendency: the first was the reorganization of school systems. As long as school districts were organized in the early New England pattern with each district containing a single one-room school, administrative duties could be handled quite adequately by the members of the board of education. However, when many of these districts were combined into areawide school systems, as was done in numerous districts during the first part of the nineteenth century, the management of the entire enterprise tended to become very demanding for boards of education made up of citizens who were volunteering their time to public service (Reller 1935, 82). This problem was also hastened by the growth of cities and of school systems. Soon, it was not a case of having a school located in each ward or section of the school district; rather, each of these schools grew from one-room schools to four, eight, twelve, and sixteen rooms each. The work of several schools in a single school system needed to be coordinated. Moreover, the financial resources of the areawide school system required allocation among the various schools in the district. Again, lay board members were beset by problems and demands on their time that caused them to seek assistance.

The growth of the centralization movement and the combining of ward schools into school districts increased so that, by 1860, twenty-seven cities or city school districts had established the office of superintendent of schools. As city school systems grew and the educational enterprise became a more important focal point for the cities, boards of education began to feel it necessary to employ a superintendent of business as well as a superintendent of education. This frequently led to a dual administrative organization with an executive for business and an executive for education, both reporting directly to the board of education. As a matter of fact, some major school systems that are organized under the dual system still exist today, including Milwaukee, Wisconsin, and several eastern school systems. As a partial response to the inadequacy of the dual system of organization, the superintendent's role began to be more and more encompassing with all functions, including the business function, housed in the office of superintendent.

The second movement that reinforced the need for the superintendency was the more recent era of specialization giving rise to the need for a generalist superintendent or chief executive officer to coordinate the activities of the various specialists employed by the school system.

A. HISTORICAL PERSPECTIVE OF THE SUPERINTENDENCY

In more recent times, the superintendent has become identified as the chief executive officer of the school system with a variety of specialists reporting to the board of education through the office of the superintendent. The superintendent is the chief executive officer of the board of education, and his/her role is to interpret the educational policy as established by the board of education. This, of course, has led to the development of the highly centralized, task-area concept of organization. The chief administrative officer, the superintendent, is by definition a generalist in school administration, while a variety of specialists perform crucial, important roles in numerous areas of expertise. These activities allow the school system to operate effectively and efficiently. The specialists report to the superintendent and, in turn, to the board of education. There are two generalist positions in educational administration: the school principal and the school superintendent. Both of these individuals have to deal with broad-based and numerous administrative concerns, yet either or both can call on a number of specialists to address unique problems. In addition to the development of the superintendency and the centralized organizational pattern, there has been a parallel development in the state departments of education with the position of state superintendent of public instruction as the chief executive of each state.

Initiative in establishing the new office of superintendent was often taken by the city council. The Buffalo common council appointed a superintendent of common schools on June 9, 1837. On July 31, 1837, the first agent of the public schools of Louisville was elected by the mayor and aldermen (Reller 1935, 82). As time went on, boards of education in some states were given statutory authority to appoint superintendents; in other states, the board proceeded to make such appointments without specific legislative authorization. By 1860, twenty-seven city school districts had established the office of superintendent (Reller 1935, 82).

Establishment of the local superintendency in noncity areas did not occur until the twentieth century. For years, noncity schools were rural schools, and, as had been true earlier in the cities, each school district tended to have a one-room, eight-grade school. Moreover, a structural plan for giving minimum supervision to those schools had been evolved in the creation of the county superintendency (Reller 1935, 82).

In time, however, the movement to combine rural school districts into larger administrative units took hold. Utah was one of the early states to move toward large consolidated school systems. In 1915 the Utah legislature mandated the so-called county unit plan of school district organization (Reller 1935, 83).

Two movements appeared to affect the organization of school districts outside the major cities. The first of these was given legal expression by the Michigan Supreme Court in 1874 in the now famous *Kalamazoo* case.

Within the next three or four decades, not only city school districts, but also rural areas began to consider ways and means by which high school opportunity could be made available to all youth.

A more recent development affecting school systems outside the cities — and the central cities, too — has been the growth of suburbia. In rural consolidated school systems and in newly formed suburban school systems, the boards of education found it desirable to employ a local superintendent of schools. The concept of this position in these more recent organizations has undoubtedly been influenced by the concepts first developed in the city superintendency. In the last two or three decades, many small, inefficient school districts have been consolidated throughout the country, resulting in a large reduction in the number of school districts in America. Originally, there were over 100,000 such school districts in America; presently, there are fewer than 16,000. This reorganization occurred over a period of fifty years, but, most importantly, it accelerated during the past twenty to twenty-five years and again supported the notion of extreme centralization of authority in school district organization.

As an example, Figure 2.1 shows a typical medium-sized school district and how it might be organized under the centralized task-area concept. As is shown in the figure, the superintendent is the chief executive officer, and, typically, there will be a deputy superintendent through whom all of the various assistant and associate superintendents report to the superintendent. For example, the assistant superintendent for business directs the activities of the director of buildings and grounds and the director of financial services who, in turn, is responsible for payroll, purchasing, and so forth; the assistant superintendent for personnel is in charge of negotiations and employee relations, as well as staff recruitment, placement, and personnel services; the assistant superintendent for instruction is responsible for all instructional programs carried on in the district, including elementary, secondary, adult, vocational, and special education programs. Certain staff positions are attached to the office of superintendent, and these, typically, include information services or public relations and evaluation services or any other unique functions that are important to the district.

Under the centralized version of the task-area concept, various divisions headed by assistant superintendents deal with special functions across the total district. Therefore, the business office handles all of the finance, buildings and grounds, and business needs of the total school system — school by school. The assistant superintendent for personnel and his/her office recruit, assign, and evaluate teachers besides conducting all of the necessary negotiations with employee groups. The assistant

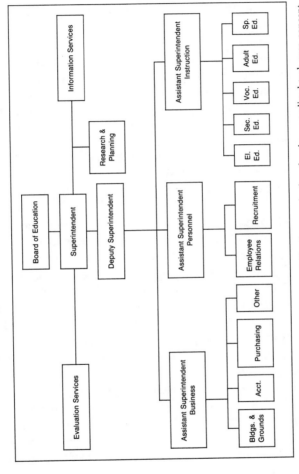

FIGURE 2.1 Typical medium-sized school district organized under the centralized task-area concept.

superintendent for instruction deals with systemic as well as the building-by-building instructional delivery systems and planning as well. Usually, under such an organizational schema, there is a planning office that deals with facility planning and perhaps some research and development efforts and is attached to the office of the superintendent.

Decisions affecting the total school system are made at the superintendent's cabinet level. Typically, the cabinet consists of five or six professionals who meet on a regular basis to make decisions concerning the whole system. Individual buildings must respond to edicts transmitted from the central office. Programs are prescribed by the central office and must be implemented on a building-by-building basis according to a particular edict. Under such a system, which incidentally works best in a relatively homogenous setting, all schools have basically the same curricula; all schools are provided basically the same services and the same resources; and all students can easily transfer from one school to another and not miss a page of a prescribed textbook, because citywide decisions are made downtown and are standard throughout all the schools of the system.

There are, of course, many tangential operational organization patterns that have been developed over the years but primarily under a highly centralized concept. The superintendent's office issues directives that affect all of the schools equally and impartially. The support staff and/or cabinet-level staff of assistant superintendents divide their obligations according to particular specializations. So, under the model posed in Figure 2.1, there are, in fact, two generalists at the central office, the superintendent and the deputy superintendent, as well as a host of specialists, each dealing with a particular function of the school system.

If consistency is the goal and if the school system happens to be relatively homogenous, this arrangement works very well. If, however, as is typical of school systems today, the school is composed of a variety of different people, if the clientele is pluralistic in nature, and if needs differ in every section of the school system, homogenous programming creates a real difficulty in terms of addressing emerging student needs. Therefore, such a highly centralized organizational pattern is neither appropriate nor necessary to achieve the educational goals of the typical school system.

B. DECENTRALIZATION—TASK-AREA CONCEPT

As the size of the school systems continued to grow and as the distance between the central office and the operating units of the school system became greater, it became apparent that efforts had to be initiated to decentralize these huge bureaucracies to provide flexibility so that school systems could respond to educational needs in particular areas. These needs could very well be different from one area to another in the district. A variety of works and studies have been published indicating the optimum size of school districts. Campbell, Cunningham, Usdan, and Nystrand (1975, 303) recommended that districts should have a size of no fewer than 2,000 students, but that 10,000 students would be preferable. They also explain that, in large school systems of more than 40,000 students, size becomes a potent variable in creating a bureaucracy that is almost impenetrable by citizens and unwieldy to professionals (Campbell et al. 1975, 303).

Citizens increasingly are demanding that the huge central bureaucracy be broken up into smaller, more workable units that will give them the opportunity to have input into the decisions and that will respond effectively, efficiently, and quickly to demands and pleas being heard from the clients. These units must be close enough to the citizenry to allow for an ongoing dialogue between the school administration and the people who support the schools. A number of large metropolitan school systems, such as New York, Chicago, Detroit, Philadelphia, Cincinnati, and others have attempted decentralization by creating subdistricts based on task-area concepts that do, in fact, provide a hierarchy of school administration at a level closer to the citizens. Figure 2.2 is an example of how such a decentralization plan might be organized.

As Figure 2.2 indicates, the decentralization model developed is quite cumbersome. It decentralizes the school system according to task areas. Typically, when a large school system decides to decentralize, it creates subsystems within the original system so that, where originally there was one superintendent for the entire system, there are now a number of subdistrict superintendents. As the model shows, four district superintendencies are created, and each of these persons has task-area support personnel, typically one assistant for business activities, another for personnel, and still another for instruction. All of these assistants have their own highly specialized staff to work with the twenty to thirty schools in the subdistrict. In addition, the superintendent's office, or the central office, retains the bulk of the specialists because it must deal with the totality of the school system so that one finds a support staff relationship (advisory in nature without supervisory responsibility) at the central office rather than a line relationship (direct supervisory relationship with super- and subordinate relations). These specialists all deal with the areas of specialization now found at the subdistrict level as well.

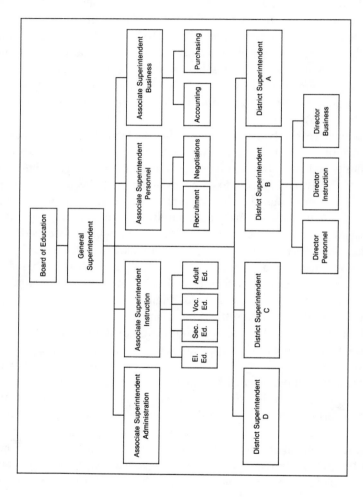

FIGURE 2.2 A typical decentralization plan.

This kind of decentralization merely creates another level of bureaucracy, another hierarchy to cope with in terms of operating the system, and thereby insulates the central office still farther from the activities and realities of the field. In many of our school systems, most prominently Detroit and recently Chicago, legislative action caused this particular kind of decentralization to occur. In Detroit, as in other large school systems, regional or subdistrict boards of education were created to set educational policy for a particular subdistrict. This is an excellent concept, theoretically, but unfortunately, the realities prove to be quite different.

For example, while subdistrict bureaucracies are created to deal with subdistrict problems and to plan and deliver subdistrict educational programs, fiscal control was retained at the system level so that, to date, very little capacity exists on the part of each of the subdistricts to set priorities and to direct resources towards the addressing of those particular priorities. In other words, what has happened is that the responsibility for educational programs has been allocated to persons outside the central office, but the control of resources so vital for programming has been maintained at the central office. Although, theoretically, this has potential for development, in actuality it stifles the initiative and drive of the various regional or subdistrict offices.

The realities of such decentralization are compounded by the hard fact of racial isolation in many of the larger school systems. Political opportunism has caused most of the subdistricts to be created along racial lines, thereby accelerating racial isolation rather than resolving the desegregation issue. Typically, because of the housing patterns in most school districts, the natural boundaries developed for subdistricts include vast majorities of particular racial groups in a subdistrict so that any hope for desegregation of a particular school system is shattered by the fact that the decentralized districts become relatively homogeneous and reinforce one another to forestall any desegregation activities that might be appropriate. In effect, what occurs in many instances is a complete balkanization of a school system into subunits that are very tightly homogenized into one group or another.

Although, historically, central office administrators have resisted attempts to decentralize authority, many have been attracted by the opportunity to be further insulated from the field as a result of the decentralization and have changed their minds about the realities and difficulties of decentralization because it provides still another scapegoat to blunt the thrust of community groups who are asking penetrating and difficult questions. Probably the strongest impetus towards decentralization grew out of the business sector of the American social order, because many corporations began to see vast opportunities available to them through the decentralization vehicle. As Chris Argyris (1962, 2) indicated in his discussion on the decentralization of large firms, "Fundamentally, decentralization means pushing down authority and responsibility to the lowest possible level. The aim is to have decisions made at the lowest possible point in the organization." Argyris (1962, 3) further pointed out that decentralization occurring within the context of the traditional pyramidal structure does not mean that people "on top" may delegate their accountability. If someone below makes a poor decision, the people "on top" are still held responsible. For decentralization to be effective, the various levels of the organization must be staffed by technically and professionally competent individuals. The organization must have solid policies that spell out the lines of communication and authority.

C. SITE-BASED MANAGEMENT—
RESPONSIBLE AUTONOMY

One approach to the centralization/decentralization dichotomy involves the development of a concept entitled responsible autonomy or site-based management. Site-based management (responsible autonomy) means achieving a balance between accountability and freedom in all parts of the educational system. Both are essential in public education. Without accountability, a system may become self-serving; without freedom, people lack a sense of personal responsibility, self-worth, and involvement. The positive elements of accountability and responsibility must be clarified and combined. For the individual professional to be both accountable and responsible is merely an assumption stemming from the appropriate definition of a professional educator.

The primary idea is that the greatest possible improvements in the school system will be attained when local schools are given the freedom to solve their own problems. Each individual school community should have the freedom to set educational objectives consistent with school system goals and to act towards the attainment of those objectives.

Site-based management or responsible autonomy stimulates individuality; it also acknowledges diversity; it encourages constructive competitiveness; it relies on the release of the total resources of all who engage in renewal at the building level; it makes it clear that teachers, administrators, parents, and students at the building level are the curriculum builders, appraisers of performance, and providers of instruction.

It is clear that educational improvement will be achieved only through the efforts of dedicated teachers, staff specialists, administrators, counselors, parents, and students working in good faith on the problems they have. The evolution of relevant curriculum, for example, and the reorientation of instructional strategies will occur in the field at the building level.

The role of the central office in the evolution of site-based management is as a support agency. It must assist in the planning and development, in providing alternative strategies, in helping to devise appropriate evaluation mechanisms, in procuring resources (both financial and human), and in stimulating local units in their own development. This new role is a dramatic departure from the traditional role held by central office personnel. Without acceptance of the new role by the central office, the entire process of decentralization cannot succeed. The first concern of the entire system must be for its people: students, paraprofessionals, custodians, teachers, administrators, and parents. The school districts exist for people—black, brown, white, red, and yellow—not for materials or things. The quality of the relationship among people will determine the quality of the educational fabric.

Organizational rigidity is the greatest inhibitor of change. Among the major items needing attention as rigidity is attacked are the following:

(1) Major authority for the administration of programs and the development of objectives must be vested in individual schools. Overall, the functional necessity of centralization of most things that take place in schools is usually overrated. However, some balance between centralization and decentralization will help minimize tendencies towards rigidity.

(2) Teachers should play a much greater role in setting program objectives and in other school matters. This means that the status schism between teachers and principals should lessen and that the administrator's role would change from one of control and unilateral direction to goal integration, articulation, and facilitation.

(3) Teacher performance should be measured by product rather than style.

(4) Structures must be developed for articulating objectives at all organizational levels, and serious efforts to determine learning needs must be undertaken.

(5) Greater in-house research and evaluation capacity must be organized and developed in order to provide research support and training to all buildings.

(6) Parents and other citizens must be provided the opportunity not only to participate more fully in school affairs, but to share certain powers with educators at both the school and school system level.

(7) The search for and the provision of alternatives and options to students and parents, either within or outside the system, must continue. The school system does have the responsibility to effect learner success.

(8) The task of true individualization of instruction must continue. This is a task worthy of complete dedication and attention.

(9) A united posture on the human quality of our profession must be developed. Education is a human and humane endeavor.

In order to address the larger concern regarding the need for school system responsiveness to individual students, the central administrative staff must utilize a slightly different perspective. The first task is to define the major functions of the school system so that it can be organized according to these functions. Second, it should be organized in such a manner as to provide the impetus for system-wide decentralization at the local building level.

As the activities of the school system are analyzed, seven basic functions are identified, and staff can begin the very difficult task of addressing a reorganization pattern to allow these functions to proceed. One of the key considerations is that, historically and traditionally, most organizational schemata have produced a highpoint pyramid where the chief administrative officer, or superintendent, has the obligation to respond to just about everything and everyone in the school system. In order to provide fast responses to diverse needs and to allow for a more moderate span of control, a more horizontal schema is suggested.

The following functions are identified as being the primary functions of the school system:

(1) Programs must be planned and developed based upon a needs assessment.

(2) The delivery of these programs becomes a very important function, which in this particular system is called the operations function. Its task is the delivery of programs to clients in the school system.

(3) The continuous and ongoing evaluation of the planning and delivery

effort is a major function. Therefore, the evaluation function is a key function for the school system.

(4) Communications, both internal and external, becomes a most important function as one plans, implements, and evaluates programs.

(5) The finances necessary to enable the prior four functions to continue are also essential.

(6) The instructional support function includes such activities as health, speech, psychological, and sociological services.

(7) No school system can exist without the noninstructional support function, which includes maintenance, custodial services, food services, personnel, data processing, and so forth.

Figure 2.3 shows a schema of a school system organized according to the site-based management concept. For administrative ease, the system is divided into three divisions.

The first of these divisions is the planning and noninstructional support services division; the second is the delivery and instructional support services division; and the third is the division of finance and evaluation, which includes across-the-board activities and is housed under the direct control of the superintendent of schools. In addition, the school system is charged with operating the public library system, so the library reports to the superintendent of schools as well.

Each of the two major divisions, planning and noninstructional support services, and delivery and instructional support, is headed by a deputy superintendent. The planning and noninstructional support division consists of three subdivisions: noninstructional support, planning, and personnel services. The following services are provided under the heading of noninstructional support: data processing, physical plant, transportation, and food services. The planning category includes curriculum planning, financial planning, state and federal relations planning, facilities planning, and research planning. These groups exist to serve the total system by enabling planning thrusts to be coordinated as the system proceeds in the implementation of this organizational structure. The directors of the various noninstructional support services and planning activities, as well as the personnel director, report to the deputy superintendent for planning and noninstructional support services.

The delivery and instructional support services division comprises elementary education, secondary education, continuing education, and instructional support services, each of which has a director who reports directly to the deputy superintendent for delivery and instructional sup-

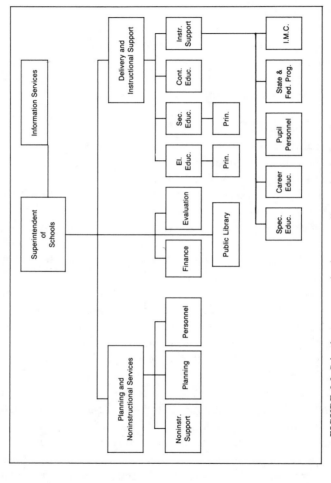

FIGURE 2.3 School system organization according to the site-based management concept.

port services. The instructional support category can be further subdivided to include special education, vocational education, pupil personnel, federal programs, and school media centers, all of which are headed by directors who report to the director of instructional support services. In addition, K–12 consultants work as instructional support personnel and also report to the deputy superintendent for delivery and instructional support services through the director of instructional support services.

In addition to the deputy superintendent for planning and noninstructional services and deputy superintendent for delivery and instructional support services, the following heads report to the superintendent: the director of information services, who is responsible for the communications function; the director of evaluation services, whose department performs the total evaluation effort for the school system; the controller, whose department provides all of the financial services needed to operate a school system; and the director of the public library, which serves the entire community and, in addition to the main library facility, also operates two branch libraries and a mobile unit.

One of the most difficult and recurring tasks is to implement a changed role for the central office personnel vis-a-vis the decentralization effort of the school system. Historically, school systems have been administered from the top down, and a filtering process was utilized to indicate what the priorities were, again always from the top down. If site-based management has merit and if the concern is the provision of adequate educational services to the students of the school system, then it seems that the top-down process is totally inappropriate. Rather, there should be a two-way process, so that the bottom-up as well as the top-down process, or, more preferably, a circular process could meet the needs of the students wherever they might be in the school system. For this reason, the concept of responsible autonomy or site-based management is developed, suggesting that there are both highly centralized and highly decentralized activities that are very appropriate for a school system. In this particular case, the ongoing attempt is to determine a decision-making matrix that defines at which level of the school system appropriate decisions are made concerning specific kinds of charges.

For example, this hypothesis states that school systems engage in some activities that can be very highly centralized, indeed at the state level or even regional levels in the country. These functions or activities might include purchasing, data processing, payroll, and all of the mechanical, repetitious activities encountered by school systems. At the same time, certain decisions are best decentralized, even to the individual classroom teacher if that's possible. These decisions properly include educational program delivery, program planning at the building level, staff selection, assignment of students, and so forth. In other words, those activities that directly impact the students on a day-to-day basis must be determined as close to the students as possible. This, briefly, is the decentralization concept shown in Figure 2.3.

There are, of course, many difficulties that surface as the school system addresses this particular decentralization effort. The first of these is the dramatic change in the role of the central office personnel and of the principals. Central staff, historically and traditionally, have been in a position to make decisions rather unilaterally. Yet these decisions impinge upon what happens at every building in the school system so that the tremendous task faced is to redefine the role of the central administration. The new role of the central administration is to be of service to the clients and personnel of the school system. Client in this context means the people that the central staff must serve, those people being building principals and staff, as well as the students and parents. The most formidable and ongoing task for the central staff to address is the provision of services to individual buildings by the particular division or department without imposing bias or obsolete guidelines on the buildings. According to the definition of site-based management, guidelines that have historically been appropriate are no longer viable. Those decision prerogatives are now the province of the individual buildings.

In order to grasp this concept, a decision might be to start with the board of education goals. These goals define the parameters under which all buildings in the school must operate. The first task is to define more sharply the goals of the school district by developing a series of systemic objectives that further narrow the parameters for individual school buildings. Since the objective is a systemic one, it is one that the individual campuses may not change at their discretion. The systemic objective becomes the overarching objective of the entire school system, particularly in the skills area. However—and this is very crucial—each campus has the obligation and the opportunity to develop variations in delivery systems that will allow the campus to best meet the systemic objective of month-for-month cognitive growth while recognizing the strengths of the indigenous staff, the needs of the community, and the best deployment of scarce resources. The delivery system is an obligation and a development charged to the campus level under site-based management. It is important that, as campuses set priorities and develop delivery options, the central staff be participants, particularly in the planning process in order to provide planning expertise and in the setting of priorities and program objectives in order to assist the building in establishing baselines for evaluation. In this way, the central staff can help the campus determine the effect of a particular delivery system and be of assistance in the recycling and/or restaffing process.

As can be discerned from the preceding discussion, the linchpin of the entire operation of the school system is the planning process. Coordination of strategic planning and a recognition of its importance permits the optimization of scarce resources.

Subsequent chapters of this book will consider the various functions described earlier. Because of its immediacy and crucial nature, strategic planning will be addressed in the next chapter. Following the strategic planning chapter, the other six functions identified earlier will be addressed. A final chapter will offer comments about the governance of the site-based management system as it impacts all levels of governance and of the requirement for staff retraining in order to successfully implement the site-based management concept.

SUMMARY

This chapter has reviewed the various organizational patterns found throughout the American school systems. It has also established a site-based management organizational pattern for consideration by the reader. The site-based management schema was used by the author in two school systems where he served as superintendent of schools and is the result of almost twenty years of serious consideration, implementation, and adjusting. The ultimate determiner of success or failure is the capacity of the staff of the school system to embrace the concept and to develop the new roles required of the participants. For that reason, the resources allocated to staff development are the most crucial budgetary allocation to be made. Experience suggests that the school system desiring to explore the site-based management concept do so by providing a healthy amount of resources for the training of staff and for the development of planning expertise in order to redefine all of the role changes needed.

CHAPTER 3

Strategic Planning for Site-Based Management

A. HISTORICAL PERSPECTIVE

School systems have had planning efforts for a long time, but these efforts have been focused primarily on facility planning. There has been, unfortunately, very little interest in and regard for the gestalt of planning or strategic planning. Strategic planning includes program planning, organizational planning, financial planning, and cooperative planning between and among the many agencies that are located in all communities. Most large school systems have an office of school planning that concerns itself with the physical plant needs of the school system. In the immediate post World War II years, with the population explosion and the dramatic and rapid growth of school enrollments, the office of plant planning was kept busy planning for new facilities to house the mushrooming school-age population. As the growth of public school systems in the country peaked and began to show a decline in the late 1960s and 1970s, the school plant planning office became increasingly concerned with the rehabilitation and remodeling of buildings that had lived a productive and useful life during the immediate post World War II era. The office of facility planning typically devotes its energies toward enrollment and demographic projections by identifying where the students are, how old they are, and where they live and toward correlating facilities to match the need as it evolves throughout the school system.

By coincidence, more than by design, facility planning does involve, at least peripherally, some attention to programs that are to be housed in the newly developed or newly remodeled facilities. By virtue of a primary interest in school plant design, the school facility planner involves himself with the program needs of a particular area or a particular grade level of the school.

Also peripheral to facility planning is some involvement in fiscal planning because, as the facility planning division develops specifications for a new or remodeled facility, there has to be a concomitant development of a plan to pay for the facility. Most of the time this plan involves the sale of bonds of sufficient value to pay for the total cost of the facility(ies). The bond issue is to be sold on the open market, and the proceeds are to be used to remodel and/or build new facilities. In turn, the bonds will be redeemed over a specified time period. The local taxpayers pay sufficient taxes to meet annual principal and interest requirements.

It is then somewhat accidental that the existing concept of school plant planning does involve the planning division in a variety of planning efforts, including curricular and financial planning. This is because the facility cannot be planned in isolation from the program needs, the size needs, and the financial requirements to pay for that particular development. Beyond that, of course, the facility planner becomes involved with the development of data, including physical plant data and equipment data, so that there can be some matching of student needs with facility data and with the facilities that are available.

Typically, the office of school plant planning concerns itself almost exclusively with the physical plant and equipment and only peripherally with those areas that impinge upon plant and equipment needs. Although data developed and generated by the plant planning division provides valuable information upon which the superintendent and other cabinet members can base appropriate decisions, the plant planner does not necessarily involve himself with the quality or quantity of those decisions. More recently, there have been efforts towards the strategic planning processes which do, in fact, open the planning division to a more important and comprehensive role in terms of the totality of the school system and of the area it serves.

There are other historical perspectives of the planning process that should be kept in mind as one considers planning for site-based management. One of the more important and cogent planning efforts, both historically and currently, has been military planning. Military history is laden with tales of planning, for example, planning for battle, planning supply lines for support of troops, and total planning. Napoleon, for example, was defeated when his planning process went awry, and he stretched his supply lines to a point where he could no longer support his troops. The military history of the United States is rich with military men who were successful because of their expertise in the planning process.

Considerable effort is made to train military personnel to assimilate and utilize the planning tools. Indeed, at the war college located at Fort Leavenworth, an entire building serves as the planning think tank. There, people utilize simulations and historical perspectives to learn the techniques of planning. It is important to note that, when one is dealing with something as vulnerable and valuable as human life and the very existence of a country, careful attention to planning is a vital initial step.

Another sphere of American life where planning has become viewed as an appropriate and worthwhile activity is in other governmental bodies and agencies. There are few, if any, cities that do not have a department of city planning. Indeed, most states have planning departments; villages and towns have planning departments; and counties and groups of cities bind themselves together cooperatively into regional planning bodies. Through the auspices of the federal government, great attention has been focused on the planning process in every sector of governmental activity, ranging from the planning of water districts and the provision of utilities across geographic areas to the planning of housing developments, traffic patterns, and the delivery of social services to clients wherever they may be located.

Great emphasis was placed on urban planning as a result of massive federal grants in the 1950s and 1960s dealing with the urban renewal process in the major cities of the country. These planning activities led to the formation of huge city planning departments that accomplish everything from social planning and delivery of programs to needy clients to the brick and mortar physical planning of an area of a city or, indeed, an entire city. In order to assure compliance with intent of legislation on urban redevelopment, the federal government has compelling interest in the city planning process. Monitoring the planning process is one of the ways that the federal government can assure that monies are utilized for their intended purpose.

The typical city planning department encompasses a variety of planning skills and planning specialists. These can range from the architectural/engineering person, who does the physical layout and physical planning for a city or area, to the health planner, the social planner, the legal planner, and the fiscal planner, all of whom address their particular specialty in light of the overarching objectives and goals of a city or municipality.

In recent years, other quasi-municipal and municipal agencies have also become involved in the planning process. Again, as a result of federal stimulus, health care planning is being accomplished on a regional basis. This is being done because of the overabundance of available hospital beds and because of the runaway cost of medical care. Now that population growth has stabilized, we cannot go on constructing the multitude of hospital facilities that are on the drawing boards. Therefore, under the auspices of the federal government, an attempt is being made to curtail the building of facilities to conform to the needs of the population. It is also a way to begin to regain control of the dramatic acceleration in the costs of health care by limiting the amount of new hospital construction that is permitted. It is interesting to note that, although this coordinated health planning process has been in existence for a number of years, the net impact is still to be felt, for hospital construction is generally dependent on the prevailing political mood of a region. Very little, if any, attention is paid to the health planning cadre, although health planners can exercise the veto power given to them by law. At any rate, health planning is another attempt to utilize planning as a way of creating alternatives and options for decision makers.

For many decades, the Department of Housing and Urban Development (HUD) has been very actively involved in the planning process. They have created, through their fiscal policies, a multitude of city planning centers. Additionally, recreation departments have been increasingly subsidized by their planning efforts. Again, this reflects federal-level concerns over increasing leisure time and the need for more programs and facilities to provide worthwhile leisure activities for the population of the United States. Other municipal bodies that have well-defined planning expertise include local police departments, state police departments, city, state, and regional governments, and so on.

Finally, in terms of historical perspective, no overview of the planning process is complete without some attention being given to the planning efforts being utilized in business and industry. Most corporate bodies have sophisticated, large, important, and powerful planning arms. General Motors, for example, consciously plans actions several years in advance that include decisions on the type of automobile to be produced, the size of the automobile, the plant at which it is going to be produced, the interchangeability of parts, the amount of decentralization to be allowed, and, finally, the price at which this particular product will be sold to the public. Because of planning decisions over the past decade, General Motors has suffered severe losses in both prestige and in sales. Their corporate planners did not believe what the public was saying, and, as a result, Japanese and European automobile manufacturers gained an important niche in the American market.

The uproar in the past decade over the interchangeability of engines among General Motors' divisions was no accident. It was a conscious and deliberate decision made in order to be able to reduce the unit costs of a particular set of automobiles. Incidentally, one of the strengths of a corporate body like General Motors is the attention paid to careful planning that allows for the interchangeability of parts and specifications so that the unit cost of a product can be dramatically reduced and the profit margin can be maintained at its projected level.

General Motors is but one of many corporate bodies who devote conscious effort, energy, and money to the planning process. Certainly, no one can quarrel with the success of such corporate structures as General Motors, AT&T, Sears, Ford, and many of the other corporations that have legitimized the planning process for business and industry in the United States and throughout the world. In these planning exercises, careful attention is given to the clientele to be served, to their needs, to their economic status, to the potential for marketing of a particular product, and to the desirability of and the need for that particular product. Planning efforts go so far as to create a need where none existed through the vehicle of advertising. All told, the business and industrial planning model is the most sophisticated, most highly refined and developed arm of a particular industry.

It is fair to conclude that education has been a late addition to the planning mode. Only within the past decade has an understanding of and the need for strategic educational planning been recognized in the educational systems of our country.

B. STRATEGIC EDUCATIONAL PLANNING

Assuming that it is appropriate to have planning activities that proceed in a systematic, orderly fashion, the school system must then organize itself so that planning does occur. Planning activities are unique in that they should not be the final determination of whatever action the school system takes, but rather they should provide a variety of options and alternatives from which decision makers can choose appropriate actions. Planning schemes must have the flexibility to return to the drawing board at any point in time to create other options for the decision maker to consider. Therein lies a most important point, for all too often the planner becomes so enamored with a particular point of view that he or she cannot fully comprehend the various nuances that impinge upon decision making. The planner tries to assume the role of the decision maker without the concomitant responsibility that goes with those decisions.

In most school systems, planning activities should proceed together with efforts to provide mechanisms for decisions to be made as close to the level of the student as possible. This implies that the optimal point of planning for students should be at the building level.

In the last decade, a number of school systems have chosen to define planning as a crucial component of the total operation of the school system. Anything that is attempted in the school system should begin with the planning function. It might be well to share here the definition of planning: what it is, what it can do, what it should do, and what it should never attempt to do. The planning function must be objective. Its most important task is to gather data from any source — data that is clear, objective, and to the point. Interpreting the data and transforming it into a series of options and alternatives from which decision makers can select responses to particular issues is what planning is about. One of the issues that arises, of course, is the fact that planners are human beings, and no matter what kind of an organization they are planning, they tend to internalize the planning function and want to dictate the priorities of the organization rather than assist in the priority development. We must repeatedly remind ourselves that the role of the planner is not to make the decisions but rather to provide the data on which the decisions will be based. The author has had many occasions to blend the planner's data with political realities in order to make the appropriate decision. These political realities are not readily apparent to the planner for he/she does not confront such activities on a regular basis while the chief executive must constantly be attuned to these nuances.

It is important, as one engages in strategic educational planning, to establish parameters that allow the planning process to advance. It is vital that the people doing the planning, as well as the consumers of the planning effort, know what these parameters and limitations are. For example, one parameter that must be considered in strategic educational planning is federal law and the resulting decisions. Every year, case law, as a basis for educational decisions, is growing around the country. In the years since the *Brown I* and *Brown II* decisions made in 1954 and 1955, a whole body of case law and federal legislation has evolved dealing with equal educational opportunity, with school desegregation and segregation, and with equal employment practices. More recently, there have been conflicting opinions, as defined by the *Bakke* decision involving the University of California Medical School. At any rate, these legal mandates are very real parameters for the local school system planner to consider.

Many circuit and Supreme Court decisions involving pupil assignments have been rendered. These decisions must certainly be considered as one begins to develop educational plans for the students of a particular school system. The assignment of pupils without regard to race or ethnic group is not the best advice one can follow. It appears, given the *Brown* decisions and the equal opportunity laws, that some balance of racial, ethnic, and socioeconomic groups must be a serious consideration in making student assignments. Beyond that, the whole issue of due process for students is a very important point when developing educational programs for students.

Additionally, the screening, selection, and assignment of staff have implications for observing existing federal court decisions. The employment of minority staff members in accordance with the Singleton principle of relating to the approximate ratio of minorities to be found in the geographic area is an important concern for the school administrator as the planning process unfolds.

There are other federal laws and decisions relating to such disparate concerns as school food services, due process, the provision of services and programs directed at particular student groups as a result of the Elementary and Secondary Education Act, the provisions of Public Law 94–142, and other similar federal legislation that certainly inhibit, if not direct, planning efforts.

Another parameter to be observed in local school system planning is the multitude of state laws and mandates that emanate from the state capital. Because education is not specifically mentioned in the Constitution, it becomes a purview of the various states. Indeed, local boards of education and local superintendents are not local officials at all but merely arms of state government and, as members of state government, are liable and vulnerable to the whims of state law and state mandates. Typically, most states are awakening to the realities and relative importance of the educational system. With the dramatic increase in state participation in the funding for education, an awareness of the state role in education is becoming much more prevalent. State legislatures are asking for data about the effective use of state funds and are increasingly placing restrictions on the use of state resources.

Among the generally mandated and legally enforced expectations in education are the requirements that state government be taught, certain health facts, i.e., the evils of tobacco, drugs, and alcohol and so forth, and that certain minimal standards be met in terms of the various disciplines to be included at the local school level. Additionally, most states provide lists of acceptable textbooks and other materials for the local school systems. A local school district may not deviate from those lists but may select from the books approved by the state so that there is still some flexibility left. Many states are getting into the minimal expectation testing movement and, as a result, are requiring that school systems meet basic expectations in reading, arithmetic, and other basic skills. A number of states are involved in the competency movement and are providing exit tests in order to ensure that persons finishing high school can meet minimal expectations as defined by the state legislature.

Many states provide mandates, rules, and regulations that require the teaching of certain subjects and the provision of certain services. Since school lunch and vocational education activities are funded through federal pass-through monies, they require state plans that encompass the intent of the federal legislation that provides the resources for the program. Finally, a local parameter must be recognized and that is the local board of education that governs the school system in which the planner operates.

Many local boards of education meet periodically to establish educational priorities and to review policies dealing with those priorities. Out of this generally comes a listing of concerns that reflect the needs of the school system, as well as the biases and priorities of each board member. These policies, as indications of need, are the final parameter to which the educational planner must respond. For example, it is probable that, in a school system committed to site-based management, a compilation of concerns and needs identified at the campus level can be merged, collated, and massaged to create a listing of some ten or twelve priorities for use by the school system staff. Issues such as arts and humanities, basic skills development, affective education, bilingual education, community school, counselling, declining enrollment, finance, education of the gifted, special education, at-risk students, energy conservation, and the like can all be addressed in the rank order assigned by the board. (State legislatures and state boards of education can also mandate items to be given a higher priority.) It is unusual to ignore board of education policy and board of education priorities because the board is the legal governing body of the school system. The effective planner will also assist the board to recognize other needs and obligations of the school system.

Another parameter that can be identified and must be considered is the negotiation of contract agreements with various employee groups. Certainly, if the work day, the work week, and the length of the school year is spelled out in the contract, it does little good for the planner to suggest in-service activities that carry on beyond the contracted time. The nuances of contracted agreements must be considered as one begins to engage in strategic educational planning. Additionally, the realities of fiscal limitations must certainly be observed, as well as the particular idiosyncrasies of the geographic and/or political context in which the planning is done. The process of identifying local barriers can be a most complex one and is generally accomplished through a series of interlocking planning efforts with various segments of a particular community that are involved in the planning process. It should be clear that blind adherence to imagined parameters does nothing to promote strategic educational planning. It is indeed impossible, through the planning process, to expand the parameters particularly as new needs are identified and new innovative approaches to delivering services are created. At any rate, the imaginative and adept strategic plan will address the parameters as they are currently perceived and expand those parameters to allow appropriate responses to be made to the students of the school system.

The main prerogative of site-based management involves planning in a context called "responsible autonomy." The idea of "responsible autonomy" is to allow the local sites to respond to particular needs as the needs are identified and as resources can be gathered to address those particular needs. By dealing with site-based concerns as the primary focus of the planning effort, the school system develops greater capacity to manage the change process and to initiate change at the level of the student.

C. THE PLANNING CYCLE

The planning cycle as it impacts the development of a strategic educational plan is best explained by Figure 3.1. As shown by Figure 3.1, the planning process is identified as a developmental process model. It starts with the gathering and examination of all the data available about a particular building or system. It also includes consideration and recognition of the board of education goals and feeds those in through the community involvement process into a context. The context examination deals with needs assessment, the establishment of priorities, and the school's response to the priorities. This leads to input analysis that defines, or attempts to define, the program thrusts and identifies planning teams that develop time lines, a monitoring chart, and a delivery system. Next in the cycle is process analysis that is really the monitoring function of checking the startup and the implementation of the program. The final analysis is product evaluation that is an examination of whether or not the desired objectives and goals have been met leading to a recycling of the program into a more appropriate thrust if needed. The planning cycle as identified in the foregoing section is the CIPP model of decision making developed for the Phi Delta Kappa Thrust on Evaluation. The CIPP model lends it-

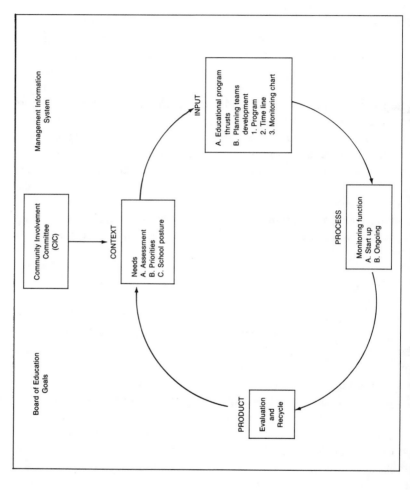

FIGURE 3.1 Educational planning: a development process model.

self to the planning effort as it provides the capacity to change at many points in the planning cycle. It is a most flexible and appropriate planning tool.

Before site-based management can be planned and before site-based programs can be delivered and implemented and certainly before they can be evaluated, a rather comprehensive context analysis must take place. Part of the context analysis is a needs assessment done on behalf of the students to be served. Any analysis of context will present data related to the socioeconomic level of the students as well as information regarding the racial composition of the student group. Income levels, Aid to Families with Dependent Children (AFDC) levels, and all of the pertinent socioeconomic data are part of the context analysis. Included in context, of course, must be the particular building and the staff of the facility. Identified should be the indigenous resources, staff strengths, staff weaknesses, community resources, and so forth. Once the context is well identified, it is then possible to initiate the input analysis at that level. Delivery components or programs are defined and devised to meet the particular educational need. Priorities are established leading to the diversion or conversion of certain resources into program realities. Time lines and monitoring charts are also developed, leading to process analysis.

Process analysis is essentially a monitoring activity that provides data for the product evaluation. The product evaluation quite simply determines whether the program efforts were successful or not. If they are not successful, product evaluation should indicate appropriate recycling considerations or a complete discarding of the existing program. The planning cycle is crucial because it does not stop at the point at which the program is implemented but rather continues through the entire implementation process to allow for recycling, revision, or discarding. In other words, planning is not an isolated activity, but is an ongoing fact of life in the school system choosing to utilize the planning approach.

D. STRATEGIC PLANNING

In order to address the planning needs of an educational system, a format must be developed with which to provide consistency, continuity, and cooperative efforts in the planning. The term *strategic planning* is used to indicate total comprehensive planning. In range planning, the short-range efforts are in the one-year time span, medium-range are two to three years, and beyond three years are long-range efforts. Site-based management efforts must start with the development of site strategic plans that are directly related to systemwide goals, objectives, and strategic plans. Site plans reflect the particular and unique needs of a particular locale. Our earlier discussions dealt with the identification of roles within the total system and an awareness of the parameters within which the planning process takes place. There are easily identifiable decision points across the system. Some decisions are made at the systemic level, others at the building level, still others at the classroom level, and many that are a combination of the three levels. Within each of these decision bases there is a need for the planning activity. Therefore, the strategic planning form that identifies the priority, the board goal that it relates to, the needs assessment showing the need for that activity, and whether it's a short-, long-, or medium-range effort is an important document for tracking purposes. It identifies a program goal, the delivery system to be utilized, and whatever variables and constraints are in operation at the time. In addition, this form identifies elements of planning including the evaluation of the objectives and the total evaluation strategy. Personnel needs, facilities needed, and finally the supplies and materials that are necessary to enable the plan to be implemented are designed. The form provides for costs to be defined and whether those costs will be in addition to or part of the ongoing operation of the campus, department, or system (see Figure 3.2).

Consistent with the wide variety of decisions possible in a school system and with the various decision points, planning proceeds at every level of the system. Strategic planning involving the board and central office staff provides the gestalt for the many interlocking and supporting planning efforts. Planning proceeds bilaterally from classroom to building to system as well as from system to building to classroom.

The teacher plans a program for the students he/she serves. Individual student and topic plans are the framework for site-based planning. Site-based management is predicated upon plans developed to meet the needs of the students of a particular or group of buildings. Certainly, the most fundamental and basic of all plans are the classroom plans. Teacher-made plans involve the day-to-day, week-to-week, and month-to-month activities of the children in a particular classroom or set of classrooms. These are the individual plans or plans for groups of students dealing with particular learning objectives or goals. These are predicated upon student needs as identified by the teacher.

The next level of planning is logically at the campus level or the site-based level. At this level, a much more sophisticated, more articulated needs assessment is accomplished, utilizing not only the students, but the

STRATEGIC PLANNING FORM

School _____ Date reviewed by CIC_____

Submitted by _____ Date submitted _____

Planning liaison_____

Priority #1, 2, 3, 4   Board Goal(s)
(Circle one)

Needs Assessment:

short (0–1) yr, medium (1–3 yrs), long (over 3 yrs)

Elements of planning

I. PROGRAM
   A. Goal
   B. Delivery system
   C. Variables
      Constraints

ELEMENTS OF PLANNING	SHORT	MEDIUM	LONG

II. EVALUATION
   A. Objectives
   B. Strategy			

III. PERSONNEL
   A. Professional-
      certificated
   B. Para-professional
   C. Contracted services
   D. Support personnel			

IV. FACILITIES
   A. Renovations, additions
   B. Furniture, equipment			

V. MATERIALS A. Supplies			

VI. FINANCE
   A. Cost of program
      (budget)
      1. Personnel
      2. Materials
   B. Source of funds
      1. Building
      2. Special project			

FIGURE 3.2 Strategic planning form.

parents and community as well. The needs of a particular community are spelled out in some detail and the corresponding resources and strengths and weaknesses are also identified. Out of this effort comes a series of priorities to be addressed by the educational program at that particular campus. The planning proceeds to the implementation stage where specific objectives are identified and specific delivery mechanisms are developed to meet those objectives. This is a relatively straightforward process but must also involve not only the local staff and community, but resources from the central office and state as well. It is entirely possible that, through rigorous planning activities, proposal development can take place to generate an expansion of the resource base to enable far more productive programs to be implemented at the building level. In other words, good planning generates marketable proposals with which to garner additional resources.

The final and, perhaps, the most sophisticated planning activity in the school system is at the systemwide level. At this level, the board of education goals and objectives are addressed as the parameters for the planning activity. All of the various campus-level and department-level plans are assimilated into a cohesive and coordinated thrust towards meeting the board of education goals and objectives. The usual product of such a planning activity is a school system handbook which could be entitled "Strategic Planning Report" and explicates the short-, medium-, and long-range plans for the school system and its member components.

The strategic planning report quite often is most useful for the immediate year in which it is produced because, as further planning is accomplished during the subsequent years, enough of the variables are redefined and changed to cause a skewing of the original medium- and long-range activities as they were projected. It's important to note that the planning process is a continuing one and that, while the product of the planning efforts reflects the needed changes, the process itself repeats with little change.

Among the issues to be considered during the planning process are those that deal with the pressures of change and its impact on education. The continuing social transformation is causing many revered notions to be questioned or even to be discarded. Educational planning no longer is a linear process involving the simple extension of known data on a one-dimensional and constant projection. The many nuances of social and political forces must be considered in any attempt to plan for the future in education. There are dimensions which can be described and discussed by any group that is concerned with the future, including classroom teachers, specialists, building administrators, parents, students, and others in the community. A taxonomy of social and political impact issues to be considered includes the following:

(1) The economy of the nation, state, and community
(2) Action of the Congress and/or the state legislature
(3) Nation, state, and local educational trends that include many thrusts, i.e., back to the basics, religion in the schools, desegregation, at-risk students, gifted and talented, and so forth
(4) Community pressures
(5) Local and state office holders and their impact
(6) Informal political forces

There are other impediments but to place unwarranted faith in the technology of planning without due regard for the aforementioned issues would be totally unrealistic. Planning at the school-site level must also consider many political intricacies related to departments and personalities. They can be known only to those who function within those confines.

While the art of educational planning is still in its infancy, it should be generally accepted that its function takes on the tasks of establishing goals, gathering and organizing data, defining activities, describing options, and making decisions. Certainly in this process, techniques are borrowed from other forms of planning. It should be kept in mind that the purpose of planning is found in a desire to improve. The key to educational planning is to provide the incentive, the setting, the background, and the tools to cause planning to be accepted by teachers, principals, support staff, parents, community, students, and all levels of administration. Those who have responsibilities for operations should have planning involvement. Planning should be done *with* people—not for them—and at a level as close to the learner as possible. Therefore, the emphasis on site-based planning is vital to the development of site-based management procedures.

E. COORDINATION WITH OTHER AGENCIES

As the strategic planning process is implemented at the local school level, it becomes important for the planner or planning group to initiate cooperative ventures with other agencies in the community. Included among the other agencies to be involved in the planning process are the city, the county, the variety of social agencies found in any community, and other private or quasi-public agencies that function in the community, including the various churches and the United Way agencies.

The coordination of educational planning with the planning efforts of other agencies is important because, as scarce resources are being identified and allocated, it becomes important not to duplicate efforts already mounted by other agencies but rather to provide supplementary activities in order to maximize the utilization of those scarce resources. It's entirely possible, for example, that other agencies are organized to provide for the health needs of students, and therefore the school system need not duplicate those efforts but should merely identify the health related needs of the students and then refer the students to the appropriate health agency. In this manner, scarce resources are more appropriately allocated and focused on the specific need that is to be addressed.

All too often, the educational system attempts to provide an inordinately broad range of services to students. It fails because it simply does not have the expertise or resources needed to meet the particular needs that are manifested by the diverse clientele of the school system. It would be far better to identify those needs and refer the student to the appropriate agency that provides program assistance in the area of need. One of the criticisms rightfully levied against the school system is that it has expanded its efforts far beyond the normal definition of education and attempts to be all things to all people. By coordinating the planning efforts of the multitude of agencies in the community, a grid or taxonomy of support services can be identified along with the agency providing the particular support activity so that the clients in need of a particular support service can be referred to the specific agency offering the service.

F. THE SETTING OF PRIORITIES

Strategic planning engenders a series of priorities and options for the decision makers to consider. It is probable that from the campuses, from an examination of the needs assessment process, and from a series of board conferences dealing with objectives and goals, a set of priorities can be established. This is a tentative list that was culled from the efforts of one school system (Forth Worth Independent School District, Forth Worth, Texas 1984). The needs are summarized as follows:

(1) Schools are expected to teach the basics.
(2) Technology will assume an increasingly greater role in our lives. For schools, this means a greater emphasis on coping skills.
(3) Humanization of instruction will have to continue as government becomes larger and more monolithic.

(4) Educational options and alternatives will continue to be part of the educational system.

(5) Changing societal expectations regarding the role of women and of the family will cause a revision in the traditional curriculum.

(6) A rethinking of the role of the teacher, especially as he/she relates to technology, is essential.

(7) Interdisciplinary curriculum planning seems to be an emerging trend.

(8) Staff development will be even more essential than is currently the case.

(9) Concern for sensory, hands-on educational experience continues to mount.

(10) Schools will continue to increase the range of services to meet the increased responsibilities for early childhood education, health, and nutritional needs.

(11) The teaching of parenting will become increasingly important.

(12) Learning will become a continuous, permanent, and lifelong process.

The above are the result of a series of "futures" workshops convened to provide planning direction. Out of the broad goals and objectives listed, a series of specific planning activities leading to program thrusts are being developed.

The relationships of needs assessment results at the campus level are examined in light of the forecast "future" needs to sort out the similarities and/or discrepancies. Based upon the degree of agreement concerning specific needs, program planning can proceed. In those areas where little unanimity exists, a gestation process can be initiated. This process can alert the various planning levels, i.e., classroom, campus, and system, that a particular forecast should be examined with some awareness of its possible impact on the total program. Such sharing of information provides additional data on which to base plans.

Priorities thus established are addressed through program development and delivery. The cyclical nature of the planning process permits — indeed forces — focus on the priority until a need is met or redirects program resources if it is not sufficiently resolved.

Finally, the planning process forces attention on the best possible use of systemic resources. Because financial limitations are very real in every school system, planning expertise can assist in the systematic and optimum use of fiscal and human resources by the identification and establishment of priorities for student programs.

SUMMARY

This chapter focuses on the planning function as one of the most important functions of the educational system. It traces the development of the planning function in other noneducational organizations and draws upon the planning success in these other areas to develop a strong rationale for the inclusion of the planning function in the educational sphere.

Strategic planning is as important to the school system as it is to the military, to business, and to government agencies. The need for comprehensive educational planning becomes even more important when one considers the rapidly changing environment in which we now find ourselves. The time is past when a long-range plan could serve the school system for a number of years. Today, the most one can hope for in terms of plan accuracy is one to two years. After that, the rapidly changing environment makes such projections very questionable.

While the data from which plans are drawn change rapidly and dramatically, the process of planning does not change, and this chapter attempts to establish the process for use by the practitioners. Planning, as a function of the school system, should precede every developmental activity of the school system. The best use of talent and scarce resources depends on the wise use of planning expertise in the school system.

CHAPTER 4

Delivery of Educational Programs

The delivery function is, quite naturally, a progression from the planning activity. Once educational programs are planned, they must be delivered to the students of the school system. This is done through a variety of means and organizational structures common to many school systems. Because the emphasis of this book is on site-based management, the focal point of this discussion will remain on the individual campuses. The only departure from this mode is in the case of special programs, i.e., special education, adult education, career education, etc., where, for reasons of economics and/or law, delivery is planned on a systemic basis rather than on a campus-by-campus basis. The conscious effort of centralizing certain activities while decentralizing others permits optimum use of scarce resources, allows for combining limited enrollments into efficient-sized groupings, provides specialized activities at reasonable cost, and protects those students who would be overlooked because of their unique and different needs.

The school system that is committed to the development of a site-based educational delivery and management model must initiate its implementation with a process that allows such development to take place. The board of education must examine and review policies that would preclude such a decision process. Board of education policies allowing local principals, staffs, and communities to exercise autonomy, to make program decisions, to recommend personnel, to deviate from past practice, and to accommodate local needs are a precondition to the development of site-based management (SBM).

Given the political and legal realities within which local boards function, the development of enabling policies is not to be taken lightly. For example, in most states the legal parameters for local boards are very rigid. Any deviation from state mandate is difficult, if not impossible. Yet, in order that SBM be implemented, certain license with existing rules and regulations may be necessary. It is therefore good strategy to include the state department of education in the planning effort so that the special "exclusionary" permits may be forthcoming in order to initiate an effort at improvement of delivery services.

Once board policy is revised to encourage or permit SBM, the task of the board becomes one of developing systemwide objectives and priorities that become the parameters under which local units develop programs. *It is important to note* that these objectives, expectations, and policies are not negotiable but rather are the product expectations that are constant across the school system. The board of education must establish product objectives so that the quality and quantity of educational services are consistent and equal for all students.

SBM fosters the capacity of the local unit to develop and implement the processes and methodologies needed to deliver educational programs to students. It allows the local administrator, working in conjunction with the staff and community, to develop the best strategies for program delivery consistent with local needs, strengths, weaknesses, resources, and board of education objectives and priorities. SBM encompasses the highest order of accountability because it places the responsibility for serving students where it belongs but does so while permitting (demanding) indigenous solutions to problems so that local needs, strengths, idiosyncrasies, and capacities are incorporated with a minimum of dislocation to the student(s).

A. THE ELEMENTARY SCHOOL

In a decentralized educational system, the local campus becomes the focal point of most educational program planning and delivery. Because of the age range served and the fact that elementary schools are generally much smaller and less diverse than secondary units, the capacity of the elementary school to work closely with parents and community is greatly enhanced. While secondary units enrolling over 2,000 students are not uncommon, elementary schools generally serve from 250 to 600 students. Campuses serving a larger number of students are quite unusual and rare.

The very nature of the elementary program, with the bulk of the delivery responsibility delegated to the classroom teacher (supplemented by specialists and support staff), reinforces the close collaborative efforts between school and home. The staff of the elementary school is generally able to establish effective lines of communication with the patrons and parents of the school attendance area. Indeed, the school staff often is personally close to the school community and draws upon the community for a wide range of support activities and services on a regular basis.

What then are the mechanisms utilized as the decentralized elementary school provides educational services to the students in the attendance area? Following is a vignette of activities and strategies undertaken by such a school as the needs of students are identified and melded into a program of education for serving the community.

BOARD OF EDUCATION OBJECTIVES

The starting point for delivery of all services and programs is (or should be) the statement of educational objectives (expectations) as developed by the board of education. These objectives are the parameters within which all programs are planned, developed, and delivered. The statement of the board of education objectives should be reviewed and updated annually by the board working with the superintendent and staff.

Board of education objectives are definitive statements of expected outcomes drawn from the broader and more encompassing goals statements incorporated in board of education policies. As an example, an appropriate goal for a board of education might be that, "The program of instruction will provide the opportunity for each student to develop his/her reading ability to the optimum level." An objective related to the goal statement might be, "Any student enrolled in the school district shall exhibit month-for-month growth in reading as a result of his/her matriculation." The specificity of the objective becomes the rubric under which educational plans are developed. *It is imperative that board of education objectives be directed toward product rather than process!* If this is not the case, there can be no system of site-based management because decisions will be handed down from above. The capacity of the local elementary school to address student needs is dependent upon the capacity of the school to devise unique and creative methodologies for the delivery of services. Using the reading objective as an example, let us proceed to the actual process that might be utilized in developing the campus plan for reading instruction.

CAMPUS PROGRAM PLANNING AND DELIVERY

In the development of a program of reading instruction, the elementary school staff initiates its plans from the point of examining all available data in terms of month-for-month growth (i.e., growth in reading ability will parallel time spent in school). The product (month-for-month growth for all students) expectation is not negotiable. The building staff must devise a system of delivery that will produce "month-for-month" growth for all students. Among the data used are previous scores, socioeconomic data, health data, community educational level data, personnel data, home ownership data, employment statistics, and other related information. The gathering and analysis of the data is really a context analysis (from CIPP model) or needs assessment.

Out of the context analysis comes a variety of proposals directed at the reading needs of the students. Included might be such items as a listing of appropriate materials to be incorporated into the program, an indication of staff preferences as to basal and supplementary materials, an identification of the seriousness of the need, a prioritization of the reading need as compared to other curricular requirements, a listing of needed additional supplementary supplies and equipment, an identification of special staff needs, an estimate of classroom time needed for the reading program, a cost estimate to implement the planned program, and, finally, an estimate of the length of time needed to meet the product expectation for the program. Working with the community, the staff, under the direction of the principal, comes to an agreement as to the type of reading program to be implemented, the materials to be used, the time allocated to reading instruction, the resources available for program delivery, and the specific reading objectives to be used as the evaluative criteria.

The program, as developed, becomes a range plan for reading at the particular campus. Additionally, the components of the delivery cycle encompass the CIPP decision model (content, input, process, product). The reading effort is implemented and continuously monitored to see that the objectives are met. Individual student records are kept to ensure that *all* students are served. Regular reports to staff and community provide current information on program success. Adjustments are accomplished as the need arises since the process decisions are made at the campus level. There is great flexibility for staff to respond to individual needs and differences. The community, because of its ongoing involvement in program planning and evaluation, provides additional resources in the form of volunteers to assist in mundane as well as instructional activities. (One district known to the author generates well over 1.5 million volunteer hours a year.)

The process just described is repeated for every area of the curriculum. Each instructional plan is related to a board of education objective. Appropriate building-level process objectives are determined in concert with community and staff. The context analysis (needs assessment) determines the severity and scope of the deficiency and helps establish a priority for the curricular area. Once context analysis and process decisions are established, input decisions, such as resource allocations, are initiated. These resources are both human as well as financial. They include staff and community resources as well as supplies, materials, and equipment. The monitoring effort (see Chapter 5) is constant and ongoing, involving evaluation staff as well as campus staff (teachers and administrators) and community. As a result of the continuing planning/evaluation efforts, the recycling and/or redirecting of instructional efforts to more clearly focus on student needs is more quickly and adequately accomplished.

In addition to establishing delivery processes for programs mandated through board of education goals and more specifically identified by the board of education objectives and priorities, the SBM concept encourages the development of particular programs to meet student needs unique to a school campus and/or community. If, in the course of a context analysis, a special and specific need is identified, the appropriate instructional effort can be quickly developed for delivery. Such concerns and student needs as the arts, academically talented programs, cultural/ethnic diversity, large muscle development, preschool programs, substance abuse, and others can be resolved as a result of campus priority identification.

The staff of a single building or group of buildings can and should cooperate to resolve common needs. The grouping of campuses identifying similar priorities is accomplished through the planning division and the resultant cooperative delivery of programs ensures efficient use of scarce resources as well as broadening the number of participants to allow for increased diversity and creativity in responding to a student need. Such collaboration also permits the development of project proposals to be submitted for special funding to the various private and public funding sources. This, too, expands the resource pool available to the students, staff, and community.

As is becoming clear, the delivery of educational services can occur at or, rather, can be initiated from three distinct levels of the school system.

At each level, a different order of need is addressed and a range of specificity is identified and resolved. Each level supports and complements the other with the desired result being a much more comprehensive and personalized program.

CLASSROOM LEVEL DELIVERY OF PROGRAM

The ultimate and primary provider of educational services is the classroom teacher. (S)he really is the person upon whom most of the success or failure of the delivery process must rest. Elementary teachers, because of the structure of the elementary school and program, have great power of determination over the students located in their classrooms. It is crucial that the planning of instructional programs be concentrated at the classroom level. While the broad systemic needs can be and are identified at the school district level and unique campus needs are highlighted through the context analysis, it remains for the classroom teacher to develop specific delivery mechanisms to resolve individual student needs and to personalize the instructional program so that students are served.

While the obvious and persistent goal is to provide the capacity to respond to individual student needs, reality suggests that complete individualization is virtually impossible given the vagaries of finance, teacher-pupil ratios, state requirements, and local capacities. It is therefore appropriate to consider the notion of "personalized instruction" which suggests the possibility of responding to personal needs by utilizing the many methodologies, grouping strategies, and technologies now available. The capable classroom teacher, utilizing already existing mechanisms, can provide a number of activities to address specific and unique instructional needs for a very diverse and varied student clientele. This implies that the appropriate role for the classroom teacher is one of diagnoses and prescription and one of developer and manager of the instructional delivery system(s).

The idea of classroom teacher as the provider of resources, as the instructional planner, as the personalizer of instruction, and as the diagnostician suggests a different sort of educational professional than once was the case. However, master teachers have always been capable of and, in fact, have always done those things mentioned in the previous sentence. True, while these skills were generally developed "on the job" and without the benefit of formal course work, they were nonetheless part of the teacher's complement of skills. More recently, colleges and schools of education have increasingly incorporated the provision of such skill development as part of teacher-training programs.

The author feels that, while such training is an important part of teacher education, certain prerequisites to success are also important. These prerequisites can be grouped into a general category called "personal qualities" that cannot be taught. The selection of teachers who embody these qualities may be the most important task to be accomplished by the administrative leader. Such qualities as empathy, tolerance, commitment, genuine love of children, respect for others, and the like are important to success as a classroom teacher. It is a paradox that those most important of all qualities cannot be taught, yet, without them, success is simply not possible. Education is a people business, and the capacity to deal with and relate to others is a most important trait.

The reality of an SBM system, while not changing the professional behavior of the classroom teacher, does provide flexibility and legitimization for those behaviors long embodied in the master teacher. Assuming that the staff selection process is such that the majority of campus personnel possess those personal qualities described previously, what additional technical skills are needed and how are classroom teachers provided the opportunity to acquire those skills?

First, the capacity to diagnose student needs on an individual basis is very important. This includes the ability to generate and interpret all of the available data in order to perform an accurate diagnosis. Second, the classroom teacher must be able to perform the educational planning function. This involves creating delivery processes appropriate to the immediate and year-long educational needs of the students. Third, the classroom teacher must provide instruction to the students under his/her charge. Finally, the teacher must be able to generate special and unique delivery methods if student needs demand them. This involves (among other things) matching student needs with human resources provided by staff and/or community, utilizing all materials and equipment available, and designing special instructional strategies to serve special needs.

To fully implement the SBM concept, a variety of program support efforts should be mounted by the school district. Included among these are the following:

(1) Active solicitation of support and cooperation from institutions of higher education, particularly in the training and retraining efforts. Most institutions are anxious for symbiotic relations with local schools.

(2) The development of a supporting relationship with the state department of education. The needed flexibility may require certain exemption from state rules. In addition, many diverse talents are available in the state level.

(3) The creation of a local support services cadre which can, on demand, be available to individual teachers, groups of teachers, campuses, and combinations of campuses. This cadre of master teachers should be available to assist teachers as they plan and deliver "personalized" instructional programs. Among the techniques and skills to be emphasized are classroom management, instructional management system utilization, program planning, student needs diagnoses, and the understanding and use of growing amounts of educational technology.

Additionally, specialized educational personnel must be available to supplement the classroom teacher in the delivery of instruction. Such professional staff as library (IMC) staff, physical education, art, music, and other specialists are important to elementary teachers as they plan and deliver personalized programs. These programs can assist in program development, indirect instruction, and in helping the classroom teacher develop skills in the particular discipline. Many strategies are employed including the presentations of "microlessons," role-playing, and demonstration.

The elementary classroom instruction task is a difficult and demanding one because of the generalist nature of the elementary position(s). The bulk of the instruction is provided by a single teacher (self-contained) or a small group of teachers (team approach) for a defined group of students (25 to 100). SBM, while providing the capacity to participate in determining and developing programming responses to student needs, also requires expanded participation and responsibility on the part of the classroom teacher in total school operation. Direct involvement in planning and in the management of the instructional program is a demanding but rewarding activity. The capacity to impact the educational process is one of the intrinsic rewards of the education profession. SBM provides the opportunity for committed teachers to have expanded impact on students.

B. THE SECONDARY SCHOOL

The delivery of instructional programs at the secondary level is somewhat different than the process utilized at the elementary school level. The general context of the secondary school is such that many differences between secondary and elementary schools are apparent. For one, the organization of the secondary school is usually along specific disciplines with teaching staff trained in the particular curriculum area, i.e., mathematics, science, history, English, German, etc. For another, the differences in numbers of faculty also serve to complicate the organizational difficulty. Faculties of over 100 persons are not uncommon among secondary schools while elementary facilities generally number fewer than 25. There is, therefore, a loss of the personal identity and internalization that is more easily established at the elementary school. Furthermore, the very size of the typical secondary school, both physical because of specialized facilities as well as in the numbers of students housed, precludes the more informal organizational approach so common to elementary schools.

Because students are older and because their educational needs and interests are much more diverse and varied at the secondary school level, the typical secondary school organization tends toward a more formal, more highly regulated activity. Students generally feel a participatory right to the governance structure, and most secondary schools provide instruction at every level of achievement and ability and, in addition, meet the nonformal needs of the student body. Typically, this is done through a variety of cocurricular or extracurricular activities that include athletics, drama, clubs, music, travel, the arts, and other areas of student interest.

Community involvement, too, is generated and accomplished differently. At the elementary level, parents are easily and regularly in attendance at the school for a variety of activities ranging from PTA and school carnivals to teacher conferences and school programs. By the secondary level, parents and students are much more reticent about such intimate and direct involvement, and the community participates in other ways. Perhaps the most direct form of community participation is through attendance at athletic events, productions, and other cocurricular activities. The task of the secondary school staff is to extend this form of "spectator" participation into direct participation in the ongoing activities of the school. Many mechanisms are utilized to do this. Some are quite traditional and institutionalized. These include such activities as the PTA or PTSO, the various booster organizations such as the athletic or band parent groups, or other similar vehicles for involvement. Other methods include increasing the number of ad hoc and ongoing advisory committees becoming institutionalized across the country. As with the elementary delivery effort, community participation in needs assessment (context analysis), planning, priority setting, and evaluation is equally important at the secondary level.

Since the typical secondary school covers a much larger attendance area than the elementary school, the process for community involvement is more complex and difficult. In addition, it is common to include student representation in community involvement activities at the secondary level. The author has found that a more formalized procedure of representation, which guarantees that all geographic areas, all ethnic and racial groups, and all grade levels are included, seems to be most effective. The establishment of a quasi precinct or ward system for such representation is one strategy to be considered. One of the realities to understand is that parents and other community representatives are busy and cannot be expected to spend inordinate amounts of time in nonproductive activities. They are usually quite willing to be in attendance provided the meetings are conducted with some degree of organization and focus on specific issues. Generally, community representatives are quick to respond during crises situations and when priority decisions are to be made. At other times, the prevailing feeling seems to be that the school staff is doing their job and any great intrusion by the community is unwarranted. The principal, as the instructional and administrative leader of the school, sets the tone for the quality and quantity of the involvement process. Most successful principals have done well at getting the community to participate in the educational process of the school. School site-based management procedures mandate active participation by the community in order to be successful.

By virtue of size alone, the educational planning process is more complex at the secondary level. Typically, the organizational schema of a junior high school or high school is along departmental lines (Figure 4.1) As Figure 4.1 shows, the secondary school structure is well-defined with the various department chairpersons assuming much of the responsibility for the delivery of instructional services. The number of departments generally reflects the degree of comprehensiveness at the school and also the systemwide decisions on delivery of services. Typically, the secondary school that is organized along departmental lines will encompass departments in the following areas:

(1) English
(2) Social Studies
(3) Mathematics
(4) Science
(5) Foreign Languages

(6) Physical Education
(7) Office Skills
(8) Industrial Arts
(9) Human Ecology (formerly Home Economics)
(10) Music
(11) Arts

Additionally, specialized areas such as vocational and technical education, advanced placement, drama, dance, and the like are potential inclu-
sions under the departmentalized structure. It becomes a departmental
responsibility to accomplish a needs assessment (context analysis) dealing with the particular discipline as it relates to the gestalt of student
needs. Consideration of not only individual differences as to readiness
but also the variety of depth of offerings must be reflected in the planning
process. It is not unusual to have the community involved with the principal and staff to develop broad instructional guidelines that reflect board
of education goals and objectives and establish departmental parameters
that will provide the basis for instructional planning at the departmental
level. In that type of operation, the departments utilize community and
students to assist in educational planning and priority establishment.
Such involvement assures diversity of scope and sequence. It is essential
that the principal's office remain informed and involved to guarantee that
board objectives and school priorities are addressed in departmental
planning. The well-established and effective secondary school provides a
balance in its programmatic efforts. It reflects the diversity and capacity
of the student body. It should also reflect the quality of educational opportunity provided the students. Because the principal is the person
responsible for the educational delivery process, (s)he must be actively
involved and, ultimately, make the decisions on the viability of the
various recommendations.

There are, of course, a number of school organizational patterns. They
usually reflect local preferences and desires and/or school system guidelines. Figure 4.2 is a model that suggests a different form of school organization. In Figure 4.2, the departments are grouped into four general
areas with the lead teacher providing the coordinating and directing func-
tion(s). As Figure 4.2 indicates, the student services and administrative
functions remain as originally posed in Figure 4.1, but the principal is
much more directly involved with the instructional delivery by virtue of
the close reporting relationship to the lead teachers. What the organizational structure in Figure 4.2 provides is closer coordination of the instructional delivery system and an opportunity to encourage cross disci-

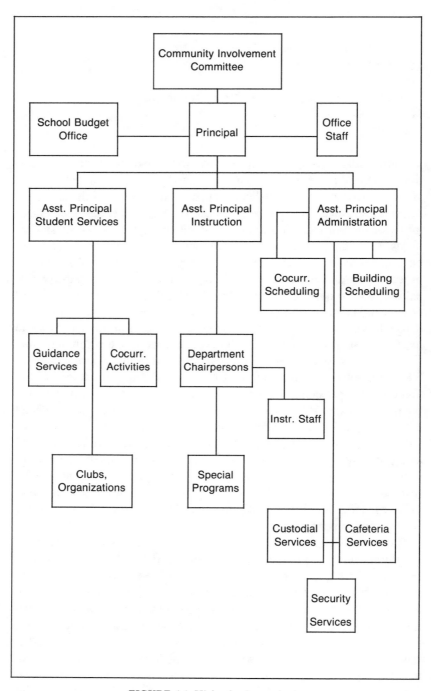

FIGURE 4.1 High school organization.

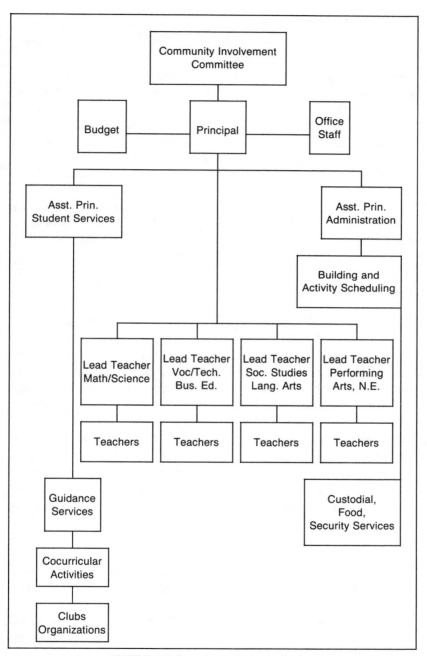

FIGURE 4.2 Secondary school organization.

plinary activity. It (Figure 4.2) forces increased recognition of students as individuals and tends to diffuse the strict and rigid lines so often found in the traditional departmental structure.

Over the past decade, many school systems have provided a series of alternative programs and/or schools to serve students who either cannot function in the traditional school or who have special needs best met by a nontraditional approach to education. The variety and scope of these services is limited only by the limits of human creativity. They range from storefront academies to sophisticated "magnet" schools. Programmatically, they cover the waterfront from the "open" or unstructured curriculum to very highly specialized and formal course activity.

Under the SBM concept, the movement of students from the traditional school to one of the alternative programs results in a reduction of funds available to the original campus of enrollment. Large numbers of student transfers would cause a serious loss of operating revenue and ultimately a loss of teaching staff. Principals generally recognize this reality and attempt to plan a broader program in order to meet the educational needs of students requiring nontraditional approaches. Under SBM, it is not unusual to find a school within a school approach whereby unique programs formulated to meet specific needs are offered in concert with the more traditional programs. Such individual idiosyncrasies as personal time of day preference, learning style differences, and other concerns are increasingly being addressed at the local campus. However, systemwide special purpose programs are and will remain important for reasons of efficiency, effectiveness, and equal educational opportunity.

Increasingly, the secondary schools are providing students opportunities for advanced placement, job-related curriculum options, independent study, testing out of certain course requirements, contracts for specific courses, and other innovative alternatives to the traditional course structure. Also expanding is the modular scheduling and grouping process that departs dramatically from the one-hour-per-day, five-days-per-week approach. It is not unusual to find groupings as large as several hundred for lecture purposes and as small as six for seminar activities. Modular scheduling provides the opportunity to efficiently utilize staff to provide the diverse groupings necessary to contemporary secondary education. A parallel and equally important development is the expanding use of sophisticated technology including computers, television, and other electronic equipment. Increasingly, the technology is being developed to enable greater program diversity and to expand alternatives for students.

The evolution of the middle school as a hybrid between the elementary school and secondary programs is indicative of the concern for the school organizational patterns to more closely reflect student growth patterns and needs. Increasingly, student groupings more compatible to the maturation levels of the students are being attempted. Age groupings from ten to fourteen or eleven to fourteen are more advantageous than eleven to fifteen or twelve to fifteen. Additionally, the fifteen- to eighteen-year-old age grouping is also appropriate. This suggests either a non-graded approach to complement the nongraded elementary or a 5 to 8 or 6 to 8 grade structure. The high school structure becomes grades 9–12. Systems that have committed to the middle school concept are generally organized on a K–4, 5–8, 9–12 or a K–5, 6–8, 9–12 basis. Proponents claim this approach to delivery of educational services is much more responsive to the prepubescent needs of children and allows for a more natural transition to adulthood.

Secondary education is in the process of undergoing considerable change. There have been many reasons presented for the need for change. It appears that a number of traditionally sacred notions are now being questioned and altered. The "comprehensive" high school is now being reconceptualized and it appears that a number of variations will ultimately emerge. The author believes that SBM will be a component of any future model of secondary education. It is becoming increasingly clear that the huge size and enormous enrollments of today's secondary schools is one source of the difficulties being manifested in the secondary schools of the country. A serious plea for personalization of instruction suggests that smaller, more manageable units are appropriate considerations. It also appears that specialty instruction, i.e., vocational–technical, business, etc., will be increasingly provided as a result of public–private sector cooperation. In addition, the expanded use of media and computers will negate the need for huge physical structures. All of this, of course, is in the future and will unfold over the coming decades.

C. ADULT/CONTINUING EDUCATION DELIVERY

School districts are increasingly being called upon to provide educational services to the adult and out-of-school population. The range of educational services requested and needed is most diverse and broad. Sizable numbers of adults are in need of basic education, i.e., elementary education and basic literacy skills. Another large segment of the adult population needs high school completion activities in order to meet either vocational or personal goals. Still another group of adults are in need of training/retraining opportunities in the myriad of business–technical–agricultural arenas. A final and sizeable group desires the multitude of leisure time and enrichment activities that range from flytying, bridge, and belly dancing to chess, investments, and furniture upholstering. These latter activities are viewed as important and excellent linkage opportunities for the school system.

School systems have developed comprehensive adult/continuing education divisions that operate the many programs that may include a complete adult high school often housed in a separate facility and provide for a multitude of basic education and high school courses located at various buildings in the school system (usually secondary facilities in order that needed materials and equipment be available). The leisure time courses are provided at school facilities or other public buildings, private or church facilities, or even industrial and commercial facilities. Many private institutions, i.e., financial and commercial, provide facilities at little or no cost for community use.

The school site management concepts developed in this book require a slightly different application where systemwide delivery is attempted. The adult/continuing education division of the school system is geared toward the provision of a single, systemwide program because of the uniqueness of need, the distribution of clients, and mainly because of the economics of program delivery. Although programs can be and are housed in facilities across the school system, the program planning and delivery responsibility rests with the department of adult and continuing education rather than with the individual campus.

Typically, those programs housed in high school and/or junior high school facilities are late afternoon or evening courses so that they do not interfere or conflict with the regular day school. The needed records and program or student information is best coordinated at the adult/continuing education office so that individual students can best be served as they pursue their educational goals. Perhaps the most simplified explanation of the SBM application to the adult/continuing education department is to consider the entire school system as a single site with all activities coordinated and directed from the office of adult education. With such a consideration, all other procedures and processes can continue uninterrupted. Financial grants and personnel assignments are made by responding to the adult/continuing education department as though it were a single unit rather than a myriad of units across the school system. Of course, as the demand for adult services increases and as the enrollments warrant, some decentralization might be in order so that the most efficient and effective use of the system can be accomplished.

As with any other segment of the school system, the delivery of adult/continuing education services must begin with board of education goals and objectives. Increasingly, boards of education are recognizing their responsibility to the adults of the community by adopting policies relative to the provision of educational services to adults. Such recognition, accompanied by the development of board goals and objectives, serves to initiate the educational planning process as a precondition to the delivery of educational services.

In planning educational programs for adults, one must consider a number of unique characteristics, among them:

(1) The age of the students—while basic literacy skills may be needed, the subject matter must address adult interests and awareness.
(2) The interests of the students—adults generally have rather specific and defined interests. The planning of programs should encompass those interests.
(3) The needs of the students—the panorama of needs that exist among adults require careful attention to the provision of flexibility and diversity of educational programs. Needs as basic as beginning literacy skills and as sophisticated as advanced mathematics and science are sometimes exhibited by the same person. It is therefore difficult to provide services without considering the individual student.
(4) The previous educational experiences of the student—many adults have had negative school experiences (a major reason for their not having finished). Recognition of factors leading to alienation and hostility must be considered as programs are planned. Care must be taken to develop an institutional environment that will not reinforce previous negative experiences. Often the adult student has an extremely low self-concept and must be carefully nurtured in order to remain enrolled.
(5) The educational and personal goals of the student—high school completion is often a prelude to other personal and educational goals. Improvement of skills in order to gain vocational/occupational promotion, qualifying for admission to post high school educational programs, and personal gratification are among the reasons increasing numbers of adults matriculate in adult/continuing education programs.

It is generally true that adults are quite serious about meeting their educational objectives. It is also generally true that many have an underdeveloped educational background and are lacking basic skills as well as adequate study habits. At the same time, adults who muster sufficient courage to enroll in the basic education or high school completion program will work to the absolute limits of their endurance and ability to succeed. It is important that the staff assigned to work with adult basic education and high school completion be selected for their empathy, understanding, tolerance, and commitment to those students. Because the abilities and backgrounds of those who enroll are so different and because the needs and interests are so varied, delivery of programs in the adult/continuing education department is difficult and demanding. Individually prescribed solutions to learning problems are mandated. The ability to allow persons to "comp" out (take competency tests for credit as they reach a desired level of competency) as skills are acquired and refreshed is important. The capacity for the program to accommodate differentiated skills and learning rates is crucial to serving adults.

While some students in the normal K–12 program of most school systems are there because of compulsory attendance laws and tradition, no such formal pressure exists to force adults back to school. The motivating force for adults is largely internal to the person, although job, family, and peer pressure also contribute. In many districts, the adult/continuing education departments actively recruit students for the basic education and the high school completion programs. Indeed, in these days of decreasing enrollments, the identification and recruitment of students needing educational programs is a survival mechanism for many school systems.

Because of the unique nature of adult needs, the flexibility inherent in SBM is most appropriate for the adult/continuing education effort. The head of the department serves much as a school principal in working with staff, community, and students to establish priorities, develop and implement programs, and to evaluate efforts at various stages of implementation. (S)he must have the autonomy (like the principal) to make the many process decisions necessary to good programming. The added flexibility of permitting students to take competency examinations as they feel ready adds to the viability of the program. A number of school systems have further expanded their adult education programs by allowing — indeed encouraging — enrollments to take place any time during the year. These districts provide individual performance contracts for students and depend primarily on personalized instruction and a series of programmed devices (C.A.T., videotape, audiotape, etc.) to enable the student to proceed at their own rate. The classroom teacher assumes a diagnostic–prescriptive role and becomes more of a consultant to the student.

To summarize, the adult/continuing education department of most school systems is a relatively recent and growing unit. This department provides a multitude of services to adults of the community ranging from basic education and high school completion to the variety of leisure time/recreation activities. The programs provided are generally offered in a nontraditional mode, and flexibility is a necessary component. The capacity of a school system to respond to adult needs is perhaps one of the keys to survival in a decreasing enrollment cycle. The provision of educational activities for adults is fast becoming a most important function of the public schools.

D. SPECIAL EDUCATION PROGRAM DELIVERY

The provisions for programs to meet the special education needs of students has become much more of an issue because of Public Law 94–142. Prior to passage of P.L. 94–142, the various states had regulations and program expectations but these varied widely between and among the states. Some states like New York, California, Massachusetts, and Michigan had well-defined and comprehensive requirements for the provision of special eduction services and programs. Indeed, the federal law is patterned after those state laws in many of its requirements. However, the discrepancy between states and, therefore, between local school systems led to a need for a common expectation throughout the country. The resulting P.L. 94–142 is a comprehensive package that requires a considerable undertaking on the part of the various state education agencies as they attempt its implementation.

Besides mandating the whole range of services needed by students, the law requires a series of other actions that serve to create change in the operational pattern of many school systems. For one thing, P.L. 94–142 requires parent advisory groups that imply change. For another, the individual educational plan (IEP) will force considerable change in many school systems. There is increasing evidence that the IEP process will become an important component for all educational planning and will ultimately be a part of every student's planning process.

The mandate of P.L. 94–142 to provide the "least restrictive" environment for students is being slowly interpreted across the country. Briefly, the mandate can be summarized as follows:

(1) There is a duty to identify and locate handicapped children.

(2) Free, appropriate public education must be provided for all handicapped children.
(3) Handicapped children must be educated with nonhandicapped children as much as possible.
(4) An evaluation system to prevent misclassification of children must be developed.
(5) There must be procedural safeguards so parents can challenge actions taken.

Needless to say, the mandate has been accompanied with much rhetoric, foot dragging, and gnashing of teeth. It is being implemented, and emerging legal tests will serve to accelerate implementation. As with most federal legislation, considerable disparity exists between the intent of the law and the final rules promulgated to enforce the law. In many instances, the person(s) formulating the rules had little or no conception of the realities of the field and the result has been chaos.

In spite of the states' differing interpretations of the "mainstreaming" rule, efforts are proceeding in all areas to provide handicapped children educational experiences with the nonhandicapped. Figure 4.3, "Hierarchy of Services for Special Education Programs," presents a schematic interpretation of the mainstreaming principle. Figure 4.3 also implies the need to prevent misclassification of children while, at the same time, avoiding unnecessary expenditures and serving children with appropriate programs.

Special education programs serve a limited segment of the population and generally require the gathering of students from a much broader area to enable the most efficient use of resources and to generate sufficient numbers of similarly afflicted students to enable the delivery of services. Typically, the special education programs serve a number of local school systems, particularly those programs addressing severely and multiply handicapped students. One result of P.L. 94–142 is the decentralization of classroom-type programs to regular classroom facilities to encourage the mainstreaming process. This, of course, causes some concern, particularly among educators who have not previously been involved with special education students and/or programs.

In a SBM situation, the principal must depend upon the special education personnel for support and training. As the administrator in charge, the principal chairs the IEP committee meetings at which the student's program is defined. The IEP committee(s), which includes parental representation, determines the student program, degree of mainstreaming, support services needed, review sequences, and other special assistance

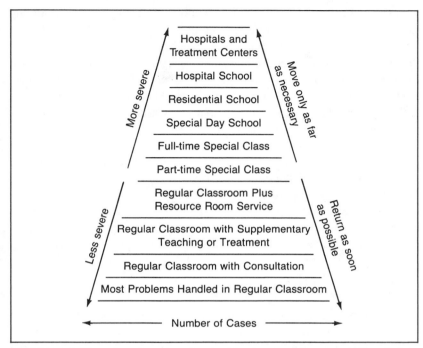

FIGURE 4.3 Hierarchy of services for special education programs. [Adapted from Reynolds, M. C., "A Framework for Considering Some Issues in Special Education," *Exceptional Children*. 37 (1970).]

that might be needed to provide a suitable program. The merging of the regular education staff and program with the special education effort requires patience and tolerance on the part of both groups. The principal must have his/her understanding of the requirements of the law, of the rules as promulgated, of the local goals and objectives, and of the IEP needs of students in order to provide the leadership necessary to successfully implement the mainstreaming mandate.

The planning process is a crucial one for the delivery of special education services. As Figure 4.3 indicates, those needs best met at the lower end of the diagram, from part-time special education classes to problems handled in regular classrooms, are very much in the mainstreaming mode and require assignment of special education students to facilities housing regular education students. Those needs requiring services listed toward the top of Figure 4.3 can be housed in special facilities and/or hospitals located to serve a much broader region.

Special education students, by virtue of their handicap, require the services of a broad range of specialists. The coordination of those services in conjunction with the mainstreaming effort causes concern among some principals. It is the author's opinion that, as the rules are revised and as a rational interpretation of the mandate emerges, the process will become much more effective and more easily incorporated into the total program. Any animosity between special education staff and regular education staff and the protective instincts experienced by those principals who feel threatened by the mainstreaming issue will gradually dissolve into a cooperative, mutually supportive relationship focusing on the needs of children. As with all programs, the key to success is the capacity of the system to remain flexible and to recognize and address the special and diverse needs of students. Historically, special education personnel have accommodated unique and different needs. It is the present challenge to extend that capacity to all students while meeting legal mandates.

E. DELIVERY OF OTHER PROGRAMS

There are a variety of other program needs that do not fit nearly into the rubric defined as an SBM system. These programs are either one of a kind, very sophisticated in terms of equipment needed, require the pooling of students from a wider area to generate sufficient numbers to warrant the program, or are best provided at a specific site as opposed to offering the program at multiple locations. In most instances, economic efficiency forces management consolidation of programs. The following is a brief description of some of these activities. The list is not intended to be exhaustive but merely indicative of the kinds of exclusions that occur.

VOCATIONAL/TECHNICAL/BUSINESS PROGRAMS

In the large, multiple high school systems, dramatic savings in personnel, equipment, and materials can accrue by planning the delivery system so that a minimum of duplication occurs. It is, for example, possible to locate related, compatible, and supportive programs at each high school so that those students enrolled in, say, electronics programs are served at one location, those interested in motor-related curriculum are at another, those enrolled in the building trades are at still another, while students interested in computer technology are assigned a fourth school. These students are housed at their home school for their basic curriculum, but are "shuttle bused" to the school providing one of the special programs for a two- or three-hour vocational block of time. In this manner, expensive equipment is more efficiently utilized, duplication is at a minimum, and sufficient numbers to warrant a full program are generated. Many such vocational/technical/business areas can be effectively provided in this way. Among those known to the author include the following:

(1) Building trades, design architectural drawing, interior design
(2) Automotive trades, body bumping, engine repair
(3) Electronic technology, computer science
(4) Business and office technology, office machine repair
(5) Quantity foods, chef's training, restaurant management
(6) Machine shop, welding, metal trades
(7) Printing, commercial art
(8) Landscape architecture, horticulture, agriculture
(9) Distributive education, sales, display, merchandizing

These areas, and others, can logically be grouped and provided at separate locations. Increasingly, the need arises for additional vocational emphasis. The school system must anticipate and provide those activities.

MAGNET PROGRAMS

The past decade has given birth to a delivery system that provides for special programs to be housed in a special facility. Many times this is an effort to utilize the attraction of an outstanding program in order to encourage voluntary desegregation of students. These schools are identified by a number of titles, among them "magnet" school, the educational "park," academy, cultural–educational complex, or by the special focus of the institution, i.e., performing arts school, school of science, academy of basic education, etc.

As implied, the "magnet" concept provides for the gathering of students from a broad area, drawn by a common educational or career interest, and provides exemplary programs. Those schools exist at either the elementary or secondary levels. Examples abound and include the following:

(1) Walt Disney Magnet in Chicago. An elementary unit serving the northern one-third of the city with a focus on the arts.
(2) The Academic Interest Center in Lansing, Michigan. A secondary center serving the entire city with one-of-a-kind programs. Included are such activities as Russian, aquatic biology, advanced calculus, music composition, and others.

(3) The Parkway School in Philadelphia. A high school using community facilities and resources as the focal point for program development.
(4) The Education Park in Grand Rapids, Michigan. A secondary program housed at the community college campus. Programs range from one of a kind to advanced placement. It serves both public and nonpublic school students.

These and many other special purpose schools abound. A slightly different but nonetheless important development is the growing alternative school movement. These institutions also serve a segment of the student body in unique ways. Typically, all of the alternative schools are devised to treat specific and unique educational needs. Alternative schools fit very well into the concepts of SBM.

GIFTED AND TALENTED PROGRAM DELIVERY

A recent and growing demand made on the school systems of the country is the emerging concern for programs directed to those students who are judged to be gifted and/or talented. The evolution of these programs is fraught with danger. Danger that the criteria used to determine "giftedness" could be unsound, that parental bias can cause confusion, that single criteria (IQ) are used, and that definitions of giftedness are not clear are all included in the number of concerns surfacing that must be considered and addressed. In addition, there is a growing concern over the segregative effects of these programs and over the questionable legality of "tracking" that occurs unless great care is exercised.

In reality, parents are becoming much more vocal in demanding that the special talents of their children be recognized and provided for. The U.S. Department of Education defines gifted and talented via a variety of criteria that include not only the traditional "intelligence" criteria, but also such traits as leadership ability, artistic ability, scholastic ability, and actual performance in order that the full range of talented and gifted students may be recognized.

In a SBM organizational schema, principals attempt to meet the needs of gifted students in a variety of ways. Locally developed "personalized" experiences are most likely to succeed with these children. Also utilized are schoolwide enrichment experiences and activities. These programs are offered during the regular school day as well as in extended-day programs. One of the benefits of SBM is the flexibility it provides. Utilizing this flexibility, groups of principals define common program goals and objectives and jointly provide for gifted and talented needs. In this manner, twenty to thirty students of special talents can be grouped on a regular basis to enable programs relating to their special interest and talent to be efficiently presented. The provision for gifted and talented experiences on an extended-day basis is in keeping with the traditional practice of providing extended-day experiences to those gifted in athletics, music, or theater via the interscholastic programs, the band, and drama programs of most school systems.

However, the gifted movement goes far beyond this schema. It is creating a major demand that produces "pull-out" programs that isolate certain students for a major portion of their educational experience. While this does appease parents and does provide special programs for those students, it also smacks of elitism and of classism that should not be permitted in the public schools. Besides, growing research shows that the pull-out type of programs are not conducive to the kind of development that is best for the students involved. There is increasing evidence to show that these types of academic activities do not provide the appropriate stimulus for the students involved. The concern for and provision for special traits and talents is important and must be recognized, but the creation of a special class and the separation of these students from their peers is cause for concern and must be resisted.

Suffice it to say that the integration of programs to meet special needs of talented and gifted students is an important responsibility of the principal, staff, and community. These special talents must be recognized and nurtured in each individual. Philosophically, the recognition that *every* child is gifted in his or her own way will accommodate much of the existing discrepancy.

SUMMARY

This chapter emphasizes the importance of the building principal in the delivery of educational programs in the SBM approach to school system organization. Because the school campus is the unit in closest proximity to the student, common sense suggests the appropriateness of the SBM approach.

It is important in the development of site-based management that the board of education initiate the process by adopting appropriate policies and goals that encourage the SBM process. In addition, the board and the superintendent must adopt objectives that are product oriented in order that campuses can develop process objectives and methodology.

It is also important that the needed flexibility and support be provided building personnel as they embark on the SBM trail. As dichotomies emerge, cooperative resolution will be needed. Principals must not feel threatened and must open up their campuses so that a variety of needs and concerns may be accommodated.

One final word. The model presented in this book is one of many, many options. The author presents this model because it is one that has been proven successful. There are undoubtedly other models that will prove equally effective and productive. The development of a decentralized system is dependent upon many variables including the mind-set and capacities of the individuals that make up the staff of the school system.

CHAPTER 5

Evaluation
Services

Evaluation is often overlooked in the day-to-day affairs of the school system. In reality, the ongoing evaluation of programs, personnel, and activities may be one of the more important aspects of the quality of effort being extended by the organization.

Programs are mandated by a variety of mechanisms: by state law, by state board of education rules, by local policy, by graduation requirements, by federal law, and by the needs of students. As programs are developed for a particular clientele, they must be delivered to that clientele and then evaluated to see if they (the programs) accomplished what the planners intended. All too often, educators initiate a program and it's left to divine judgement to determine its effectiveness.

In this day of accountability, of wise use of scarce resources, and of increasing competition for the local and state tax dollar, it is important that evaluation efforts be initiated and maintained in order to justify programs and budgets. Especially as one considers the implications of site-based management (SBM) and all that it entails, the need for a well-grounded evaluation process is essential.

As programs are planned, the evaluation process should begin. Questions such as the following should be examined as a result of the evaluation process:

(1) Is the target population being served?
(2) Is the program producing the desired results?
(3) Is the program cost-effective?
(4) Is the program compatible with other programs?
(5) Does the program support the mission of the school?

The integrity and viability of the planning process is dependent on the capacity of the evaluation design and process to stand alone as an independent function of the organization. Ideally, evaluation, while closely aligned and supportive of the planning mechanism, is independent of any other function of the school system. This independence not only allows greater objectivity of process, it also guarantees that the evaluation of any program or activity will be accomplished on its own merits and based on its own performance.

As was described in an earlier chapter on organization, the evaluation function is best performed when it is located under the superintendent and not involved with any of the other functions of the school organization. Ideally, the evaluation process gathers data and presents it in such a way that the decision maker (principal, director, superintendent, board, etc.) can interpret the data and decide the subsequent actions required of him/her.

Evaluation is a process of delineating, obtaining, and providing useful information for judging decision alternatives (Stufflebeam et al. 1971, xxv). In other words evaluation is a mechanism for generating data on which decisions can be made. If performed at its most objective level, alternative situations and data can be examined, and the most appealing and productive decision is possible for the person charged with the decision.

A. ROLE OF EVALUATION

The role of evaluation services is to permit appropriate educational decisions to be made. The making of any single decision is always a complex process. It includes four stages: (1) becoming aware that a decision is needed, (2) designing the decision situation, (3) choosing among alternatives, and (4) acting upon the chosen alternative (Stufflebeam et al. 1971, 50).

Becoming aware that a decision is needed is the first element of the decision-making structure. Awareness has many sources. It may stem from a psychological, cognitive, or experiential base. It may derive from empirical data, subjective judgement, or situational events.

Some decisions are governed by rules, laws, and/or policies. These are known as programmed decisions for they must be made regularly on a cycle. Other decisions are the result of an identification of unmet needs and unsolved problems. As these needs and/or problems surface, they must be faced and resolved. Still other decisions are made as a result of the identification of opportunities for decisions that could be utilized. This mode of awareness is the most risky and least used in education.

Once the need for a decision is evident, the decision maker must design the situation to be processed. Stufflebeam suggests a six-step process for such processing. The six steps are: (1) state the decision situation in question form, (2) specify authority and responsibility for making the decision, (3) formulate decision alternatives, (4) specify criteria which will be employed in assessing alternatives, (5) determine decision rules for use in selecting an alternative, and (6) estimate the timing of the decision (Stufflebeam et al. 1971, 50).

After designing the decision situation, the actual choosing of the decision alternative is the third stage of the decision process. The steps involved in choosing an alternative include (1) obtaining information, (2) applying decision rules, (3) reflection, and (4) confirmation of the indicated choice or recycling.

The fourth stage, that of acting on the chosen alternative involves four steps: (1) fixing responsibility for implementation of the chosen objective, (2) operationalizing the selective alternative, (3) reflecting on the efficacy of the operationalized alternative, and (4) executing the operationalized alternative or recycling.

That the evaluation process is an important component of decision making is ever more clear when superintendents are increasingly called on to justify and clarify decisions. Personal biases and propensities are often dispelled when confronted with hard data and evaluative results.

It is appropriate at this point to develop the relationship between the evaluator and the decision maker. First, the relationship is symbiotic, meaning that the evaluator goes through the same mental processes as the decision maker but does not actually make the decision. Therefore, the evaluator must have close and continuous relationships with the decision makers to be served. Second, the evaluator must provide an extension of the decision maker's resources through analysis and synthesis of data. Third, the evaluator must be aware of the decision-making setting in order to provide appropriately informative data. Fourth, evaluation must involve broad capabilities if the information requirements of decision makers are to be served. Finally, to be effective, evaluation must be a cooperative effort. That is, the evaluator must draw on all disparate parts of the school system for information and data.

B. CIPP—A PLANNING MODEL

CIPP, an acronym for context, input, process, and product types of program evaluation, was developed by Dr. Daniel Stufflebeam of Ohio State University, during the late 1960s and early 1970s. The CIPP model's relationship to decision making continues to be applied to a variety of educational settings throughout the country. According to Stufflebeam's theory, the four evaluation types serve general decision-making categories, as shown in Figure 5.1.

CONTEXT EVALUATION

Although four types of program evaluation are significant in the management of information related to educational programs and services, an understanding of context evaluation is most important to a practicing school administrator. In general, its importance focuses on three factors which oftentimes affect the success or failure of decisions related to school programs. First, context evaluation serves short- and long-range planning decisions. Planning in many school districts becomes an academic exercise of exchanging ideas between colleagues, which leads toward reinforcement of the key decision maker's position on any one of many issues. For reasons of time, lack of know-how (possibly too many staff theoreticians), and commitment (key decision makers are threatened), accommodation of the planning process may be brushed aside as an administrative frill, taking organizational energy away from the operational practices of a school district. Secondly, context evaluation is ongoing or continues throughout the life of an educational program or service. Educational programs are dynamic in nature and therefore vulnerable to change even after extensive systematic planning. If educational programs were planned, developed, and administered in a vacuum void of people, possibly the importance of the ongoing nature of context evaluation would be minimized. Thirdly, context evaluation continues to provide a reference point or baseline of information designed to examine initial program goals and objectives. It allows for a close relationship between decisions based on planned goals and objectives and final pro-

EVALUATION TYPES		DECISION TYPES
Context	services	Planning
Input	services	Structuring
Process	services	Implementing
Product	services	Recycling

FIGURE 5.1 Relationship between evaluation types and decision types.

CONTEXT EVALUATION	PLANNING DECISIONS
Focusing, gathering, and reporting useful information addressing the present and desired program by staff	Using information provided to generate alternatives addressing the present and desired programs by staff
Defining the existing setting and identifiable influences (political, economical and sociological)	Analyzing existing needs, problems and opportunities
Identifying concerns of people reflecting and communicating their values, philosophies and expectations as individuals and in groups	Studying the degree and outcomes of involvement or participation by parties affected
Recommending goas which are compatible with the setting, acceptable to parties affected and adaptable to further refinement into specific objectives	Establishing goals and objectives by which program outcomes can be assessed through the decision making process

FIGURE 5.2 General outline of context evaluation related to planning decisions.

gram outcome. School administrators have the flexibility to examine initial program goals and objectives at any time throughout a program's life, overlay them on what is presently happening in the program, and make a decision to continue, stop, or redirect the program and its resources. The result is avoidance or minimizing "after-the-fact" or "post-mortem" evaluations of educational programs and services following their completion.

Figure 5.2 lists, in general, the kinds of information a school administrator can expect to be provided through a context evaluation and types of planning activities the information services.

As an example or, rather, several examples of context evaluation, consider the typical urban system with its myriad schools and situations. One result of a context analysis is an understanding of the unique strengths, weaknesses, needs, and indigenous resources that can be identified. Because of the realities, no two schools are alike and no two context evaluations should produce like data. As a school profile is constructed, a host of planning data surfaces, data upon which to base program decisions and plans. For example, while two high schools might have similar numbers of Hispanic students, one might house a high incidence of limited English proficiency students (L.E.P.), while the other might enroll a large number of second, third, and fourth generation students whose language skills are very well developed. Consequently, while the first school requires a variety of bilingual/ESL programs, the second school would need far fewer. The school profile would provide data such as ethnic-racial data, S.E.S. data, neighborhood data, staff data, achievement data, etc.

Under the principle of SBM (Site-Based Management), the principal of the particular school would use the context analysis as a planning document to provide important data for the school's program decisions to evolve. Such data would certainly dictate program decisions, the type of internal organization required, the expectations of the clientele and community, the product expectations of the district board of education, and the existing conditions of the school and its programs.

Context evaluation provides the basis for goals and objectives. It allows planning to proceed predicated on realistic objectives and doable expectations. Context analysis allows the decision maker to answer questions related to the how, what, where, and why of a particular situation.

INPUT EVALUATION

As one moves from context evaluation to input evaluation, the focus shifts from planning decisions to allocation of resources in order to meet program goals.

Using the example of the two schools with the large Hispanic enrollment, input evaluation quickly provides data relative to the availability of bilingual/ESL programs at the school with high L.E.P. enrollment while identifying the relative absence of such a need at the second school. Such careful evaluation will provide important data on what is in terms of existing programs and activities. It also provides a good analysis of the efficacy of the existing programs. If, for example, a school's input analysis shows a great emphasis on highly academic, advanced instructional programs while the context evaluation identifies a great need for basic skills emphasis, there obviously exists a great discrepancy between what is and what the needs are. This type of input evaluation will permit the building principal to focus his/her resources on the areas of greatest need and reduce inefficient use and waste of scarce resources.

As a result of input evaluation, adjustments in both type and amount of resources, as well as a shifting of resources, is indicated. Getting back to the example of the two schools, the strategies available to the decision maker to deal with the diagnosed needs in school #1, the school with a high incidence of L.E.P. students, might be as follows:

- to redirect the efforts of the cadre of teachers trained in the more

esoteric instructional programs to the basic level of need identified in the context evaluation
- to reconfigure the staff of the school to include a number of staff
trained to provide instructional services to L.E.P. students
- to add specially trained bilingual/ESL staff to meet the needs of
the L.E.P. students

PROCESS EVALUATION

Once a course of action has been approved and implementation has
begun, process evaluation is necessary to provide periodic feedback to
persons responsible for implementing plans and procedures. Process
evaluation has three main objectives: the first is to detect or predict
defects in the procedural design or its implementation during the implementation stage, the second is to provide information for programmed
decisions, and the third is to maintain a record of the procedure as it occurs (Stufflebeam et al. 1971, 229).

Among the strategies to be followed in process evaluation is the continuous monitoring of the potential sources of failure in a project including interpersonal relationships, communications channels, and adequacy
of resources. Another strategy involves the projecting and servicing of
preprogrammed decisions to be made by project managers during implementation of the project including the choice of specific schools for particular participation in the project. Still another strategy involves the
noting of the main features of the project design, such as the concepts to
be taught and the amount of discussion to hold using this data to describe
what actually takes place. From this comes a determination of whether
or not objectives were achieved. Sometimes the lack of meeting on objective is not the fault of the design or the procedure.

It's important to recognize that the process evaluator(s) rely on both
formal and informal data collection procedures. This includes interaction
analysis, open-end, end-of-the-day reaction sheets, interviews, rating
scales, diaries, semantic differential instruments, records of staff meetings, program evaluation and review technique (PERT) networks, and
other devices.

It's also important to recognize that the process evaluation is a function
of how well the context and input evaluations have been performed. The
more adequate the context and input evaluation, the less critical is the
need for process evaluation, and, conversely, the more poorly developed
the context and input evaluations are, the more demanding and critical is
the need for an adequate and thorough process evaluation.

Process evaluation means the delineation, obtaining, and reporting of information as often as project personnel require such information – especially during the early stages of a project.

Process evaluation is the mechanism through which the project director makes the adjustments necessary to keep the project on track.

PRODUCT EVALUATION

The fourth type of evaluation is product evaluation. Its purpose is to measure and interpret attainments not only at the end of a program cycle, but as often as necessary during the project term.

While product evaluation gives an understanding of what is, policy setters often use product expectations to establish goals and objectives for particular projects and programs. The establishment of a product objective or expectation by a board of trustees or board of education certainly adds a dimension to the reality of context, input, and process evaluation.

Traditionally, evaluation meant product evaluation only, and context, input, and process evaluation are variables which must be added to enable an evaluation process that recognizes as many of the disparate components of the total evaluation contents as possible. Stated another way, product expectation is a legitimate policy matter while context, input, and process are the tools to be utilized, changed, and adjusted to meet product expectations.

Let's go back to the first high school which enrolls a large number of L.E.P. students as an example for consideration. Suppose the board of education sets a product expectation of exit from the L.E.P. program into the mainstream after a maximum of two years. Suppose the product evaluation indicates that after two years in the program, fewer than 30 percent of the students are ready to mainstream. Parallel examination of context, input, and process could reveal the considerations needed to enable the two-year matriculation process to be effective. The adjustment could be in the resources allocated, the processes used, the methodology, or the time allocated. Whatever adjustments are needed can be recommended and tried to enable the product evaluation to meet the product expectation. The data collected and used in the decision process provide important rationale for the decision itself.

Product evaluation must consider a variety of realities as it is conducted. While the results of product evaluation are relatively precise and straightforward, the context, input, and process evaluations can reveal important decision data if the policy setters have established the product expectation at a realistic level. Product evaluations can change as a result of adjustments in input or changes in process used.

To summarize, the CIPP model for decision making provides the best utilization of data and the most flexible parameters for adjustments while maintaining the integrity of the evaluation process. CIPP allows for decision alternatives to be explored and for the decision maker to project cost-effectiveness of a particular project. The use of the CIPP model can simplify the planning process while strengthening the results.

C. PROGRAM EVALUATION AND EVALUATION CRITERIA

A commitment to increasing accountability through managing a program evaluation does not begin or end at either the building or central office level of a school district's operation. A proactive, as opposed to a reactive, school district will encourage a multiplicity of programmatic evaluation activities to take place concurrently in all buildings. To organizationally accomplish the task, the central office of evaluation services must be staffed and supported as an integral part of a school district's line-staff hierarchy (see Figure 5.3).

The key consideration of the organizational chart is the direct line relationship between the director of evaluation services and the superintendent. The implication *is not* that the evaluator does not have working relationships with other central office and district administrators, but the evaluator must have the freedom to focus, gather, and report useful information as close as possible to the individual having ultimate responsibility for decisions affecting school district planning and operational processes. The direct relationship between the superintendent and director of evaluation minimizes design problems created by multiple decision-making levels within the school district, specifically those directed at selecting appropriate criteria for judging whether information provided is useful or nice to have.

In order to support (financially and philosophically) an evaluation services office, the superintendent of schools must trust and have confidence in the information received and used as a basis for decisions affecting the district. Certainly the personal relationships between the superintendent and director of evaluation will be a factor as to whether information provided through a systematic evaluation is used or placed on a shelf to draw dust. Beyond factors of the evaluator's credibility are

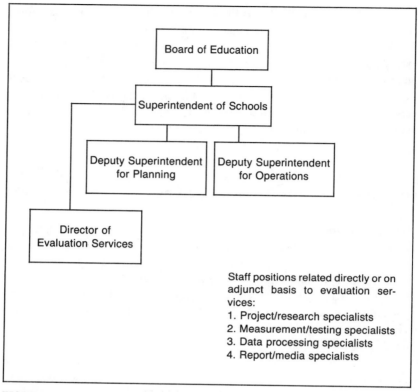

FIGURE 5.3 Line-staff relationship between Director of Evaluation and Superintendent of Schools.

other criteria or standards for determining the value of information by the superintendent.

Stufflebeam et al. (1971, 28) identifies five practical criteria in addition to credibility for judging the value of worth of evaluative information:

(1) **Relevance**—evaluative data are collected to meet certain purposes, and, if the data does not relate to those purposes, they are useless.

(2) **Importance**—a great deal of information can be collected which is nominally relevant for some purpose . . . evaluative information must be culled to eliminate or disregard the least important information and highlight the most important information.

(3) **Scope**—information may be relevant and important but lack sufficient breadth and depth to be useful.

(4) **Timeliness**—the best information is useless if it comes too late (or too soon). . . . Providing perfect information late has no utility, but providing reasonably good information at the time it is needed can make a great deal of difference.

(5) **Pervasiveness** – evaluation designs should contain provisions to dis-
seminate the evaluation findings to all persons who need to know
them.

Practical criteria are important to a decision maker when judging the
usefulness of information provided by the evaluator. Another criterion
considered by the school administrator in determining whether the information received is practical relates to costs of evaluation personnel.

The total cost of employee salaries and fringe benefits range from
eighty to eighty-five cents on the budget dollar in many urban school districts' operational budgets. If the information provided by the evaluation
office continually falls into the nice-to-have but seldom used category, the
office becomes an administrative frill and a low priority at budget preparations time.

Practical criteria are not the only standards a school administrator
should apply to judging the worth of information received from the evaluation office. The following scientific criteria, according to Stufflebeam et
al. (1971, 27–28), are equally important:

(1) **Internal validity** . . . the information must be "true." A more accurate way is to state that there must be a close, if not one-to-one, cor-
respondence between the information and phenomena it represents.
(2) **External validity** . . . refers to the "generalizability" of the information. Does the information hold only for the sample from which it
was collected or for other groups (or the same group at other times)
as well?
(3) **Reliability** . . . refers to the consistency of the information. If new
data were gathered, would the same findings result? Reliability . . .
depends to a great extent on the nature of the instruments (used in
gathering the information).
(4) **Objectivity** . . . is concerned with the "publicness" of the information. . . . Would everyone competent to judge agree on the meaning
of the data?

Figure 5.4 displays the relationship between context evaluation, activity, criteria for judging the value of information identified, and degree of
usefulness in making alternative planning decisions.

In general, the use of practical and scientific criteria is ensuring that an
evaluation process (CIPP) will reveal and communicate accurate information about the program or service being studied. The degree of accuracy by which information is judged is not only the responsibility of
the evaluator, but also the decision maker who uses or chooses not to use
any or all of the information provided.

Assuming a school superintendent is convinced that evaluative information does enhance the decisions he or she makes, the issue of install-

CONTEXT EVALUATION	INFORMATION CRITERIA	PLANNING DECISIONS
Focusing, gathering and reporting useful information addressing present and desired programs.	Practical 1. Credibility of evaluator 2. Relevance 3. Importance 4. Scope 5. Timeliness 6. Pervasiveness 7. Cost	Using information provided to generate alternatives addressing present and desired programs.
Defining the existing setting and identifiable influences (political, economical and sociological).	Scientific 1. Internal validity 2. External validity 3. Reliability 4. Objectivity	Analyzing existing needs, problems and opportunities.

FIGURE 5.4 Relationship between informational criteria, context evaluation activity, and planning decision services.

ing evaluation services as a department within a school district remains difficult. The difficulty is justifying personnel, other operational costs, and the evaluation department's goals and purposes.

D. JUSTIFYING THE INSTALLATION OF AN EVALUATION SERVICES UNIT

In many school districts the issue of installing an evaluation services unit or office is one of reorganization. For example, most central offices have units defined as testing, research, and planning services. Combining these operations to philosophically approach the focusing, gathering, and reporting of useful information for decision making could merit a change in title to office of evaluation and planning or evaluation services. Support personnel with expertise in testing and research would be an integral segment of the staff. It is conceivable the new evaluation services office could contract with other school districts in the area and thereby minimize operational costs. Reorganizing and becoming cost-effective are two methods of installation that may be saleable to a budget conscious board of education.

Equally important is the stated purpose or goals of the evaluation services office. One justifiable goal may be to provide evaluation services for systemwide programs. Another goal for the evaluation department may be to assist building staffs in designing and conducting their own evaluations of programs.

A third goal of an evaluation department may be to continually examine and test internal school district practices with agencies outside the district. The goal encourages the sharing of evaluative methodologies with smaller districts lacking an evaluation department or a state or university project requiring field-based evaluative applications. The writers are quick to caution that the three general goals of servicing central and building needs of the district must be heavily weighted with respect to the goals of working with outside agencies. Otherwise, the district may have difficulty justifying an evaluation department's existence.

In summary, an evaluation department responsiveness to school district systemwide needs for accountability based on board of education policies and goals, as well as acceptable administrative philosophies and practices, will initially justify the department's role in the organization. Continued support for the department's worth will be judged on the effectiveness of evaluators as a group and as individuals working to support other departments and buildings located throughout the district. Theoretical and technical competence of the evaluation department in areas of testing, research, statistics, report writing, and program design is assumed. The skills and ability of the evaluator to relate to decision makers at all levels is not assumed. Therefore, the evaluation director's responsibilities must include the knowledge that the school district is first and foremost in the people business. Through direct and indirect involvement with the evaluation staff and others in the district, the director must continually blend technical problem-solving skills of individuals with those of being human.

E. EVALUATION FOR SPECIAL PURPOSES

In the late 1970s and accelerating into the 1980s, many state and local education agencies began utilizing evaluation data for decisions related to sunset regulations established by state governments and/or by local policy. As the budget pinch became more severe and as the accountability movement gained momentum, many states adopted sunset procedures, whereby each program is reviewed systematically in a sequence and with evaluation results as an important part of the data to determine whether or not the program is to be extended or dropped from the funding pattern of the state.

As the chief executive officer of two urban districts during the 1970s and 1980s, the author had the opportunity to suggest a sunset policy to the board of education. The policy called for a sunset review of all programs on a three-year cycle utilizing evaluation data produced by application of the CIPP model. The data clearly showed which programs were meeting objectives, which were cost-effective, which were not productive, and which should be carefully screened and eliminated. The process works well as long as it's objective and dispassionate. However, when someone's favorite program is questioned or someone's creative idea is shown to be wanting, subjectivity prevails, and the sunset process is subverted.

Policy makers are politicians first and foremost. They create, support, and advance programs for a variety of reasons, not the least of which is political. When a politician's favorite program is judged inadequate and recommended for termination, all kinds of machinations are set in motion to preserve and protect the program. It is indeed a strong executive that can survive in the face of that reality. It is even more crucial that the evaluation process be precise and explicit with irrefutable data to support recommendations for the sunsetting of a program. In the final analysis, if the evaluations and recommendations are consistent, the executive has done his/her job and it's now the policy bodies' turn to focus on the issues.

Because the CIPP model is such an all-inclusive model, the opportunity to redirect and refocus resources at the input and process stages of evaluation can be a face-saving device to allow favorite programs to be made effective and productive rather than face the political consequences engendered by sunsetting decisions. At any rate, the CEO can recommend a variety of options, including elimination of a program, as a result of the CIPP process. At that point, the policy board takes the recommendations and alternatives and makes the final decision that includes the political considerations as well as the program considerations.

F. PERSONNEL EVALUATION

Many school districts have well-defined and developed personnel evaluation procedures. In the late 1970s such districts as Mesa, Arizona; Salt Lake City, Utah; Lansing, Michigan; and Columbus, Ohio, utilized personnel evaluations as an important step in the staff development process. Their evaluative efforts focused primarily on the use of the evaluation as a springboard to the development of a professional growth plan to enable the educator to become more effective and proficient in his/her task.

A by-product of the education reform movement of the early 1980s has been the demand to implement statewide educator evaluations and often to tie evaluation to salary. Tennessee, South Carolina, Georgia, and Texas have been among the leaders in this development.

For example, in Texas, the state legislature mandated education reform in 1984 with the passage of House Bill 72. Among the many requirements of H.B. 72 was the formal evaluation of educational personnel tied to a career ladder. The Texas Education Agency was required to develop and implement a teacher evaluation process by the 1985–1986 academic year and a management training and assessment procedure beginning with the 1987–1988 academic year. Among the requirements imposed by the legislature were a minimal skills examination for all educators to retain and/or gain certification. In addition, all entering juniors interested in becoming educators were required to pass a basic skills test and all graduating teachers are to pass an exit examination in their major and in pedagogy. In the summer of 1987, the legislature passed a number of clarifying statutes which are intended to simplify the process.

Among the requirements of H.B. 72 was the completion of a forty-hour instructional leadership training sequence along with a thirty-six-hour evaluation training program for all administrators. Additionally, teachers have to participate in advanced academic training to qualify for advancement on the career ladder. These advanced academic training offerings include graduate level classes, specific programs developed by service centers and/or universities, programs devised by statewide organizations, and programs developed by private vendors. Approval must be obtained from the state education agency before a program is certified.

In the summer of 1987, the Texas legislature passed a statute limiting the number of credit hours in education required for a baccalaureate degree to eighteen hours including six semester hours in student teaching. The statute also eliminated baccalaureate degrees in education so that every prospective teacher must declare a subject matter major. It is possible to generate group majors in language arts, social science, and science but the emphasis is to be in-depth knowledge of a particular field.

These and other developments in the education reform movement of the 1980s lend strength to the opinion that education and education governance, policies, and standards are increasingly being established at the state level by governors and legislative bodies which delegate the purvues of the local district.

The recent and consuming focus on accountability results from both the general decline in student performance coupled with a dramatic increase in education costs, most of which are generated from the state capital. With increased awareness of the importance of education to the general welfare of the state and the realization that education is the largest single expenditure in the state, the demand for accountability accelerated rapidly, culminating in a variety of state mandates for personnel and program evaluations and for a number of sunset provisions intended to force inappropriate and ineffective programs out of existence.

The intent, while well-intended and appropriate, is still in the formative stage so results of these various activities are still nebulous and tentative.

CHAPTER 6

Financial Services
(with Gary L. Wegenke)

A. PURPOSE

One of the big dilemmas facing today's educator is providing instructional services at the student's level. A few school districts are making progress in developing instructional methodologies directly related to specific needs of students by utilizing building-level budgeting. These school districts are providing increased fiscal flexibility at the building level in an attempt to heighten the impact of program decisions on individual student growth. The degree of fiscal flexibility suggested by such an effort mandates that the staff and principal of a specific building become more intimately associated with day-to-day budgeting and budget control processes.

Historically, teacher and administrative training programs have not provided teachers and principals with the background needed to understand nuances of budgeting and fiscal resource allocation. This chapter has been prepared as a basic guideline to enable principals and other educators to appreciate and understand building-level fiscal approaches associated with educational decision making and problem resolution.

The departure from traditional centralized administrative methods is possible when building principals, their staffs, and communities have the capacity to control the budget of a particular building and have the necessary expertise to continually match student needs with available resources. Underlying this document is the realization that children vary from one another. Building principals and staffs must recognize these differences (e.g., cultural, ethnic, and socioeconomic) and programmatically serve the varying levels of their students by utilizing strengths of staff and community and by deploying fiscal resources to meet priority issues. It is assumed that a carefully planned needs assessment of students be performed in the local district before building priorities are established.

Implementation of the building budget process is dependent on the principal's capacity and skill to coordinate the various planning and operational components of a total educational program. Inherent in the process is the principal's ability to work with a limited number of dollars to meet specific student educational needs.

This is not a simple process. It's new, it's different, and it will take some effort on the part of building-level administrators to redefine their traditional roles by absorbing and applying fiscal management techniques encouraged by the building budgeting process, a process that allows the building staff to be proactive rather than reactive. The process forces planning and operational educational decisions to be made at the level closest to the student: the building level. The building budgeting process also encourages imaginative principals to proceed with the development of unique educational programs. It is limited only by the professional training and capacity of principals and their staffs.

The role of central administrative staff is also dramatically changed. Central administrators become support rather than line personnel. They become facilitators to be utilized by building staffs and the community to further enhance educational concepts unique to a building's service area. Therefore, a close dialogue between community members and school staff is encouraged.

The following sections are designed to provide useful guidelines for a building-based budget process.

B. BUDGET COMPONENTS

SCHOOL BUDGET COMPOSITION

Despite the mystique that has developed around the so-called intricacy of school finance and school budgets, it is possible to simplify the process. The educational system is charged with providing educational services to its clients. This is accomplished by delivering programs directly to students. The delivery process invariably involves professionally trained educators meeting with students and their parents, either in groups or individually, to accomplish the task. In addition, the process includes the provision of support services to the direct teacher–learner relationship. These support activities are defined as direct instructional support (i.e., pupil personnel, psychological, sociological) and noninstructional support (i.e., maintenance, custodial, food service, transportation).

Approximately 85 percent of a school district budget is allocated to personnel. Another 8 percent to 9 percent of total costs are allocated to so-called fixed costs, such as utilities, fringe benefits, insurance, and interest costs, over which little control can be exercised. The remaining 6 percent to 7 percent of the total budget is allocated to supplies, materials, and equipment used in the system, including instructional as well as noninstructional materials.

It is important to the educational process to develop a mechanism that permits more than the limited 6 percent to 7 percent of resources to be used for unique student needs as identified at the building level. A growing number of educators feel this is best accomplished through a flexible system of allocating personnel and resources at the building level.

Many school districts are restricted in personnel allocations by union contracts that specify pupil–teacher ratios and determine class size. However, many union contracts permit deviation from contract language for specific educational purposes. At the very least, the specific use of professional personnel as determined by the educational needs of the student body of a particular building will allow for reasonable flexibility in utilizing personnel. The application of staff strengths to highest priority educational needs is the most important task faced by the building principal. Similarly, the allocation of nonprofessional instructional personnel (i.e., aides, clerical staff) can enhance an educational program. It is appropriate that such allocation be made at the building level.

Conversely, the application of noninstructional support services, such as maintenance, transportation, data processing, food services, payroll, and purchasing, is best accomplished at districtwide or even regional/ state levels because of the potential reduction in units costs for such services.

Since the personnel portion of the school budget is so great and since union agreements sometimes dictate size of staffs, it becomes a matter of deploying staff so program needs can be met. The building principal must have the leadership responsibility for such deployment, and it must be predicated on careful needs assessment and priority establishment.

NONSTAFF BUDGET COMPONENTS

The portion of the typical school budget allocated to nonpersonnel items is roughly 15–18 percent. Of this, some 8–9 percent is utilized to pay for so-called fixed costs over which little direct control can be exercised. Minor savings can be effected in certain areas such as utilities by setting thermostats at a lower level or by cutting the number of lights in buildings. However, even with such conservation measures, the net savings are usually much less than the increased cost of energy, which has more than doubled in the past decade.

Similarly, insurance costs, interest charges, and fringe benefits are all undergoing dramatic increases, leading to the speculation that the fixed cost portion of the school budget will continue to rise in the coming decades. Certainly, legislative mandates and contractual agreements will not lower the impact of fixed costs.

If personnel costs (82–85 percent) and fixed costs (8–9 percent) allow little direct discretionary control to the building principal, what then is the potential for exercising building-level determination over the remaining 6–7 percent of the school resource?

Significantly, this 6–7 percent must cover all nonpersonnel and nonfixed components of the school budget. Among these items are the following:

(1) Consumable supplies and materials, instructional and noninstructional. Included are paper, crayons, lab, music, shop and office supplies, custodial materials, gasoline for vehicles, carpentry supplies, and electrical supplies.
(2) Materials such as films, globes, books and other printed matter, balls, uniforms, tapes, and records
(3) Equipment, instructional and noninstructional. Vehicles, typewriters, copy machines, commercial ovens, videotape recorders, walkie-talkies, refrigeration equipment, and electronic microscopes are examples.

Typically, almost one-half of the supply/equipment allocation is used for noninstructional items and roughly one-half for instructional purposes.

Given the reality of school budgets, it is understandable that, short of staff reductions, the only way to adjust expenditure to income is by manipulating the supply/equipment portion of the budget. Therefore, it is common to delay purchase of major equipment during periods of financial shortfall. Amortization schedules, so common in business and industry, are virtually unknown in school systems, and it is not uncommon to use equipment until it literally collapses from age and use.

For the principal, utilizing nonstaff, nonfixed resources requires great skill when determining priorities and when planning ahead for major purchases. Wise planning dictates contingency funding as well as accumulation of resources for major equipment addition and/or replacement. Stretching supply dollars and procuring multi-use items are the marks of the more resourceful educational leaders.

BUDGET COMPONENT SUMMARY

Figure 6.1 outlines a summary of the components that comprise the school budget. It does not follow the prescribed accounting manual but, rather, is a recognition of the three major delineations identified in the previous discussion.

The foregoing emphasizes the restrictive nature of the school budget and the limits of what can be considered discretionary resources. The next section presents a model for building-level budgeting that permits flexibility in the allocation of resources.

C. BUILDING ALLOCATION PROCEDURES—A MODEL

STAFF ALLOTMENTS

Assuming that a school system makes a decision to share budget prerogatives with building principals, staff, and community and that after careful study it is decided that the direct delivery of educational services

---

I. Personnel (82–85% of total budget)
   A. Instructional
      1. Professional—teachers, administrators, specialists (certificated)
      2. Nonprofessional—aides, clerical and technical personnel
   B. Noninstructional
      1. Professional—engineer(s), administrators, specialists, analysts, accountants
      2. Nonprofessional—custodians, skilled craftsmen, cooks, bakers, clerical and warehouse personnel, drivers, technicians
II. Fixed Costs (8–9% of total budget)
   A. Utilities
   B. Insurance
   C. Fringe Benefits
III. Other Costs (6–7% of total budget)
   A. Supplies and Materials
   B. Equipment (new and replacement)

FIGURE 6.1 Components of a school budget.

is appropriately the purview of the building, what then can be presented as a model for such a decision? Based on the experiences of districts that have studied the process and implemented it for a number of years, it is felt that union agreements, contract language, community expectations, staff and principal capacity, and student needs all must be considered in developing a model flexible enough to serve diverse school systems. For purposes of such development, the following assumptions are made:

(1) Classroom teacher/pupil ratios are fixed by union contract or by state law.
(2) The building is led by a nonteaching principal.
(3) A variety of noncertificated instructional personnel are part of the staff.
(4) Instructional specialists in art, music, physical education, and media are available on either a full- or part-time basis.
(5) Deployment of teaching personnel can be either through self-contained scheduling or by team/departmental/differentiated procedures.

Given these parameters, how does the school system provide flexibility to principals and their staffs so that they can direct their best effort toward meeting educational needs of students?

Although the number of teachers assigned to a particular building is often based upon a negotiated agreement that specifies a ratio of students to teachers, the deployment of staff does not necessarily have to be entirely on the self-contained classroom concept at the elementary level or predicated upon each class meeting daily for one period at the secondary level. Optimum use of teaching staff is possible when professional staff are assigned to areas of staff strength and when support personnel are used for tasks better performed by nonprofessional staff.

The model proposed assumes such staff deployment, but goes beyond to include the potential of diverting resources according to specific needs at the building level. Figures 6.2 and 6.3 illustrate the proposed model for elementary and secondary schools.

Many variations of Figures 6.2 and 6.3 are possible. The model provides that buildings receive personnel resources according to contract, either in the form of staff or equivalent dollars figured at the average teacher's salary. It is important to indicate that existing staff members are not discharged to create equivalent dollars. Only when attrition creates openings is the model operable. Given normal conditions, however, such opportunities are readily available.

ASSUMPTIONS
1. Student enrollment 600 students
2. Nonteaching fulltime principal
3. Contract calls for funding at a 1/30 teacher/pupil ratio
4. Music/art/physical education/media personnel are assigned according to a district plan
5. Secretarial personnel assigned on a 1/30 student ratio
6. Instructional aides assigned on a 1/100 student ratio

STAFF ALLOCATIONS AS DETERMINED ABOVE ARE
1. Twenty classroom teachers
2. Two secretaries
3. Six aides
4. Principal
5. Assorted specialist personnel in music, art, physical education, and instructional media

Additionally, all staff allocations are based on actual personnel employed or in equivalent salary amounts. For example, an equivalent salary amount for teachers is the average teaching salary in the district. The average salary is $27,000/year.

As the staff, community and principal develop educational priorities for the program, several important plans are adopted. These include:

1. The need for consultative assistance in teaching basic skills, i.e., reading and math
2. A need for programmed materials
3. A priority for increasing the number of aides from six to ten

In terms of dollar needs, the plan calls for the following:

1. One reading specialist	$27,000
2. Materials	4,000
3. Three aides @ $7,000 each	21,000
TOTAL	$52,000

To generate the needed resources ($52,000) the building staff determines that it can provide basic classroom instruction with eighteen rather than twenty classroom teachers. Since the building qualifies, by contract, for the twenty teachers, the equivalent dollars or 2 x $27,000 is allocated to the building to be used in meeting program objectives. This amount is the average teacher's salary multiplied by the number of positions not filled. The principal is then able to hire a reading specialist and three aides and provide for programmed materials. (In the event only one opening is available, the staff could reassign an existing staff person to the reading specialist role and, with equivalent funding for one position, accomplish the same objectives.)

The potential of this example is limited only by the limits of human creativity. One district has, under this model, provided great program diversity to its elementary program.

FIGURE 6.2 Elementary staffing.

ASSUMPTIONS
1. Enrollment 1,500 students
2. Principal and three assistant principals
3. Contract calls for maximum pupil/teacher ratio ranging from 1/28 in English to 1/50 in physical education
4. Counseling staffs meet North Central guidelines
5. Vocational programs meet state/federal guidelines
6. Clerical positions are assigned on a 1/150 student ratio
7. Instructional aides are assigned on a 1/150 student ratio
8. Media professionals assigned on a 1/750 student ratio

STAFF ALLOCATIONS BASED UPON THE ABOVE ARE
1. Eighty teachers (including vocational education staff)
2. Six counselors
3. Two instructional media (library) staff
4. Four administrators
5. Ten clerical staff
6. Ten instructional aides

The building staff, community, and principal agree on the following priorities as part of the educational plan for the coming academic year:

1. The establishment of four study centers, each to be staffed by a professional trained in English, math, science, and social science as well as two aides.
2. A program of videotape material collection to be initiated at a cost of $5,000 per year.
3. Materials totaling $12,000 needed for initiation of the program.

The proposed four centers can be staffed by absorbing three teaching positions, which will generate 3 x $27,000 (average salary) or $81,000 for use by the building. Using the money generated by staff reductions, the building can meet the identified priorities as follows:

1. Assign four center leaders from existing staff $ 0
2. Employ eight aides at $7,000 each   56,000
3. Purchase center materials   12,000
4. Develop videotape libarary   5,000

    $73,000

Balance for other uses is $8,000.

FIGURE 6.3 Secondary staffing.

FOUNDATION ALLOTMENT

A second major item of concern to principals is the utilization of those resources allocated for supplies, materials, and equipment. The model provides for block grant allocations to buildings for these items on the basis of an amount per student. This allocation replaces the line item amounts generally found in school accounting procedures. The building principal, the staff, and the community determine the type and number of line item allocations. They determine how much will be allocated to capital outlay, to textbooks, to library books, and to general supplies.

Once that determination is made, the central office must be notified how the block grant has been distributed so budget control mechanisms can operate for the protection of the total system. On a periodic basis, usually weekly, buildings receive printouts indicating the status of each of the supply, material, and equipment accounts they have identified, the amount of encumbrances, and the current status of available budget. Should there be a need for shifting of funds from one account to another during the year, a simple form will handle that transaction. In this manner, funds are allocated equitably to all buildings in the school system on a per pupil basis, eliminating central office judgements as to how these resources are to be expended. The central office does oversee that building totals do not exceed the amount of the block grant.

Internal shifting of resources to meet emergency needs is the purview of the building principal. The foundation allowance provides for teaching supplies, textbooks, instructional materials, replacement of equipment, new equipment, or whatever the building educational plan calls for. Limits on foundation allowances are faced by all school systems.

CATEGORICAL FUNDS

Many school systems receive categorical funds by virtue of qualifying for one or more of the various state and/or federal programs. These may be Title I funds, Article 3 funds, bilingual funds, or migrant funds. They are devised to meet specific kinds of needs found in school buildings and school systems. All categorical funds in the model are allocated on a per pupil basis to buildings. The use of categorical funds must be incorporated into the total educational plan of the building. Typically, categorical funds are used to hire staff, to buy supplies and equipment, to hire specific consultative help, and the like. They are passed through to individual buildings in the form of block grants earmarked according to the specific category for which the funds are received. They must be utilized for that particular kind of program, but the deployment of those resources either in the form of personnel or materials is strictly the purview of the building staff.

GRANTS

School systems apply for and receive grants from a number of agencies and foundations. In addition, many school systems have devised internal grant systems for addressing particular educational needs. Much the same as the categorical funds allocation, the grant allocation is funneled to the building level in the form of a block allocation. The use and dispersal of these funds is dependent upon the educational plan devised for that building.

A model of the type just described creates a need for greater fiscal management sophistication on the part of principals. Principals, however, do possess this potential and have for decades been anxious to assume such leadership responsibility. It is, therefore, an evolving model that can be utilized and changed to accommodate the particular characteristics of a school system.

D. BUDGET CONTROL PROCEDURES

Coordination of fiscal information between the central office and the buildings is a key step in the implementation of the budget process. It is the responsibility of the finance office to develop, with the cooperation of the building principals, a budget control procedure. The procedure focuses on (1) an equitable method of distributing building funds (autonomous funds) on a yearly basis; (2) sufficient time for building principals, their staff, students, and parents to plan for the best use of available resources; (3) a systematic monitoring of all building funds; and (4) the establishment of a purchasing process to accommodate building budget expenditure requests.

DISTRIBUTING BUILDING FUNDS

Each year before the board of education accepts the school district's budget, a decision must be made as to how much money should be allotted to buildings as autonomous funds. In order to maintain equity between buildings, the amount is based on the number of students enrolled per building. Enrollment figures are projected in January for buildings and adjusted on the official final enrollment count submitted to the state for state aid monies.

Program assumptions related to dollars required also become a variable to be considered in fund allocation. A distinction between elementary, junior high, and senior high fiscal needs is one method of approaching the problem. The need to differentiate between levels of education because of higher costs associated with higher levels of education can lead to differences in basic allowances by level.

In the area of initial allowances, specialized programs requiring expensive equipment and large quantities of consumable supplies generally mandate larger allocations for junior and senior high schools as compared with elementary schools. Differences based on programmatic emphasis (e.g., an all-student requirement involving industrial arts or home economics in the junior high) will cause fiscal differences between junior and senior high program costs.

Another dimension to autonomous funds involves the unique use of personnel and the budget. A model for utilization of certificated personnel, presented earlier, was predicated on flexibility in staffing buildings, thereby allowing building staffs to design a variety of differentiated staffing arrangements.

Fiscal appropriations for additional supervision, clerical support, and extra personnel beyond normal classroom needs are important to consider when defining building programs. Supervision may vary from elementary lunchroom duties to ticket-taking at a senior high school basketball game. Funding decisions for the above purposes must consider revenues engendered locally (ticket sales, etc.) as well as contractually determined rates of reimbursement.

Because of size, elementary schools usually have more difficulty in meeting supervisory needs. A secondary school with three or four times the staff may find the task much easier. Therefore, a difference in autonomous dollars allocated for supervisory aides may vary per student from elementary to junior high to senior high. Clerical support will also vary depending on student enrollment and responsibilities unique to elementary and secondary operations. However, the unit cost of clerical support throughout the district is defined by contract.

The ability to generate revenue for paying supervisors for extra assignments (e.g., ballgame ticket-taking) is greater at the secondary level. An internal accounting system is established at all levels of building operations. Such a system allows individual buildings additional fiscal flexibility beyond autonomous funds. Monies generated by the school through athletic events, drama productions, and class and club activities are a few areas found in the internal account of buildings, the larger of which are found in high schools. Therefore, principals and their staffs are charged to plan the wise usage of both autonomous and internal account funds to meet student needs.

PLANNING THE USE OF FUNDS

In order for building principals to involve staff, parent organizations such as the Community Involvement Committees (CIC) or PTA, and student organizations in the budget process, initial direction and ample time must be provided by the central finance office. The degree of group involvement in the budget process will vary based on the management abilities of the principal.

Projections made the previous year are the basis for original allocations. Final budget revisions are made according to the official final enrollment of each building. Most building principals have learned to prepare for a slight gain or loss in monies by placing from 10 to 15 percent of their projected budget in a contingency account. The impact of gains or losses is felt in the contingency account and not necessarily in accounts affecting building operations.

As an example, a secondary principal and his staff plan courses based on projected enrollments. If more students are actually taking a course on final enrollment day, an adjustment is made internally to provide the instructor with extra resources. On the other hand, a decrease in a specific course's enrollment would cause a proportionate decrease of funds. The particular secondary building makes per pupil adjustments not only on the final enrollment day in the fall, but also on an internally designated enrollment day in the spring semester.

Once adjustments for enrollment are made, a regular monitoring of the budget is accomplished with the aid of data provided by the finance office. The details of the monitoring process are discussed later. Using detailed budget reports identifying building accounts and monies budgeted, encumbered, and expended, the principal, staff, CIC, PTA, and student organizations can begin to note trends between projected budget figures and actual expenditures. Decisions are made during the year to revise original budget projections in accordance with actual budget expenditures. The principal is held accountable by the finance office for any budget revisions made while the budget is being implemented. A few principals have delegated budget monitoring to their head secretary and/or building treasurer.

As semester and fiscal years pass, budget histories are established.

These financial histories, based on monies budgeted and expended are useful in providing fiscal projections for succeeding years. Building account histories coupled with finance office direction early in January provide the basic information and time needed to complete budget projections by the end of May.

Between January and May, building principals and staffs are busy with day-to-day operational matters. In order to involve staff, parents, and students in the planning of next year's budget, a time line must be established by the building principal. The time line is determined by the data available, staff awareness of student needs, existing resources, and community expectations. Building priorities are established through extensive dialogue among the various publics and must be consistent with school district goals.

In April or early May, final decisions related to the new budget must be arrived at by all parties concerned. Although all members involved in the budget process may not agree with final allocations, they must at least understand the rationale for projecting next year's budget. The final budget document must reflect (a) adequate time and information for determining client needs, (b) school district goals and building priorities, (c) use of past fiscal budget information (reports), and (d) a concerted effort by all parties to operate within the budget for one fiscal year.

MONITORING BUILDING FUNDS

Once a building budget has been approved by building planners and revised in accord with student enrollment, the monitoring process becomes extremely important. Fiscal accountability between a building and the finance office (central administration) is based on a successful routine information flow between both parties.

Aiding the fiscal information flow process requires an extension of most school districts' accounting systems to include autonomous fund accounts at the building level. Secondly, a direct relationship between accounts and data processing must be established. Finally, internal auditing procedures must be established at the district and building levels to make certain expending of the autonomous budget takes place as planned.

One district uses a six-digit accounting system which supplies fiscal information to decision makers at the board of education, central administration, building, and outside agency levels. Building principals report budget figures on a document which allows for a differential in excess of 250 accounts. The sizeable number of accounts available to buildings for budgeting purposes permits principals and their staffs to more adequately monitor their own expenditures. For example, a differentiation among monies budgeted for repairs, supplies, and equipment in a typing class can be quickly identified by looking at a building's account structure.

A biweekly budget report from the finance office is sent to each building principal. The building code number precedes the account number, followed by a brief description of the account. Monies budgeted, encumbered, and expended are itemized on the biweekly report. Close monitoring of the report allows a building's budget committee to make revisions (transfers of monies) at any time there is a need to do so. Generally speaking, revision needs occur when planned expenditures exceed monies budgeted. The correction shold be made within the specific account structure. For example, if the supply account in industrial arts/woods becomes overdrawn, the deficit should be handled from funds within the same industrial arts account structure. The managing of deficits in this manner puts part of the pressure of fiscal management on the staff member directly involved with the account.

In some instances, unforeseen circumstances cause certain accounts to become quickly overdrawn. An example is the home economics supply account. Alternatives are (1) transferring monies from another home economics account or (2) carrying the deficit over into the next fiscal year. As the reason for the deficit is discussed in budget projection meetings, the need to increase an appropriation may surface, thus covering the prior year's deficit.

Carryover is a unique feature of the autonomous fund budget process. All funds allocated to buildings but unexpended are carried over from one year to the next. This allows buildings to accumulate funds in order to purchase items which exceed any one year's allocation. For example, a $2,500 copy machine for office use may be purchased after funds in the office's equipment account have been carried over for a two- or three-year period. Principals have the option of carrying over funds in specific accounts or transferring such funds to a general building account for carryover purposes. These monies can then be reapportioned on the basis of need by the building budget committee. Without the carryover budget feature, long-range planning takes a back seat to a traditional building fiscal philosophy which implies, "Spend it now on anything; otherwise, you may not have another opportunity."

ESTABLISHING THE PURCHASING PROCESS

After planning, budget allocation, account code assignment, and record bank establishment, the building begins to identify items to be purchased. Items identified are generally categorized as supply, text-book, furniture, equipment, or repair. A purchasing form is filled out at the building level. The proper account number, brief description of the item, vendor, and cost is determined. Once signed by the principal, or his designee, the form is forwarded to the purchasing department. There a purchase order number is assigned after all other segments of the form have been double-checked for accuracy.

A situation occasionally exists when sudden price changes necessitate cost column revisions. If this situation occurs, buildings are notified immediately before the purchase order is submitted to the vendor. The total purchasing process from building to purchasing department to vendor takes from three to four days. When a situation necessitates much quicker action, a telephone transaction between the building, the purchasing department, and the vendor may take place. All telephone transactions are quickly followed up with the appropriate paperwork. Generally, equipment breakdowns requiring immediate repair are permitted as a verbal transaction.

The purchasing department is an integral part of the building's fiscal planning process. Annual requisition forms identifying items commonly used by all buildings (e.g., pencils, theme paper, first aid supplies, machine oils, etc.) are sent to buildings in the spring. Although autonomous funds are used, large quantity buying of items by the purchasing department permits buildings to receive a lower cost per item. Central supply and warehousing capacity are essential for such economy of scale. In summary, the purchasing department staff serve as expeditors between buildings and vendors, maintaining credibility between the school district and vendors on items requiring the bidding process. Additionally, good business procedures are maintained by developing standardized equipment, supply, and material lists for use by all schools.

E. COMMUNITY AND STAFF INVOLVEMENT IN BUDGET PROCESS

The budget process varies little from other sound management techniques implemented by school administrators. Management processes designed to provide useful and timely information to educational decision makers become the framework upon which school districts succeed or fail. Activity in the areas of planning, operations, communication, evaluation, and finance in educational programs offered by the district is continually assessed, adjusted, and/or discontinued based on information matching available resources (e.g., monies, staff, facilities, etc.) to current student needs. Constantly keeping abreast of existing student needs requires the district and individual school buildings to involve as many stakeholders as possible (e.g., parents, staff, board members, community leaders, and students who share common interests in the educational process directed by a school district or building) in decision-making processes that affect educational programs.

An administrator cannot afford the luxury of rationalizing away the need for community involvement. In such cases, program decisions have a tendency to be made in a semi-educational vacuum. Involvement of staff and community is best accomplished through organized activities. Techniques utilized to involve stakeholders will vary by situation. Some schools utilize the PTA (or PTSA) as the vehicle, while others develop formalized mechanisms such as CIC or CAC (Community Advisory Committee). It is crucial for the building to have such participation. Following is a brief outline of events that make a point of involving various stakeholders in the budget process.

DEFINING THE LIMITS OF DOLLARS AVAILABLE

The finance office must serve as a catalyst to the other four general areas of the district by projecting expected revenues and anticipated expenditures over a period of one to three or more years. In the process, fixed factors (e.g., enrollments, staff salaries, utility rates, etc.) may be considered by groups like the board, citizen advisory committees, bargaining units, and building involvement committees (e.g., PTA, CIC). Once the big picture of financial resources related to fixed charges (generally 93–94 percent of a total budget) is communicated to stakeholders, decisions related to the other 6–7 percent of a budget can be made. To make the best use of the remaining portion of the projected budget, an amount must be allocated to meet overall district concerns and priorities while the balance is distributed to buildings.

INVOLVING STAKEHOLDERS AT THE BUILDING LEVEL

Once dollars per student have been clearly defined for building administrators, they in turn can begin involving stakeholders in preparing the building's budget. Generally, the building budget committee is comprised of teaching staff representatives, CIC or PTA delegates, and selected students (more common in secondary schools). The committee's charge is to plan a program budget keeping in mind the school district's goals and student needs assessment information. As weeks of the process unfold, time is spent discussing points of view of all stakeholders related to a building's program priorities. Initially, dreams requiring far more money than is appropriated to a building give way to short- and long-range allotment of funds. Negotiation skills are quickly learned by all involved parties. Ultimately, the spin-off has usefulness in other areas of the building's decision-making process. If the budget process allows for meaningful involvement, the result is a committed group of stakeholders ready to see the successful implementation of programs based on a budget arrived at through mutual agreement.

MEMORANDUM

TO: Building Principal
FROM: Building Budget Committee
DATE:
SUBJECT: Proposed Budget Appropriations Based on Enrollment Adjustments

Last year's total autonomous fund budget ($42,900) was based on ten classes per student and allocated as follows:

I. Last year's allocations ($33 per student x 1,300 students):

A. Contingency (10–11% of total budget)	$ 4,595
B. Industrial arts—834 students @ $8.74	7,289
C. Business—340 students @ $4.50	1,530
D. Science—685 students @ $3.17	2,171
E. Math—1,242 students @ $1.59	1,975
F. Driver education—402 students @ $6.61	2,657
G. English—2,239 students @ $2.68	6,001
H. Physical education—1,357 students @ $.90	1,221
I. Foreign language—93 students @ $1.39	129
J. Social science—1,930 students @$2.56	4,941
K. Art—361 students @$5.15	1,859
L. Music: Instrumental—179 students @ $2.37	424
Vocal—138 students @ $1.25	173
*M. Vocational and special education—3,000 @ $.50	1,500
N. Counseling (3% of total budget)	1,287
O. Office expense (4% of total budget)	1,716
P. Instructional media (8% of total budget)	3,432
TOTAL	$42,900

*Funds do not include supplemental funds utilized to buy equipment and supplies unique to vocational and special education courses.

FIGURE 6.4 Budget appropriations and enrollment adjustments.

A 5% decrease in enrollment is expected next year. Ten classes per student will serve as a factor for projections. Following budget study meetings by committee members next year's projected budget ($44,460) is allocated as follows:

II. Next year's allocations ($36 per student x 1,235 students):

A.	Contingency (10–11% of total budget)	$ 4,668
B.	Industrial arts—792 students @ $8.30	6,574
C.	Business—323 students @ $4.28	1,382
D.	Science—651 students @ $3.01	1,960
E.	Math—1,180 students @ $1.51	1,782
F.	Driver education—382 students @ $8.64	3,300
G.	Physical education—1,291 students @ $.86	1,110
H.	English—2,127 students @ $2.55	5,424
I.	Foreign language—88 students @ $1.32	116
J.	Social science—1,834 students @$2.43	4,457
K.	Art—343 students @$4.90	1,681
L.	Music: Instrumental—209 students @ $6.15	1,285
	Vocal—131 students @ $2.91	381
M.	Vocational and special education—2,850 students @ $.50	1,425
N.	Counseling (3% of total budget)	1,334
O.	Office expense (4% of total budget)	1,778
P.	Instructional media (8% of total budget)	3,557
	SUB TOTAL	$42,214
*Q.	Emergency School Aid Act (ESAA)	2,246
	TOTAL	$44,460

*Monies to cover supplies and part of an aide's salary in a project (ESAA) whereby the school district no longer receives federal support at the secondary level.

FIGURE 6.4 (continued) Budget appropriations and enrollment adjustments.

MEMORANDUM

     TO: Elementary Principal A
  FROM: Finance Office
   DATE:
SUBJECT: Building Financial History

Following is a four-year history of autonomous funds your building has received and amounts carried over:

YEAR	AUTONOMOUS FUNDS	CARRYOVER
1982/83	$8,100	$ 0
1983/84	7,975	1,255
1984/85	7,969	2,124
1985/86	7,950	3,368

This year's projected funds based on an enrollment of 314 students is $7,404 and $4,972 in carryover.

We hope the information will help in finalizing your budget.

FIGURE 6.5 Financial history.

MEMORANDUM

TO: Elementary Principals and Staff
FROM: Finance Office
DATE:
SUBJECT: Autonomous Funds

Attached is a schedule showing your building's final allocation for autonomous funds. Component parts and bases are shown merely to indicate how the total was derived. Decisions on the allocation of the total are yours. Explanations for component parts and bases appear below.

ENROLLMENT

This is the official fall enrollment on which all per student allowances have been calculated.

BASIC

The basic allowance is $ per student. This represents the initial allowance of $ plus the allowance for repairs, maintenance contracts and field trip transportation as shown below:

ALLOWANCE	AMOUNT
Initial	$
Repairs & maintenance contracts	
Field trips	
TOTAL	

SUPERVISION AIDES

The allowance for supervision aides for those buildings with a hot lunch program has been calculated on total enrollment at $ per student. As soon as participation figures are firm, the total allowance will be redistributed.

The allowance for supervision for those buildings with a sack lunch program has been calculated on the basis of average participation in each building.

OFFICE AIDES AND SUBSTITUTES

The allowance for office aides, overtime and substitutes is $ per building plus a $ allowance for coops in buildings where an area principal is located or where enrollments are between 500 and 600.

CLUSTER SCHOOL ALLOWANCE

The cluster school allowance is $ per cluster school. This amount is to be redistributed to all buildings in the cluster. The costs of coops working in cluster schools continue to be a part of this allowance.

OTHER

The allowance for buildings participating in the State University Student Teacher Program is $

FIGURE 6.6 Projected elementary and secondary autonomous fund memorandums.

The allowance for buildings with aides remaining from the BRL or Project READ program is $. This allowance will *not* be repeated.

The contingency fund allocation of $ will be distributed to individual buildings based on applications approved by the Elementary Contingency Fund Committee.

SUB TOTAL

This amount represents the total of $ autonomous fund allowances.

ORIGINAL ALLOWANCE

This amount represents initial allocations based on anticipated enrollments and programs of individual buildings.

DIFFERENCE

This amount represents the difference between original allocations and the revised total of $ autonomous fund allowances. Amounts stated parenthetically will be deducted from your general appropriation, account 1XX.000. Other amounts will be added to account 1XX.000. Such deductions or additions may require your subsequent redistribution of appropriations. Please use a Budget Transfer Request form to accomplish your transfers.

CARRYOVER

This amount represents the cumulative balances of prior years and has already been posted to the account(s) of your choice.

Any allowances for differentiated staffing programs and/or carryovers for same will be over and above allowances on the attached schedule. You will be contacted individually for differentiated staffing budgets.

cc: Superintendent
    Deputy Superintendent—Operations
    Deputy Superintendent—Planning
    Director of Elementary Education

FIGURE 6.6 (continued) Projected elementary and secondary autonomous fund memorandums.

MEMORANDUM

TO: Secondary Principals and Staff
FROM: Finance Office
DATE:
SUBJECT: Autonomous Funds

Attached is a schedule showing your building's final allocation for autonomous funds. Component parts and bases are shown merely to indicate how the total was derived. Decisions on the allocation of the total are yours. Explanations for component parts and bases appear below.

ENROLLMENT

This is the official fall enrollment on which all per student allowances have been calculated.

BASIC

The basic allowance is $ per student in junior high schools and $
per student in senior high schools. This represents the initial allowance plus the allowances for repairs and maintenance contracts as shown below:

AMOUNT

ALLOWANCE	JUNIOR HIGH	SENIOR HIGH
Initial		
Repairs & maintenance contracts		
TOTAL		

EXTRACURRICULAR

The allowance for extracurricular salaries is based on the expanded positions and salary base schedule as outlined in the September memorandum, a copy of which is attached.

The allowances for field trips and other expenses of extracurricular activities includes the additional girl's athletic supplement of $ per building at senior high and $ per building at junior high. In addition, $ per building has been provided at junior high for the football program first aid supplies.

AIDES

The allowance for aides is $ per student in the junior high schools and $ per student in senior high schools. The cost of instructional aides, clerical aides, co-ops, secretarial substitutes and overtime continue to be a part of this allowance.

FIGURE 6.7

124

OTHER

Amounts parenthetically stated represent transfers to the reentry budget for students placed in that program this year-to-date.

The driver education supplement will be used to cover the actual cost of vehicle rentals.

The athletic fund supplement will be transferred to individual buidlings at year end based on a formula of total athletic revenues and expenditures.

The allowance for the Academic Interest Center includes all normal autonomous fund allowances plus $ for the start-up of the humanities program.

The contingency fund allocation of $ will be distributed to individual buildings based on applications approved by the Secondary Contingency Fund Committee.

SUBTOTAL

This amount represents the total of $ autonomous fund allowances.

ORIGINAL ALLOWANCE

This amount represents initial allocations based on anticipated enrollments and programs of individual buildings.

DIFFERENCE

This amount represents the difference between original allocations and the revised total of $ autonomous fund allowances. Amounts stated parenthetically will be deducted from your general appropriation, account 1XX.000. Other amounts will be added to account 1XX.000. Such deductions or additions may require your subsequent redistribution of appropriations. Please use a Budget Transfer Request form to accomplish your transfers.

CARRYOVER

This amount represents the cumulative balances of prior years and has already been posted to the account(s) of your choice.

Any allowances for differentiated staffing programs and/or carryovers for same will be over and above allowances on the attached schedule. You will be contacted individually for differentiated staffing budgets.

cc: Superintendent
    Deputy Superintendent—Operations
    Deputy Superintendent—Planning
    Director of Elementary Education

FIGURE 6.7 (continued).

BUILDING	ENROLLMENT	BASIC	SALARIES	EXTRACURRICULAR FIELD TRIP & OTHER EXP.	AIDES	OTHER	SUB TOTAL	ORIGINAL ALLOW.	DIFFERENCE	CARRY-OVER
Senior High										
"A"	1,684	$ 58,030	$ 35,613	$ 8,839	$ 11,721		$114,203	$114,230	$ (27)	$ 33,453
"B"	1,687	58,134	35,613	8,839	11,741	(64)	114,263	112,988	1,275	26,571
"C"	1,387	47,796	35,613	8,839	9,654	(32)	101,870	99,713	2,157	9,384
"D"	1,542	53,137	35,613	8,839	10,732		108,321	106,983	1,338	9,466
Driver ed supplement						11,000	11,000	11,000		
Athletic fund supplement						15,000	15,000	15,000		15,000
A.I.C.	2					14,700	14,700	14,700		
SUBTOTAL	6,302	$217,097	$142,452	$35,356	$ 43,848	$40,604	$479,357	$474,614	$ 4,743	$ 93,874
Junior High										
"1"	1,107	$ 39,752	$ 17,004	$ 2,836	$ 12,498		$ 72,090	$ 72,157	$ (67)	$ 3,941
"2"	1,507	54,116	17,004	2,836	17,014		90,970	91,037	(67)	20,820
"3"	1,476	53,003	17,004	2,836	16,664		89,507	86,552	2,955	12,526
"4"	1,245	44,708	17,004	2,836	14,056	(68)	78,536	76,168	2,368	8,741
"5"	1,554	55,804	17,004	2,836	17,545	(34)	93,155	91,395	1,760	7,103
SUBTOTAL	6,889	$247,383	$ 85,020	$14,180	$ 77,777	(102)	$424,258	$417,309	$ 6,949	$ 53,131
Contingency fund						$15,000	$ 15,000	$ 15,000		$ 265
TOTAL	13,191	$464,480	$227,472	$49,536	$121,625	$55,502	$918,615	$906,923	$11,692	$147,270

FIGURE 6.8 Autonomous fund allowances — secondary buildings.

MEMORANDUM

TO: Secondary Principals
FROM: Finance Office
DATE:
SUBJECT: Cocurricular Positions and Salary Bases

Below are listed the details of authorized cocurricular positions which make up the cocurricular salary base part of your autonomous funds. This schedule shows the recently authorized expansion of positions for girl's athletics and the assistant athletic director. Stipends have been adjusted accordingly and your autonomous fund budgets will be adjusted for the revised total along with other adjustments necessitated by the fall official count.

TITLE	AUTHORIZED POSITIONS	% OF BA BASE	COST	EXTENSION
Senior High				
Athletic director	1	17%	$3,400	$ 3,400
Asst. athletic director	1	10	2,000	2,000
Head football	1	17	3,400	3,400
Assistant football	4	10.5	2,100	8,400
Football, extra week	5		175	875
Head basketball	1	16	3,200	3,200
Assistant basketball	1	10	2,000	2,000
Cross-country	1	8.5	1,700	1,700
Head swimming	1	12	2,400	2,400
Assistant swimming	1	8	1,600	1,600
Head wrestling	1	12	2,400	2,400
Assistant wrestling	1	8	1,600	1,600
Golf	1	8	1,600	1,600
Head baseball	1	10.5	2,100	2,100
Assistant baseball	1	8	1,600	1,600
Head track	1	12	2,400	2,400
Assistant track	1	10	2,400	2,400
Tennis	1	8	1,600	1,600
Equipment manager	1	6	1,200	1,200
Girl's intramural & cheerleading	2	8	1,600	3,200
Girl's sports	7	8	1,600	11,200
Debate & forensics	1	9	1,800	1,800
Band director	1	9.5	1,900	1,900
Choir	1	7.5	1,400	1,400

FIGURE 6.9

127

TITLE	AUTHORIZED POSITIONS	% OF BA BASE	COST	EXTENSION
Dramatic productions	2	4	800	1,600
Yearbook	1	6	1,200	1,200
Newspaper	1	4.5	900	900
Business advisor for:				
Newspaper & yearbook	1	4.5	900	900
Book custodian	1	5	1,000	1,000
School treasurer	1	7.5	1,500	1,500
TOTAL				$72,475
Junior High				
Athletic director	1	8%	$1,600	$ 1,600
Asst. athletic director	1	5	1,000	1,000
Football & assistant				
football	3	7	1,400	4,200
Wrestling	1	7	1,400	1,400
Swimming	1	7	1,400	1,400
Varsity basketball	1	7	1,400	1,400
Junior varsity basketball	1	7	1,400	1,400
Track	1	7	1,400	1,400
Volleyball	1	7	1,400	1,400
Intramural	1	7	1,400	1,400
Girl's sports	6	7	1,400	8,400
Girl's intramural &				
cheerleading	3	4.5	900	2,700
Book custodian	1	3	600	600
Band director	1	5.5	1,100	1,100
Orchestra director	1	3	600	600
Choir	1	3.5	700	700
Dramatic productions	2	4	800	1,600
Newspaper advisor	1	4.5	900	900
School treasurer	1	6	1,200	1,200
TOTAL				$34,400

Please remember that component parts of building autonomous funds are strictly bases. Decisions on the allocation of the total budget are to be made by individual buildings.

FIGURE 6.9 (continued)

128

MEMORANDUM

TO: Secondary Principals and Staff
FROM: Finance Office
DATE:
SUBJECT: Building Budget Appropriations

From the total autonomous funds granted to your building, please indicate the amount you wish to have allocated to each account (even dollar amounts only—no cents). The building principal should sign this form on the last page and return it to the finance office by June.

BUILDING NAME: _____

BUILDING NUMBER: _____ TOTAL AUTONOMOUS FUNDS $_____

ACCOUNT NUMBER	DESCRIPTION	AMOUNT
_____.000	General appropriation	$_____
_____.005	Office aides and overtime	_____
_____.009	Contracted scheduling services	_____
_____.010	Office expense	_____
_____.034	Instructional aides, general	_____
_____.035	Clerical aides, general	_____
_____.036	Noon supervision aides, general	_____
_____.041	Contracted instructional services, general	_____
_____.043	Field trip transportation, general	_____
_____.044	Textbooks, general	_____
_____.050	Instructional supplies, general	_____
_____.842	Contracted services, other	_____
_____.843	Supplies, other	_____
_____.844	Equipment, other	_____
_____.845	Transportation, other	_____
_____.853	Clerical aides, counseling	_____
_____.855	Contracted instructional services, counseling	_____
_____.856	Counseling supplies	_____
	TOTAL	$_____

_____
Signature of Building Principal

_____
Date

FIGURE 6.10 Building budget appropriation form.

BUILDING AUTONOMY BUDGET REPORT
_____ SCHOOL DISTRICT

JULY 1, 19   TO JUNE 30, 19

ACCOUNT	BUDGETED	ENCUMBERED	EXPENDED	AVAILABLE
ELEMENTARY SCHOOL A				
SCHOOL ADMINISTRATION				
120.000 General appropriation	$ 2,115	$	$	$2,115
120.005 Office aides & overtime	341		324	17
120.010 Office expense	731		323	408
TOTAL	$ 3,187		$ 647	$2,540
GENERAL INSTRUCTION				
120.043 Field trip transportation	$ 225	$	263	38
120.044 Textbooks	215		187	28
120.049 Student supplies	789		421	368
120.050 Instructional supplies	3,660	39	2,219	1,402
120.055 Furniture & equipment maintenance contract	341		109	25
120.056 Furniture & equipment repair	287	20	257	10
120.058 Furniture & equipment addition	609	35	278	296
TOTAL	$ 5,919	$ 94	$3,734	$2,091

FIGURE 6.11 Sample page printout for monitoring a building budget.

ACCOUNT	BUDGETED	ENCUMBERED	EXPENDED	AVAILABLE
INSTRUCTIONAL MEDIA SERVICES				
120.109 Library books & binding	$ 834	$107	$ 708	$ 19
120.110 Library periodicals	181	3	172	6
120.112 Audiovisual materials	54		5	49
TOTAL	$ 1,069	$110	$ 885	$ 74
MATERIALS FOR SPECIFIC PROGRAMS				
120.210 Textbooks, reading	$ 41	$	$ 24	$ 17
120.211 Instructional supplies, reading	233		141	92
120.236 Instructional supplies, English	34		23	11
120.311 Instructional supplies, art	38	10	26	2
120.386 Instructional supplies, math	364		343	21
120.411 Instructional supplies, science	115			115
120.486 Instructional supplies, phys. ed.	261		242	19
TOTAL	$ 1,086	$ 10	$ 799	$ 277
GRAND TOTAL	$11,261	$214	$6,065	$4,982

FIGURE 6.11 (continued) Sample page printout for monitoring a building budget.

MONITORING AN APPROVED BUILDING BUDGET

Periodic budget reports should be available to any group of stake-holders throughout a fiscal year. Openness expressed by having a budget report at faculty meetings, student meetings, and PTA or CIC sessions is a key to seeing that the money is expended as planned. Invariably, unforeseen expenditures over a fiscal year will require revision of building budgets. A building that predicated the preparation of the budget on involving stakeholders and continued a policy of open review throughout the year will have little difficulty in explaining the need to revise initial budget priority projections. In contrast, a lack of management skill by the building administrator as he or she prepares and monitors the budget process generally leads toward allegations of misappropriation and misuse of public funds and ultimately a lack of trust in the administrator as a professional.

In conclusion, involvement of stakeholders in the budget process will lead toward a feeling by the community in general that they do have a say in how their dollars are spent in educational programming. Staffs operating in buildings are no longer totally dependent on central administrators providing instructional materials, supplies, and equipment for meeting the needs of students they are teaching. And, most important, students in a building or classroom have the benefit of a planned process to identify their unique needs and to provide available financial resources to meet those needs.

For the convenience of the reader, following are a series of sample forms, reports, and memorandums utilized by one district that has accomplished a building-level decentralization (see Figures 6.4–6.11).

CHAPTER 7

Communications

A. INTRODUCTION

As one of the basic functions of any educational (or other) organization, communications play an increasingly important role in the success and/or failure of the system. Considered in the perspective of the educational system committed to site-based management and decision making, effective communications is crucial to survival.

The educational system moving toward site-based management is, at the same time, moving toward a much more participatory management system. In terms of systems theory, such a movement would be categorized by Rensis Likert (1976, 71) as a move from a System 1 or 2 type of organization toward a System 4 type of organization. The involvement of an expanded number of persons in decisions and the departure from a top-down process reinforces the need for positive and continuous communications. According to Likert, those organizations falling into System 1 or System 2 classification are best characterized by little teamwork, by top-down communications, by decisions made at the top and handed down, by control concentrated at the top, by rare participation by subordinates, and by covert resistance to organizational goals. Conversely, those organizations classified as System 4 organizations are identified by much subordinate trust and participation, by excellent two-way communications, by great involvement in decisions, by group involvement in goal setting, and by little resistance to organizational goals (Dowling 1978, 52).

Communications results from the interaction of a complex of visible and invisible human variables. Figure 7.1 illustrates some of the variables in simplified form (adapted from Berlo 1960).

S	M	C	R
Source	Message	Channel	Receiver
Communications Skills	Content	Seeing	Communications Skills
Attitudes	Treatment	Hearing	Attitudes
Knowledge	Code	Touching	Knowledge
Social System	Structure	Smelling	Social System
Culture	Elements	Tasting	Culture

FIGURE 7.1 A model of some of the ingredients in communication.

Frequently, people seek a single, simple cause to understand communications when a variety of causes are inevitably present. Behavior and meaning result from forces operating in a variety of directions within the total life space of an individual.

People have a perceptual filter through which they perceive the behaviors of others. Communications is an extremely difficult human act because of the complexity of human interaction. An individual, sometimes unawarely, transmits messages, but, because of the perceptual filter of the receiver, the clarity of the message is unknown to the sender. The receiver may have distorted and/or changed the intended message.

Leaders who wish to improve interaction must be aware of their own behavior as well as the behavior of others. Behaviors, both verbal as well as nonverbal, convey powerful messages to members of the organization and to the community at large.

B. COMMUNICATIONS TECHNIQUES AND MODES

Because the salient implication of site-based management (SBM) is the extended involvement of many persons, the communications processes utilized have great significance to the members of the organization and to the community served. A variety of communication modes and styles must be developed in order to reach the total community and to engage clients, patrons, and staff in meaningful dialogue. The next section will present and explain some of these communications avenues.

ONE-ON-ONE

Perhaps the most effective means of communications is the one-on-one dialogue. In this manner, both verbal and nonverbal (or body) language can be utilized and reactions and responses to a message can be instantly transmitted. The identification of issues to be resolved can proceed directly, and resolution is quick and effective. Personal dialogue and contact, while certainly the most effective means of communications, is a tedious and lengthy process, especially if large numbers of people are involved. There also exists the danger of message distortion for it is difficult to repeat all nuances and nonverbal items time after time. It is therefore appropriate to restrict the use of the one-on-one communications technique to those situations where small numbers of people are involved and/or where certain key persons are singled out for special communications effort. Most effective use of one-on-one communications techniques in the educational organization are in small group situations (i.e., departments, small schools, neighborhood meetings, etc.) or when specific issues arise that involve small numbers of persons.

TELEVISION

Another communications mode that utilizes the verbal/visual technique is the use of television to convey a particular message. At the present time, this technique does not allow recipient response so the communications is strictly one-way and not a dialogue as the one-on-one personal relationship provides. However, emerging technology suggests that it may soon be possible to engender audience responses through electronic wizardry. At any rate, the use of the television media requires communications skills different from those utilized in one-on-one interplay. For one thing, the presentation must be well prepared and rehearsed in advance to enable maximum effectiveness and impact. A certain stage presence and theatrical capacity is viewed as beneficial to those who use the television as a mode of communications. It is said that the camera is a stern task master and brings out the absolute worst in people. Organizational leaders who effectively use the television as a source of communications have learned the many and various skills needed to effectively project themselves and their message. Increasingly, school superintendents are utilizing the television media to transmit information, to explain issues, and to provide a reporting mechanism for the citizens of the school district. Many school districts have acquired cable television channels and therefore have ready access to television as a communications media. In addition to the variety of educational programming provided by the school system, the use of the channel for information/communications purposes is a natural extension of service. As the availability of cable television channels increases, more and more districts are developing the necessary in-house expertise to exploit this communications media. Capacity to produce, videotape, and transmit programs is rapidly becoming a reality.

In addition, many school systems are using commercial television channels for the transmission of school district information. Increasingly, commercial stations are allocating a share of required public service programming to the school district's use. This sharing provides the station with a ready mechanism for meeting Federal Communications Commission (F.C.C.) public service requirements and provides the school system with professionally trained personnel to handle the production, direction, and camera (recording) activities. This alternative is especially attractive to those districts not having access to educational television channels.

A real difficulty that is sometimes associated with school district assumption of total responsibility for a channel allocated solely for educational use is the tremendous cost of production that is also assumed. The preparation of a single thirty-minute program can take upward of forty hours and can require the participation of a number of specially trained, high-priced personnel. The temptation to cut corners and produce programs more inexpensively leads to amateurish quality and soon alienates the viewers and becomes a negative vehicle for school system communications. In addition, the demand for fresh programming, the expectation of professional quality, and the constant pressure of hours to be filled all create difficulty for an organization whose primary task is the delivery of educational services and that is not equipped to serve primarily as an information/entertainment agency.

As a result, school districts are developing expertise in television production and are creating staffs whose responsibility is the production of videotapes and live shows. Additionally, school districts are entering cooperative arrangements with other public bodies, i.e., cities, libraries, community colleges, etc., to share the public channels and the accelerating cost of production. Also being developed are commercially produced educational tapes that can be purchased as part of a videotape library and used as the need arises. All of the above mechanisms tend to provide a more professionally oriented public television capacity, one that will attract and hold viewer interest.

Typically, regularly scheduled reports to the community about school system matters, live or taped board of education meetings, special reports on crucial educational issues, call-in programs such as "Ask the Board" or "Ask the Superintendent," and other planned and/or spontaneous programs are televised. School systems are becoming increasingly sophisticated in production and programming and have learned a variety of scheduling tricks long utilized by commercial stations to gain maximum exposure and increase the audience. Techniques like scheduling the transmission of important school information before, during, and immediately after high-interest productions like athletic contests, music programs, and/or dramatic productions are now commonplace. Rewriting news releases to the interest level of the particular audience is also being accomplished to the advantage of both the district and the viewer. Use of the television media is just now emerging as an important communications tool and projections are that this mode of communications will continue to grow in popularity and effectiveness.

RADIO

Many school systems have had local radio stations (FM) for many years. These FM stations have been used in conjunction with secondary school curricula in communications arts. Typically, these low-wattage stations are restricted to a minimal number of hours of broadcasting. They do reach the homes of the school district and provide music, news, live game and show broadcasts, and other programs of local interest.

The existence of these many stations is almost taken for granted and their full potential is often overlooked. The capacity for positive utilization of school district-owned radio stations must be carefully examined by school organizations. Among readily apparent advantages are the relatively low cost of production, the already existing production expertise, the increasing popularity of radio as a communications media, and the ease with which radio shows can be produced and taped. Many school districts are presenting regularly scheduled news and views programming and are exhibiting great skill in developing such presentations. Additionally, such productions can easily be taped and shared with commercial stations or even adapted for use by commercial stations as part of their "public interest" programming.

Again, as with television, school systems are beginning to achieve greater sophistication and expertise in scheduling and in production so that programs utilizing specific objectives and techniques are directed at specific audiences.

SCHOOL GROUPS AND MEETINGS

The use of school parent and patron bodies as forums for dissemination of information has long been a primary communications technique of school administrators. The PTA, PTSA, CAC, CIC, Superintendents Advisory Committees, Title I Advisory Committees, and other such groups are regularly utilized as important communications tools for dialogue between the school system and its patrons.

The great advantage (or disadvantage) is the face-to-face personal nature of the communications. Proper use of communications techniques can and does improve the understanding between school and community. In-depth discussions and presentations, unencumbered by time limitations, are possible. Indeed, the temptation to become too wordy and lengthy is often the greatest danger and serves to alienate the audience. Persons skilled in this form of communications technique are able to accomplish a great deal at regularly scheduled activities. Of primary importance is the recognition that such meetings are not intended to be passive information dispensing one-way communications devices, but rather forums for two-way dialogue and for resolution of issues. They can be invaluable as consensus building activities, and the astute school administrator recognizes the potential for positive relations that accrue from such groups.

Of significant importance is the use of this communications mode to open the school to the community. For too long, educators have maintained an aloofness, a separation from the community, so much so that many communities are suspicious, wary, and even hostile toward the school and its personnel. For that reason, the effort toward expanding school meetings must be a carefully planned, low-key, non-threatening activity. The community must realize that the schools belong to them and not to the educational bureaucracy. They, the community, must be convinced that they can and should have considerable impact on what the school is about. School personnel, too, must recognize that they are at the institution to provide educational services for the community and not to use the institution as a personal tool.

As school meetings become more effective and better attended, a variety of subgroups can and should be developed in order to more personalize the contact between the school and the community it serves. The use of patrons as volunteers serves a variety of purposes, ranging from the provision of needed services to enrichment, and as still another mechanism for assisting the patrons to learn more about the institution.

While the locus of this communications technique is best exploited at the building level, astute superintendents create systemwide groups in order to provide similar forums to focus on the gestalt of the school district. Advisory groups of every size and description are in existence, ranging from curriculum advisory groups in the great variety of vocational/technical/business/distributive education areas to the many cultural/ethnic/racial advisory committees to the diverse ad hoc study groups who study demography or finance or instruction or facilities with a charge to assist in the development of action plans. Most recently, the mandated Title I advisory groups and the special education advisory committees have had great impact and have made great contributions to the operation of the school system. It is the position of the author that an informed, involved citizenry is a most supportive and satisfied citizenry as well.

COMMUNITY ORGANIZATIONS

In every school district there are a great number of community organizations that are interested in the educational institution. These groups range from fraternal groups to self-interest organizations to social and religious groups. They are comprised of citizens of the community and therefore patrons of the school system. School personnel are to be found in every one of these organizations, often in leadership positions for educators are respected across the spectrum of activities. Systematic cultivation and utilization of the communications opportunity presented by this duality of membership is often overlooked by the school system and a great opportunity for dialogue is lost.

Because most of the above organizations, be they the Rotary Club or NAACP or the First Baptist church or the local block club, are either directly (as parent or client) or indirectly (as taxpayer and patron) concerned with the school system, careful expansion of the communications opportunity is called for. Periodic educational presentations, reports, and information sessions can lead to extended dialogue about major educational issues facing the community. The prevailing attitude of these organizations is generally a supportive one, and, with full sharing of information, the initial feeling of support can grow to a position of advocacy for the system. As with school and school advisory groups, great pains must be taken to convey the reality that the schools belong to them (the community) and not to the bureaucracy. The school system must become an open system and be willing to stand the test of close scrutiny and examination by the various publics if it is to engender the kind of support and cooperation needed to surmount emerging issues.

NEWSLETTERS

Most school systems make concerted efforts to publish regularly scheduled newsletters directed to the patrons of the school district. These efforts, published weekly, monthly, quarterly, and/or annually provide an opportunity for the school district to convey information, news, explanatory material, and other educational items to all of the households of the district on a regular basis. Generally, these newsletters are printed on quality newsprint and are attractively laid out in order to present a favorable view of the school district. The development of the newsletter is a quasi-journalistic activity, and most school systems have staff persons trained in journalism who are assigned the task of producing the periodic newsletter. The inclusion of pictures plus multicolor print provides a most attractive format and encourages greater readership.

Information dealing with the school calendar, enrollment procedures, school closings, curriculum offerings, special educational opportunities, review of requirements for graduation, calendar of special events, and the introduction of new personnel are among the purposes to which the newsletter is committed. Additionally, news about cocurricular activities, i.e., sports events and results, plays, music activities, club activities, and other events, are announced in the newsletter. Many newsletters include minutes of board of education meetings as well as schedules of future board activities.

As the one regularly published and distributed printed material that the district offers, the newsletter is the primary source of information about the school district for many households. For those school districts also providing television and radio programming, the inclusion of information regarding television and radio programs are means utilized to increase viewers and listeners.

In addition to the districtwide newsletter, many school systems encourage and assist local buildings and departments in publishing periodic newsletters and/or similar printed materials. These newsletters serve both the school and school-based organizations, i.e., the PTA, PTSA, advisory groups, school booster clubs, etc., as outlets for information directed at the school attendance area.

The school newsletters range in quality from mimeographed sheets to professionally printed, highly sophisticated efforts. The special benefits that accrue from the publication of a school newsletter is that much more detailed and minute explanations can be included. Additionally, concerns unique to the attendance area can be explored and dealt with.

Increasingly, departments within a school are developing a newsletter format to use with their special clients and patrons. Music and athletic boosters make extensive use of the newsletter, and departments such as distributive education provide placement services and advertising through such a vehicle.

ANNUAL REPORT

Publication of an annual financial report is a legal mandate in most states. The astute school district utilizes this opportunity to have the annual report be an all-encompassing report to the community. The annual report, published in the largest daily newspaper serving the school district, provides an excellent opportunity to tell the story of the past year's accomplishments in a most favorable light. Extensive use of photographs of children in learning situations along with various graphics provides an attractive, easily understood report. Some school districts use the annual report to highlight specific educational developments, i.e., facilities, programs, cocurricular activities, etc.

Because the annual report is a once-a-year opportunity to enter every household in the community, great care must be exerted to assure that it is a high-quality, attractive, easily understood document. Often, special consultative assistance is engaged to assist in its development.

SPECIAL REPORTS

Most school districts produce a series of special publications ranging from curriculum documents to reports about a variety of program offerings. Board meeting summaries are quickly produced and distributed to interested parties.

Among the interesting documents produced are those periodic documents utilized to inform financial institutions about the school district prior to offering a bond issue for sale. These bond brochures or financial brochures are extremely well done and include a wide variety of information about the school system.

Certain publications are utilized to publicize board policy and legal mandates as equal employment policies, purchasing procedures, school lunch participation requirements, Title IX regulations, and the like.

NEWS CONFERENCES

The news conference is a communications tool used by most organizations including school systems. The news conference is most helpful in explaining particular occurrences and for providing background information to media personnel. The news conference is also a useful technique to provide important data of an emergency nature so that all media are treated equally and fairly. Because the electronic media can broadcast immediately while the daily paper has time deadlines, care must be exercised in scheduling news conferences in order not to exclude the print media from participation.

NEWS RELEASES

Periodic news releases are developed by the appropriate office. These must deal with important and relevant topics and must extend previously unreported data to the media. This communications mode is generally reserved for extra special news and/or activities, i.e., a state championship, a major award, a serious accident (could require a news conference), a new board of education policy, the employment of a high-level official (assistant superintendent, etc.).

Any and all of the aforementioned techniques are used on a regular basis by school systems to provide communications linkages with the community. The quality and variety of communications techniques developed sometimes provide the measure of success needed to stabilize the school system. Given the reality of serious communications gaps, the use of a number of techniques and modes in a mutually supporting, coordinated manner increases the probability of success. While truth, candor, openness, and honesty are crucial, the style of presentation must also be such that the material is ear/eye-catching and must be tailored to the particular audience being reached.

C. INTERNAL COMMUNICATIONS

Many urban school systems have highly sophisticated communications departments and sponsor extensive and varied communications networks to the external publics of the organization. Yet they tend to neglect internal communications needs and, as a result, suffer institutional rigor mortis. Internal communications are too often viewed as a top-down process and all efforts are expanded to keep the system a closed and autocratic organization.

Systems theorists, most notably McGregor and Likert, make strong cases for the advantages of open organizations and participatory management. McGregor with Theory Y development and Likert with System 4 both endorse the need for active two-way communications within the organization. The development of school system goals in the context of individual member's needs and objectives is an important move toward an open organization.

Recognition of the school district as a social system with two simultaneous axes to be coordinated created increased awareness of the need for attention to the internal communications process. The work of Getzels and Guba (1957) in formulating the concept of administration as a social process and of the school district as a social system was first presented in 1957.

The model developed by Getzels and Guba (1957) shown in Figure 7.2 contains a normative (nomothetic) dimension and a personal (ideographic) dimension. Each organization consists of these two dimensions and the merging of the two axes lead to organizational behavior and thrust. On the nomothetic axis is shown the institution, its role, and its expectations while on the ideographic dimension is located the individual, his/her personality, and his/her need-disposition. Each given act is conceived as deriving simultaneously from both the normative and personal dimensions.

Figure 7.3 shows the interplay between role and personality in behavior. According to Getzels and Guba, the type of organization being examined has much to do with the relative effect of the individual personality as contrasted to the institutional role. As is indicated in Figure 7.3, the military organization tends to weigh the institutional role much more significantly than the individual personality while in an organiza-

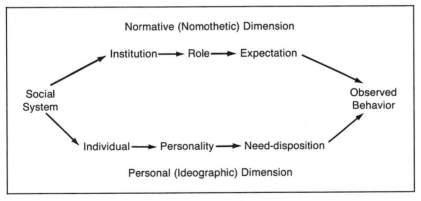

FIGURE 7.2 General model showing the organizational and personal dimensions of social behavior [Getzels and Guba (1957)].

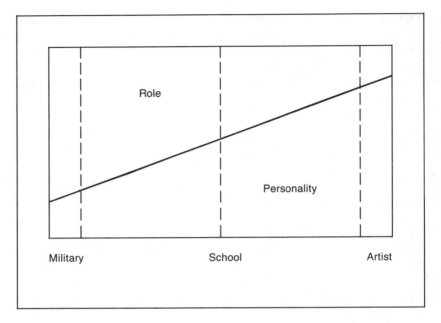

FIGURE 7.3 The interplay between role and personality in a behavioral act [Getzels and Guba (1957)].

tion committed to the arts, the personality factor far outweighs the institutional role. The school organization is viewed as approximating a balance between the role and the personality factors.

What does this mean for the approach to internal communications? First, it suggests that careful attention be given the personal dimension of the organization. The individual members of the staff, their needs, and their personalities are all important considerations. Optimum success of the institution is the result of merging individual needs with organizational expectations. The process and scope of communications is a key to the successful coordination of individual needs with institutional objectives.

Second, the institutional leader(s) must utilize the formal and informal communications networks to actively involve staff members in the formulation of organizational objectives. In this way, ownership of and commitment to institutional objectives are encouraged and often realized. It also assures that individual needs will be considered as part of the planning process.

Third, close and continuing dialogue between and among members of the organization promotes the unity and cohesiveness of the institution. Such communications permit clear identification and prioritization of client needs and encourages institutional responses to those needs. The clarification and explicit identification of client needs and the collateral planning of programs to meet those needs is a most important role for the organization. At the same time, participation in the dialogue will provide the individual with clear expectations for his/her behavior and encourage personal needs disposition efforts.

Fourth, by learning and using the informal networks of internal communications, the educational leader can learn much important data about the institution and how the institutional role and its expectations are perceived by the staff. While staff perceptions are not necessarily congruent with institutional expectations, the fact that the perceptions exist make them real and call for mitigating action on the part of the institutional leader.

The school system that chooses to embrace the site-based management concept has, in effect, committed itself on the path toward becoming a System 4 organization. Figure 7.4 shows the various organizational characteristics, as categorized by Likert and Likert (1976, 91–92). Of particular significance is the material on communications. System 4 organizations are most adept at utilization of the communications networks and show the accrued benefits of being an open institution. As noted in Figure 7.4, the flow of information, the acceptance of the validity of the information, the perception of accuracy of information, and the understanding of problems by superiors are all more positive in the System 4 organization.

As the data in Figure 7.4 indicates (Likert and Likert 1976, 94), more successful organizations are characterized by

(1) Greater confidence by superiors in subordinates
(2) More freedom felt by subordinates to talk to their superiors
(3) More frequent seeking and use of subordinate's ideas
(4) Use of involvement rather than threats
(5) Mutual confidence and trust in interactions rather than condescension by superiors and fear by subordinates
(6) Greater participation by subordinates in decisions related to their work
(7) Productivity, cost, and other accounting data used by departments for self-guidance rather than by top management for punitive purposes

	SYSTEM 1	SYSTEM 2	SYSTEM 3	SYSTEM 4
1. How much confidence is shown in subordinates?	None	Condescending	Substantial	Complete
2. How free do they feel to talk to superiors about their job?	Not at all	Not very	Rather free	Fully free
3. Are subordinates' ideas sought and used, if worthy?	Seldom	Somtimes	Usually	Always
4. Is predominant use made of (1) fear, (2) threats, (3) punishment, (4) rewards, (5) involvement?	1, 2, 3, occasionally 4	4, some 3	3, some 3 and 5	5, 4, based on group-set goals
5. Where is the responsibility felt for achieving organization's goals?	Mostly at top	Top and middle	Fairly general	At all levels
6. What is the direction of information flow?	Downward	Mostly downward	Down and up	Down, up, and sideways
7. How is downward communication accepted?	With suspicion	Possibly with suspicion	With caution	With open mind
8. How accurate is upward communications?	Often wrong	Censored for boss	Limited accuracy	Accurate

FIGURE 7.4 Profile of organizational characteristics.

146

	SYSTEM 1	SYSTEM 2	SYSTEM 3	SYSTEM 4
9. How well do superiors know problems faced by subordinates?	Know little	Some knowledge	Quite well	Very well
10. What is the character of interaction?	Little, always with fear and distrust	Little, usually with some condescension	Moderate, often fair amount of confidence and trust	Extensive, high degree of confidence and trust
11. How much cooperative teamwork is present?	None	Relatively little	Moderate amount	Very substantial amount throughout organization
12. At what level are decisions formally made?	Mostly at top	Policy at top, some delegation	Broad policy at top, more delegation	Throughout, but well integrated
13. What is the origin of technical and professional knowledge used in decision making?	Top management	Upper and middle	To certain extent throughout	To a great extent throughout
14. Are subordinates involved in decisions related to their work?	Not at all	Occasionally consulted	Generally consulted	Fully involved

FIGURE 7.4 (continued) Profile of organizational characteristics.

	SYSTEM 1	SYSTEM 2	SYSTEM 3	SYSTEM 4
15. What does decision-making process contribute to motivation?	Nothing, often weakens it	Relatively little	Some contribution	Substantial contribution
16. How are organization goals established?	Orders issued	Orders, some comments invited	After discussion, by orders	Group action (except in crisis)
17. How much covert resistance to goals is present?	Strong resistance	Moderate resistance	Some resistance at times	Little or none
18. How concentrated are review and control functions?	Highly at top	Relatively high at top	Moderate delegation at lower levels	Quite widely shared
19. Is there an informal organization resisting the formal one?	Yes	Usually	Sometimes	No, same goals as formal
20. What are cost, productivity, and other control data used for?	Policing, punishment	Reward and punishment	Reward, some self-guidance	Self-guidance, problem solving

FIGURE 7.4 (continued) Profile of organizational characteristics.

148

Additionally, these successful organizations are further characterized by

(1) Widespread feeling of responsibility for achieving the goals of the organization
(2) Mutual expectation that each person will do the job well and help others
(3) Cooperative attitudes to achieve goals rather than covert resistance to them and restriction of output

The most viable communications techniques utilized in developing internal communications are included in the following.

ONE-ON-ONE

Because of the relatively small numbers involved, particularly at the building level, every effort to approach dialogue with single individuals or with small groups is most important. The building of rapport and systemic openness is best accomplished by the dialogue and capacity for accommodation and consensus resulting from one-on-one discussion.

STAFF MEETINGS

While a certain amount of information must be dispersed through this communications vehicle, the more appropriate use of staff meeting time is for discussion and planning. Once the system has moved toward the System 4 end of the spectrum, staff meetings become fine working milieus for plan development.

STAFF NEWSLETTERS

Staff newsletters are very effective, particularly if done from the perspective of the staff. Much information can be dispensed with the newsletter. It is also an important device to improve attitudes and staff morale.

NEWS RELEASES

While this technique does little to promote direct communications, the judicious use of this mode will enable individual staff members and subgroups to feel good about their contributions and will permit other communications efforts to be still more effective. Recognition of positive contributions has the effect of creating awareness and appreciation among institutional staffs.

MEMOS

Memos to staff commending specific acts and contributions also pave the way toward responsive communications. The human animal craves recognition, and the satisfaction of the ego is paramount in creating an appropriate atmosphere for productive communications.

INFORMAL DIALOGUE

The principal or superintendent who cultivates staff by providing the opportunity for informal dialogue over coffee or during walk throughs is substantially more sophisticated in his/her approach to the communications process than are those persons whose approach is strictly formal and by use of traditional channels. Quiet, person-to-person discussion can clear up misconceptions and misinformation that spring up in institutions. In addition, the recognition of superordinates and subordinates as real people with human characteristics opens the door for additional communications.

One final word about internal communications. With the increased emphasis on collective bargaining and the rising level of suspicion that seems to afflict most urban school districts, increased effort at internal communications is an important activity in order to keep the organization focused upon the client and the needs of the community. As ideological differences rise to differentiate management from union members, a renewed emphasis on internal dialogue can refocus efforts on service to constituents. Creating and maintaining an open system becomes both more difficult as well as important as the unionization process evolves. Significant institutional priority and resources must be allocated to this purpose.

D. EXTERNAL COMMUNICATIONS

For the school district committed to SBM, the external communications are more complex and should be viewed as being multidimensional. Because of the shifting of much instructional decision-making capacity to the building level, communications networks between the local school and its constituent community must be highly effective and well utilized. At the same time, there exists even greater need to refine and improve the communications capacity at the systemic level in order that the two levels are not at odds with one another and to ensure that patrons and clients receive consistent and similar data and interpretations.

The smooth flow of communications between the school district and its many publics is a difficult, yet important task. Clients and patrons ranging from students, to parents, to citizens are most important at the individual level while groups ranging from PTAs to band boosters to community advisory groups are equally important at the school organizational level. Additionally, such external groups as city council, service organizations, church groups, fraternal organizations, neighborhood associations, chamber of commerce-type organizations, union locals, merchant groups, and other formal and informal groups must be dealt with and involved.

Because the school system is a public and quasi-municipal corporation, the external communications process takes on an even more important priority. With the recognition that all of the above groups and individuals serve as both clients or potential clients as well as stockholders in the public corporation, the importance of communications becomes more clear. On the one hand, the school system must understand client needs in order to provide programs suited to those needs and desires while, on the other hand, the corporate stockholder must know and appreciate the corporate effort and effectiveness in order to approve financial and other allocations and expenditures. Conceptualization of the community as both owner and user of the school district assists in defining the extreme importance and priority that must be given external communications.

At the building level, the direct involvement of the community in a wide variety of activities tends to enhance the communications process. Astute building-level staff and principals intimately involve the community in needs assessment, in educational planning, in priority establishment, and in program evaluation. In addition, the community serves as advisory in a variety of areas including Title I, facility planning, cocurricular activity, personnel selection, and other educationally oriented items. The use of the school as a community resource and for community meetings and activities also is an appropriate concern for the staff and community to resolve.

Extensive efforts in parent/teacher conferences provide excellent entry into school/community communications. Scheduling of conferences to the convenience of the parents (late afternoon and evenings) further emphasizes the seriousness and concern, hence commitment, the school feels for establishing communications with patrons. Utilizing the parent conference to involve the parent in the planning process further establishes trust and communication between school and home.

Astute building personnel encourage community involvement and extend communications channels by utilizing the community as school volunteers, by involving community members in a wide variety of school activities ranging from parent and grandparent days to career days, and by regularly requesting dialogue on educational matters. Easy and often overlooked avenues such as coffees, lunches with the staff and/or principal, neighborhood coffees, and similar activities can promote external communications. Active community participation in cocurricular activities such as carnivals, dinners, and other quasi-educational endeavors also assists in the communications process. Both formal as well as informal networks are utilized to maintain and improve communications linkages.

At the school district level, external communications is often along more formal lines although the development and cultivation of informal techniques must also be emphasized. Formally authorized avenues such as newsletters, annual reports, radio, and television, along with advisory groups, interest group meetings, and other formal structures, are used. Each and all of these mechanisms are important tools for the educational leader to use in establishing and maintaining lines of communications.

One often overlooked avenue of external communications is the myriad of formal and informal clubs, fraternities, organizations, and groups that include school staff as members. It is a safe assertion that almost every group in existence in a school district includes school staff on the membership roles. Many school personnel are in leadership positions in these various organizations and provide natural linkage to the school district. As members of the social system called the school district, staff are also intimately involved with a number of other social systems across the community. Most of these are quite unrelated to the school system other than in the members' individual role as client/stockholder in the public corporation called the school district.

However, although no official connection exists between say a Rotary club and the school system, each and every member of the Rotary is a client/patron/owner of the school system and therefore has concern with and pride in the educational system. Information and data regularly supplied by a colleague in Rotary is much more cogent and important than that provided through the various media channels. In addition, the ability to raise questions to an organizational colleague allows for clarification of questions and issues. Most school districts encourage staff to belong to a variety of community organizations. Indeed, some provide necessary time and expenses to allow for such participation.

As an added communications technique, many school systems recruit community members to conduct dialogue with their peers. This mode of communications is most effective when dealing with particularly touchy and delicate issues that require the members of the staff to "blow their own horn." Hearing about and learning of all of the exciting and relevant programs provided students is much more believable when it's presented by a friend and neighbor rather than by those with vested interest. An additional benefit of this approach is that those who volunteer to be the message carriers become much more knowledgeable and informed about the state of the school district and therefore more valuable as stockholders.

SUMMARY

The conduct of the communications function is of great importance to all school districts but especially crucial to those school systems attempting to introduce SBM as an operating reality. Because these districts are so dependent upon both internal and external support and understanding, the communications function assumes even greater importance. School personnel must develop skill and expertise in the many forms of communications. Educational leaders soon learn which particular mode of communications is best suited to their particular style and exploit that strength and search for assistance in developing positive approaches in the other communications techniques. The sharing of data, the inclusion of the many publics in the affairs of the school district, the involvement of staff in setting organizational objectives, the effort at providing information to all members of the school social system are all important to survival and depend on acuity in communications.

CHAPTER 8

Instructional
Support

A. INTRODUCTION

The notion of the instructional support function as one of the seven basic functions of the school system was introduced in Chapter 2. To paraphrase the materials provided in Chapter 2, the instructional support function of the school system involves a variety of activities, resources, and personnel all directed toward ongoing support of the instructional delivery system. Any school system activity that assists in the instructional program, either directly or indirectly, is considered a part of the instructional support function.

All school systems provide some form of instructional support, whether it be in the form of the principal and/or volunteers for such special instructional activities as tutorial and special programs or the complete range of special staff who provide such activities as music, art, physical education, gifted instruction, special education, advanced placement, alternative programs, and other efforts supported by the school budget.

In the system committed to the site-based management concept, the instructional support function assumes a slightly different role. Because great flexibility is allowed the individual building staff as they attempt to meet board of education product objectives, the need for and receptivity to instructional support activities varies widely from building to building, and the type of utilization made of support staff can vary from direct instructional presentations to in-service efforts to consultative relationships. The needs of the particular building coupled with the strength and capacity of the support personnel determine the extent to which they are used.

It must be remembered that any delineation of instructional support activities is not all-inclusive but rather symptomatic of the range of activities that would be considered as part of the instructional support function. The real limiting factors are the fiscal realities of school budgets and the human limitations in terms of creativity. Most probably, the financial crises now being experienced as a result of national deficits and high local tax rates, coupled with decreasing enrollments, has served to restrict, if not reduce, instructional support activities.

B. DIRECT SUPPORT

The instructional support activities that are considered to be direct support activities are primarily those that deal specifically with class-sized groups of children. Typically, these instructional activities are provided in special facilities by specially trained personnel on a regularly scheduled basis for all students. Also, typically, these instructional activities provide elementary classroom teachers with needed planning and preparation time. At the secondary level, these instructional activities are viewed as part of the normal departmental organization and are considered as key components of the total program of instruction.

However, because of accelerating costs and decreasing clientele, many school systems have had to devise other mechanisms for delivery of the variety of instructional support services. Some districts have moved toward providing such services at the elementary level by utilizing the instructional specialists as consultants to the elementary staff and as planners of instructional programs to be delivered by the regular classroom teacher. While the arrangement is not very popular with elementary personnel, it does place the burden for planning and delivering a total program on classroom personnel. It forces cooperative, building-level planning with individual strengths of teachers exploited to cover individual weaknesses. In this way, those personnel with specific strengths can extend such instruction to groups assigned to teachers who have no capacity in a particular curricular area.

In a school district having SBM as an operating reality, the provision of such special direct instructional support activities such as music, art, physical education, gifted instruction, career education, and so forth is primarily an obligation of the local staff as it develops building priorities that are predicated upon student needs. In its purest form, SBM provides resources to be allocated for specific instructional support activities as deemed appropriate by the building and community. At the very least, elementary buildings provide consultative and planning expertise for the classroom personnel. As the full range of needed instructional activities are identified at a particular building, the appropriate delivery mechanism, consistent with fiscal capacity, is also identified. As specific skills are needed, those that are not readily available on staff are procured externally, either through consultation or by engaging a person with the needed skills.

At the secondary levels, the provision of needed expertise is much more simple since most secondary teachers are subject matter specialists and are specifically trained and hired to provide instruction in a particular discipline. However, as the economic and demographic realities unfold, many specialists are having to assume instructional responsibility for a more varied program in order to justify their employment. Increasingly, teachers are expected to instruct in areas where they hold minor emphasis as well as in their major field. Increasingly, personnel selection includes attention to the diversity and variety of skills encompassed by the applicant as well as the in-depth training in a particular discipline. There is also hope for encouragement as a result of the increased concern and commitment by secondary personnel relative to the gestalt of education and for the need to assist students in their total development. The middle school movement is a particular manifestation of this recognition and is the effort of the educational profession to respond to educational needs.

Following is a partial listing of those direct instructional support activities that are most often provided in schools of the United States. Each is identified along with a series of alternative methods for delivery, culminating in appropriate considerations for the districts organized to provide for SBM.

MUSIC INSTRUCTION

Elementary Level

Elementary-level music delivery is most often through special staff trained in music (mostly vocal). The music specialist works with classroom and larger groups on a regularly scheduled basis, generally two or three times a week for periods of thirty to forty-five minutes.

In those less affluent districts, the classroom teacher attempts to provide instruction in music. If the teacher is blessed with such training, the experience is a positive one for students. If, however, the classroom teacher is completely tone deaf and unprepared, the students suffer. In many schools, attempts to develop elementary teaching teams to encompass special skills allow for students to be better served by those best trained in a particular discipline.

Urban school districts, particularly, have developed the music consultant approach to developing and implementing the music curriculum. The consultant provides training to classroom personnel and assists in the delivery of music instruction. Specific program methodologies are suggested to classroom teachers to be used in the delivery process.

In those districts embracing SBM, the local staff can call upon the music consultant for assistance in identifying and developing a delivery system most suited to the program needs of the students. Through this process, priorities are established and specific staff needs are defined. If such specific skills are not available and if the program need is of sufficiently high priority, then resource allocations should reflect it. Personnel, employed either part-time or full-time, can be sought to handle the music curriculum.

The delivery of instrumental music instruction is more complex because of the high degree of specialization involved, particularly with the stringed instruments. If instrumental music instruction is deemed a high priority, then trained special personnel will have to be found and employed. Often these personnel can double as secondary music teachers, i.e., band and orchestra directors. The teaching of instrumental music skills is a highly specialized task that cannot be subsumed by the typical elementary classroom teacher.

Secondary Level

Because of the nature of the typical secondary school, music departments with personnel trained to teach vocal music and instrumental music are developed. Depending upon the type of music program identified as appropriate, the music department provides instruction in voice, strings, brass, woodwinds, and percussion instruments. Music classes range from individual instruction to choir, band, and orchestra with a variety of special groups such as jazz band, string ensembles, quartets, madrigal singers, and so on.

Most junior and senior high schools provide music instruction. Generally, music is required for some parts of the middle/junior high school exploratory experience and is completely elective during the remainder of the junior and senior high school years.

School organizations such as band and choir provide many opportunities for students to engage in performances and to refine and improve music skills. Those activities are considered a vital part of the secondary school curriculum and are often viewed as most important by clients and patrons.

If the school system has adopted the SBM concept as an operating reality, the provision of instruction in music is dependent on a variety of variables to be resolved during the planning process. Among them are

(1) The needs assessment results
(2) The priority assigned music instruction
(3) The resources available to the school
(4) Board of education policies

Because, at the secondary level, the departmental organizational structure is so prevelant, the issue is more a function of the staff strengths and capacities rather than whether or not music instruction is provided. Most secondary schools include instrumental (band) and vocal music as components at the curriculum and an increasing number are also providing string (orchestra) programs as well.

ART INSTRUCTION

Elementary Level

Elementary art is often provided by persons trained in the art instruction field although classroom teachers are being increasingly encouraged to include art as a basic component of elementary instruction. As with music instruction, art is usually provided in specially equipped facilities, where equipment such as kilns, potters wheels, torches, and work benches are available for student use.

In those schools where neither special facilities nor trained art personnel are available, the classroom teacher works with consultative and colleagual assistance to meet the children's needs in the area of art.

Those school districts that have adopted SBM as an operating reality consider art needs in view of the total needs assessment accomplished for the school attendance area. In this way, a priority for art can be identified, and planning toward the delivery of art instruction can be initiated.

As an operating reality, the number of teachers that can provide rudimentary art instruction is far greater than those who can deliver music instruction. For this reason then, most SBM faculties tend to provide art activities with consultative assistance but feel they must engage professional assistance in the deliverance of music instruction.

Secondary Level

In the more comprehensive secondary schools of the country, art departments are very much a part of the total program of instruction and provide extensive and intensive art instruction. Art forms ranging from crayons to oils to plastics to woods to pottery and to sculpture are considered as part of the program. Again, the quality and capacity of the professional staff is the limiting factor for art programs.

Under SBM the art program of the secondary school is a function of the needs assessment and is ultimately related to the priority assigned such instruction. The level of art instruction is dependent upon the qualitative and quantitative needs of the students of the particular school.

PHYSICAL EDUCATION

Elementary Level

The delivery of physical education instructional services varies dramatically across the United States. While the more progressive and affluent school systems tend to provide such instructional activity in special facilities with physical education specialists, many school districts utilize classroom teachers for this component of the program. It is unfortunate, but true that, as a result of this, many children think of physical education as an activity devoted to kickball, relays, or some other recess type of activity. The understanding of the contributions to be realized from planned motor skill and large muscle activities is slowly increasing in this country. The use of muscle development as a method for learning basic skills is also a relatively recent development.

Because of the nature of elementary teacher training, many teachers are at least minimally cognizant of physical education program needs and, with consultative assistance, can provide a variety of instructional services.

SBM schools will be better able to meet physical education needs because of the processes utilized to determine priorities and to deliver needed programs. The building committed to SBM plans the appropriate physical education program and draws upon specialists for consultation and/or in-service assistance. If program needs are so severe that specially trained personnel are called for, the appropriate priority and resource is identified. In this manner, physical education programs are devised, implemented, and directed toward student needs.

Secondary Level

As with music and art instruction, secondary schools have supported the development of physical education departments, often for the wrong reasons. Almost every junior and senior high school includes a sophisticated interscholastic athletic program, and, as a result, the physical education department is well staffed. Occasionally, however, the physical education program is reflective of the major sports activity that is the purvue of the teacher and not a response to the physical development needs of the students. The emergence of minimal state directives in some states coupled with increased emphasis on program planning by local education agencies (LEAs) have served to stimulate the development of physical education programs that provide excellent opportunity in a variety of needed skill areas as well as the basis for the development of important health and fitness habits by students.

Secondary schools provide experiences ranging from individualized programs directed at the remediation of physical problems to very sophisticated advanced physical education skills development. In addition, the teaching of basic health concepts and physical education habits are included in most comprehensive physical education programs. Indeed, the multiplicity and variety of physical education options available to students provide for every imaginable need and aspiration, including such activities as leisure time pursuits and social dancing, as well as muscle building and gymnastics.

Under SBM, the physical education program delivery system at the secondary level is even more flexible as programs are initiated to meet the highest needs of the student population. The physical education staff of the modern secondary school must be responsive to the diversity of needs as identified in the needs assessment phase of the planning process.

SUBJECT MATTER SPECIALISTS

Many school systems include, as special personnel, persons trained to provide program assistance to teachers and students in one of any number of disciplines. In addition to the art, music, and physical education specialists, specialists in mathematics, science, foreign language, English, reading, health, social sciences, and humanities are available for either direct instruction or, more generally, to assist classroom teachers in developing program components in the particular disciplines.

In many instances, the specialist will utilize classroom groups of students to demonstrate a particular teaching strategy and/or skill. Often the demonstration lesson is presented as a model for groups of classroom teachers to observe and share. As a follow-up, the specialist visits teachers, on request, to observe and assist in technique refinement.

In the SBM concept, the use of subject matter specialists is directly related to student needs and staff strengths. As an example, if a math specialist discovers that students in a particular elementary building are largely underserved and inadequately prepared in mathematics, then the specialist becomes directly involved in a number of remedial activities. Among them might be a careful examination of materials and existing program components to discover reasons for lack of success, class visitations to observe teaching strategies and techniques, review and revision of mathematics objectives, the development of a mathematics delivery system in cooperation with the staff, in-service activities to assist the staff in learning methodologies and strategies, and, finally, monitoring and evaluation to assess the efficacy of the program. This final activity is also accompanied by a systematic recycling process that continues the improvement effort.

Similarly, the subject matter specialists provide direct building-level support in all areas of the curriculum.

At the secondary level, these direct support activities are much more oriented toward providing subject matter expertise for departmental staffs. As an example, a high school mathematics department identifies a student need for advanced calculus. The math specialist works with the department to develop the appropriate delivery system, to identify materials to be utilized, and to develop the course methodology. Similarly, the mathematics specialist can be involved in the development of applied mathematics programs to be integrated into the auto mechanics curriculum.

The provision of such specialists, while expensive, enables SBM school systems to more effectively and efficiently develop programs to meet unique and diverse student needs. As total school programs are developed, the use of subject matter specialists to provide expertise in planning specific educational experiences is crucial to the viability of the program. In addition to such invaluable planning assistance, the subject matter personnel can provide tremendous support in the form of in-service activities directed at implementing the delivery mechanism.

Persons trained in specific disciplines have the expertise needed to enable program planning to be directed at student needs as they are identified. As specific and individual program needs become known, the specialist can most efficiently and effectively diagnose those needs and suggest program options for the classroom teacher.

C. OTHER INSTRUCTION SUPPORT

Included as instructional support activities are a variety of services that are to be found in most school districts. Some of these activities are nonteaching acts although all are directly related to the instructional process. Indeed, some of the activities provide the basis for instructional decisions that impact students, particularly those students with special needs.

Because the scope of this book is to define and delineate rather than to provide in-depth discussions of the totality of the school system, the following is a brief descriptive analysis of these support activities and their appropriate function in the system committed to SBM.

PSYCHOLOGICAL SERVICES

These activities cover the range of services from special psychological assessment and testing of individual students for placement into appropriate special education programs to general psychological support provided classroom and other staff as a result of involvement of psychological personnel in the in-service program of the school system.

Psychological services personnel provide both diagnostic and treatment services to the students of the school system. While psychologists are most often involved in the multitude of special education and individualized education plan (IEP) activities, they are also crucial participants in the support system provided all students and staff of the school system. In addition to the activities already mentioned, the psychological services staff participate in on-going assessment and other activities including liaison with medical agencies and social service agencies as well as interpreting assessment results to parents and other interested parties.

The rapidly accelerating demands of the Education of All Handicapped Children Act (P.L. 94-142) has expanded the duties of the psychological services department. Preparation of data for IPE decisions, the various assessments and test batteries that must be administered, the coordination of a variety of efforts by various specialists, the interpretation of data to parents, and the final placement of students add a complexity and volume never predicted or expected. With the increased emphasis on mainstreaming and all it implies, the myriad of duties imposed upon psychological services personnel are dramatically expanded. With the SBM emphasis on program development and delivery at the building level, the obligations of the psychological services staff are expanded and require more intimate knowledge and understanding of particular building idiosyncrasies and needs. Psychological services staff must respond to their client buildings in a variety of ways in order to properly serve the students.

SOCIAL SERVICES

The social services staff of the school district provides a multitude of services and support activities to the clients and teaching staff. The school social worker is the most direct and constant communications linkage with the homes of students. The school/home cooperative efforts needed to successfully meet student needs are largely the responsibility of the school social worker.

Urban school systems and urban children are exposed to and suffer from any number of stress conditions ranging from poverty to the pressures of population density. The vastness and impersonal nature of the city also weigh heavily on the environment in which the urban youngster lives. Pressures that disrupt the nuclear family are especially high in the urban centers of the United States. Increasingly, barriers to success in school are the result of nonschool related conditions and realities.

The number and scope of social, religious, and governmental agencies that provide assistance and services to citizens is truly mind-boggling. One of the school social worker's principle tasks is to coordinate this multitude of services such that the student can function in the educational setting. Family, neighborhood, and individual conditions do impinge upon and help determine student needs. Academic programs that do not consider the environmental and sociological factors operating within the student's life are doomed to failure. The social worker is therefore an important source of data for program planning purposes as well as an important provider of support services to students, staff, and families.

Typically, the urban school system includes a high proportion of students from families whose incomes are below the poverty minimums, from single parent homes, and/or from homes where social disorganization is the norm rather than the exception. In many urban households, child abuse is not unknown, and the normal patterns of parental support are totally ignored—indeed, are not even recognized. In situations such as these, where undermployment and unemployment are considered normal, the school social worker provides an important stability in the life of the children.

In SBM situations, the capacity for the building to call upon the social services staff for support is often the difference between success and failure for the student.

HEALTH SERVICES

The provision of comprehensive health services is another support activity that is important to the school system. Because of the cycle of poverty effects on urban children and because of the many factors already discussed in the preceding section, the backlog of health related needs that mitigate against academic success are more prevalent in the urban centers of the United States.

Statistical data on infant mortality, on incidence of childhood disease, on accidents, and on safety related hazards like fire and/or crime rates all point to increased risks associated with central city residency.

The school health department typically comprises a number of school nurses reinforced by dental, medical, and other health professionals who serve in a consultative relationship with the school system.

In addition to providing direct health and emergency services associated with health care, the school health service department provides curriculum development advice on health instruction and, in many instances, offers direct teaching services for particular health topics that are to be presented to students. The health services personnel also conduct vision and hearing tests, provide preschool health checks for parents and children, arrange for a variety of medical examinations for students who require such attention, and handle medical referrals made by classroom teachers. Regular and routine examination for communicable diseases, providing immunization clinics, and maintaining health records are also part of the task of the school health service professional.

Such seemingly unrelated activities as scheduling athletic team physicals to the solicitation of orthopedic services for children with serious spine curvature all fall within the purvue of the school nurse. Dental examination and referrals also are demanding tasks. Because of the extreme poverty found in many urban households, the school nurse must find ways of providing medical and health services at no cost to the families involved.

The health professional is a crucial element in the planning of health instruction at every grade level. Emerging thought suggests that preventative efforts take higher and higher priority and that the basic life-styles be changed to incorporate good health habits and practices. The school nurse must be a participant in such program planning and must be viewed as a subject matter specialist in the field of health.

VISITING TEACHERS

The provision of instructional services to homebound students is a task assigned to the visiting teacher. These staff members, fully certified, are trained to provide instructional services to homebound students on a short-term basis. Typically, this staff serves students who are recovering from accidents, surgery, or debilitating illness. The services are often initiated during hospitalization and continued during home convalescence.

The visiting teacher works with the school on attendance and with specific teachers to provide the appropriate instruction. If the need arises, visiting teachers arrange for a specific instructor to accompany them to the student's home for special assistance. Because of the unique and varied demands placed upon the visiting personnel, long-term situations are not conducive to academic success, and such absences are addressed through other names.

PUPIL PERSONNEL SERVICES

There are a myriad of support activities that are typically considered to be a part of the pupil personnel services arena. A few of these areas are presented in the following sections.

Student Testing

The entire administration of standardized and special tests fall under the rubric of pupil personnel services. Most school districts provide a sophisticated and varied student testing service designated to provide important data to classroom teachers, building principals, central office personnel, curriculum designers, parents, and board of education members. In addition, college placement and aptitude tests are routinely offered to students. Such highly specialized tests like music aptitude to such sophisticated instruments like the various preference instruments are administered, scored, interpreted, and presented to interested parties.

More recently, states have entered into the testing derby with state assessment batteries being imposed upon school systems. The pupil personnel division has increased responsibility in the interpretation and presentation of state assessment data in its most favorable light.

Student Guidance and Counseling

The overall direction of the guidance program is a responsibility of the pupil personnel division. While guidance personnel are assigned specific buildings and become part and parcel of the professional cadre of that building, the coordination of a systemwide network of guidance services is the task of the pupil personnel office. The identification of community resources and the provision of options and alternatives for students is best accomplished in the pupil personnel office.

Student advising on program options and on career requirements are basic guidance duties. Additionally, building-level test administration and crises intervention consume major amounts of guidance resources. Assistance to teachers in working with students having unique problems is considered an important role for the school counselor. The typical school does not suffer a lack of student-related concerns for the guidance personnel to resolve. Both staff referrals as well as self-referrals are sources of client identification. Other data such as grades, absences, discipline notices, student disruptions, and referrals from other agencies are utilized to develop case files. The guidance department provides invaluable data and insight into the needs assessment process. The involvement of guidance personnel in program planning improves the viability of the delivery system.

The guidance office, besides providing information on almost every activity and option available to students, is also a stabilizing influence on students who need consistency and direction. It is the one place in the institution where student confidentiality is paramount and where students can bare their souls. In many schools the guidance professional often acts as the student advocate and smooths potentially disruptive situations.

Student Referrals and Assignment

The pupil personnel division provides the building staffs with referral support. Students that cannot be assisted by the local building staffs are referred to the pupil personnel office for evaluation and placement. Many school systems have a network of special programs ranging from alternative schools to special schools to storefront schools to tutorial options. Students in need of such special assistance are placed through the pupil personnel office.

Every school system has the need for a clearinghouse of relationships with other agencies that involve students. The juvenile court system, the police department, and other municipal and governmental agencies are concerned with the provision of services to youth. The logical place to address such multifaceted concerns is the pupil personnel office. By concentrating all such activities in this office, the due process requirements can be carefully monitored so that the student is protected. It is also possible to coordinate the variety of available resources into a cohesive assistance package for particular students.

The pupil personnel office often gets involved in investigative activities. These generally revolve around truance issues but sometimes are much broader than that. For example, investigation of child abuse, child labor charges, and child neglect are not uncommon investigative arenas.

The development of systemwide student rights and responsibility documents, as well as assistance to buildings in their interpretation of such policies into building codes, is also an important pupil personnel function. It is under this rubric that student transfers, suspensions, and occasionally expulsions are made.

The pupil personnel office often is charged with attendance boundary development and with maintaining relatively balanced student assignments: balanced in terms of numbers, race, and socioeconomic level. This is increasingly a more demanding and difficult task, particularly as court and legal requirements are handed down.

Routine Student Services

The handling of requests for work permits, screening for job placement, assistance in college application, compiling of student academic, attendance, and related records, and other routine yet necessary tasks are ongoing components of the task(s) of the pupil personnel office. The development and maintenance of student archives places additional demands on the office. Requests for historical data are seemingly inexhaustible and must constantly be filled. Microfilm, computer storage, and other mechanical means are being utilized to more adequately address this particular issue.

Other Pupil Personnel Tasks

Among the more demanding and consuming activities of the pupil personnel office is the preparation of the voluminous reports for the many state and federal agencies. These reports deal with enrollments, attendance, grades, courses taken, demographic data, and any other pupil concerns. Many states conduct audits of enrollment and attendance data in order to verify state financial solvency.

With the increased court activity concerning student rights and responsibilities and with due process requirements becoming more strongly recognized, the pupil personnel office is increasingly being requested to present data in court cases and to other agencies. Child custody cases are particularly demanding of time and energy.

The logistics of keeping track of thousands of students in an increasingly mobile society is a fierce task for the pupil personnel staff. Student transiency is accelerating in most urban centers, and it is not unusual for a building to have a student turnover of more than 250 percent during the course of an academic year (Dezavala Elementary School, Fort Worth, Texas). Maintaining a record of such rapid change in domicile is an important yet often overlooked task of the pupil personnel division.

MEDIA SERVICES

The term instructional media is a fairly recent addition to education. It is used to indicate the evolution of the traditional school library into an instructional support activity that encompasses all forms of printed, visual, and aural materials appropriate to the instructional program. The instructional materials center has become the focal point for most instructional activities conducted in the school. Media personnel must be skilled in the use of multimedia techniques.

With the technological explosion of the past decade, instructional media services have taken on a new and dramatically expanded role. Technology has evolved to a point where it is possible to maintain visual and aural communications anywhere in the world and beyond. The rate of knowledge development is such that the volume of knowledge is doubling every five years. Storage and retrieval capacity has exploded with the invention of microchips and printed circuits. The age-old reliance on printed materials has been rendered obsolete and in its place has come the combination of multimedia options. Instructional media support personnel must not only know about and utilize the variety of media techniques already in existence; they must also be able to create and develop media presentations to fit every instructional mode and need.

As program planning proceeds under the SBM concept, the instructional media personnel have major responsibility in the development of materials needed to accomplish the diverse educational objectives that vary from student to student. Instructional media can be equated with the tools of teaching. Much like the carpenter uses woodworking tools and the painter uses brushes, the educator must use the multimedia processes as tools for educating students. Included as educational tools are books, printed matter, globes, models, tapes, records, cassettes, films, film-strips, videotapes, pictures, relief maps, cards, microfilm, and disk storage.

Part of the emerging media services role is the production of television programs and videotapes. Many urban school systems are allocated public service channels and/or cable channels and the programming responsibility usually falls upon the media department. Completely equipped production studios are the norm rather than the exception in most urban school systems.

The school librarian of the 1950s, 1960s, and 1970s has become the coordinator of the multimedia technology of the 1980s. In addition to possessing the many talents and skills ascribed to the school librarian, the media staff member must be an expert in every communications form known to mankind and must additionally be able to direct and produce a variety of programs.

There are, of course, any number of additional instructional support services that can be identified. The preceding list was intended to be a sampling of a more exhaustive list of such activities. Not included were such services as volunteer services, tutorial activities, community-based instruction, work study efforts, and many other unique efforts toward quality education.

D. ORGANIZATIONAL DEVELOPMENT (TEACHER CENTER)

An important support activity for the school system that has committed itself to the SBM concept and all that SBM implies is the retraining necessary to enable staff to develop the expertise needed to function in the expanded autonomous mode. Historically and traditionally, educational decisions, when made at all, have been handed down from top to bottom, with procedures tightly drawn and usually inflexible and rigid. In many urban school systems the organizational development function is housed in the emerging notion of teacher centers. The term *teacher center* is the result of federal legislation that proposed such developments.

The conceptualization of the teacher center to serve as the organizational development support service in a district engaged in SBM activity requires that great flexibility be provided the personnel assigned to the teacher center. Because they, the staff, are on call to all building and to all staff, they must have the capacity and freedom to set their own operating style and agenda. Of course, top priority must be given to assisting buildings in the development of in-service activities that address school system objectives and needs. Beyond that, the priorities must include assisting individual teachers and groups of teachers in developing instructional expertise and techniques.

Personnel assigned to the teacher center must be commonly recognized by all staff as master teachers. These persons are drawn from all segments of the school, i.e., primary, elementary, middle, and high school, as well as special education and vocational-technical education. Assignment can be either on a short-term basis (one month to one year) or on a permanent basis (less desirable). Peer recognition of master status is essential to success.

If possible, a marriage between the school district and an institution of higher education adds quality and credibility to the teacher center. The assignment of mutual staff on a cooperative basis allows for extended flexibility. Additionally, graduate credit and advance degree possibilities are also potential outcomes of such cooperative arrangements.

Once credibility is established, largely due to the obvious quality of selected staff and operational autonomy of the center, the demands for service skyrocket and become impossible to satisfy. As buildings identify areas of concern and weakness, the teacher center staff can draw on strengths from other buildings and develop sharing programs that effectively provide in-service activities.

The advantages provided as a result of short-term appointments are manyfold. First, such an arrangement allows for involvement and recognition of many additional personnel that should improve staff morale. Second, as particular in-service needs arise, specific staff who encompass strengths in the area of need can be assigned the task. Third, rotating teacher center personnel allows more staff to "learn about the total system." Fourth, the persons who have a teacher center experience return to their home school as stronger contributors to the SBM process. Finally, it is healthy for the clients and patrons to know that there are many high-quality professional educators on the staff.

An added bonus of the teacher center concept is that those persons who are selected are generally persons who exhibit leadership capacity. They are much respected by their peers and are opinion setters in the district. Their service as teacher center staff allows careful assessment of their leadership ability and can be considered a training experience for future leadership (administrative) assignments.

An important consideration for most effective organizational development activities is to strive to locate the bulk of the in-service efforts at the buildings where the participants are assigned. In this manner, operational realities cannot be ignored, and direct application of techniques can be observed. Also, it is possible to directly involve the community in the development process, thereby enhancing community acceptance of the educational program.

Although many school systems resist allocating scarce resources to the organizational development function, this area is quickly becoming a very important activity because the rate of turnover and replacement of staff has dramatically slowed. Because of decreasing enrollments and also because of increased salaries, turnover rates have reduced a great deal. Therefore, the ability to generate new ideas and inculcate new methods through new staff members is significantly altered if not negated. Organizational development and in-service is the emerging method to generate program change and improvement.

An appropriate dollar figure to allocate to organizational development is between 1 and 2 percent of the total budget. If the development of the teacher center concept is consistent with local priorities, it would not be inconsistent to assign from 0.5 to 0.7 percent of the teaching staff to that activity. Such allocations would provide resources to allow for significant staff involvement in training activities conducted in a variety of locations while also providing resources to invite outside experts to come to the district to supplement the local staff resource.

Organizational development and in-service education is a continuing concern and must become institutionalized in the urban school system. Assimilation of emerging educational ideas and the creation of new approaches to solving education needs is an ongoing problem for the educational system. Rapid examination and quick responses to issues offer a big advantage and expanded potential. Institutional lethargy can be dispelled through commitment to such a process.

E. OTHER SUPPORT

Located in proximity to the school system are a number of institutions, agencies, and governmental units that can be considered support possibilities. For example, governmental agencies, i.e., city government, police and fire departments, state agencies, courts, etc., are all potential instructional support organizations. Any and all of the forementioned can provide instructional support services to students and staff of the school system. What better way to study government than by interning at city hall or at the state capital? The intricacies of law enforcement are best learned by working with the police department.

In much the same way, the multitude of business, industrial, commercial, and financial organizations located in the urban center also provide instructional support potential to the school system. Participation by members of all of these organizations in the various curriculum advisory committees provides direct linkage between the school system and the private enterprise. It also provides a reality orientation to the programs being developed to serve the particular occupation and/or business.

There are a number of educational institutions that are directly involved in providing instructional support to the urban school systems. Among them can be included the following.

LOCAL AND STATE UNIVERSITIES

Urban centers generally have a number of public and/or private universities located in close proximity to the city. Most of these universities have departments and/or schools of education that need the urban school system as a laboratory to provide field experiences for education students. In addition, the staff of the school system is a significant consumer of graduate opportunities and courses provided by the university.

Research interests and activities of university faculty are fueled by the urban school district. Close liaison and cooperative efforts are a natural result of close relationships, possible because of the commonality of interests and the potential for field testing that exists in the school system.

Use of the university staff for in-service activities, for planning of programs, for educational studies, and for instructional support are obvious advantages that accrue the school system.

A largely untapped resource are the noneducational segments of the university. Examples are only limited by the limits of human creativity. School districts have developed relationships with medical schools and health departments to provide diagnostic and remedial health activities. The development of collaborative relationships with the department of agriculture is a tremendous added resource for urban children. Programs such as 4-H are positive influences on urban children. It is also possible to develop other relationships with university schools, such as business, engineering, and law, to provide added instructional support. It has been the privilege of the author to have received the utmost cooperation by university officials to assist the local school district.

STATE DEPARTMENTS OF EDUCATION

The 1960s and 1970s saw a mass infusion of federal funds into the development of state departments of education. Because of such massive federal programs as the Elementary and Secondary Education Act (ESEA), the Education of All the Handicapped Children Act, the Vocational Education Acts, and other federal efforts to support LEAs, the need to train department of education personnel grew. As a result of federal resources, state departments of education have added staff and trained existing staff in the provision of consultative services to LEAs. Specialists of every persuasion and discipline are now available to LEA personnel. These state department staff members assist in program development, provide in-service efforts, monitor state mandated programs, and generally offer assistance to LEAs.

In addition to performing the myriad of mandated services needed to assure that the necessary reports, demographic data gathering, fiscal audits, program audits, and state mandates are followed, the staff of the department of education provides curriculum guides, program objectives, assessment instruments, evaluations, in-service activities, community development efforts, and countless other services to the LEA. While not always appreciated, these support services are important to the clients of the LEA and ensure that minimal standards of educational quality are met.

The authorization of federal pass-through funds to the LEA is another important state department of education function. As these funds are allocated to the LEA, compliance requirements are monitored by the state department of education staff. This, of course, guarantees that the intent of the federal legislation is followed and that the designated students are served. Often, special assistance program funds designed to serve particular groups are distributed to districts housing significant numbers of children needing a particular program. In these instances, it is not unusual for state department personnel to become actively engaged in program planning, client identification, program delivery, and program evaluation. Included are the training of local staff and extended community involvement in the program.

Many state departments have developed sophisticated data gathering and storing capacity so that assistance is extended to the LEA in terms of planning and in developing management information systems as the basis for sound planning efforts.

State departments of education perform a variety of support roles. First, they are charged with the monitoring responsibility to ensure all state and federal legal mandates are met. Second, since education *is* a state responsibility, the state department of education has a directing responsibility to ensure that programs are available to all children in the state. Third, and much more recent, the state department of education provides a multitude of direct and indirect instructional services to the staff, students, and patrons of the LEA. Many were mentioned above but many more are provided both formally as well as informally.

As the burden of financing education steadily shifts from local property taxes to state revenues and as legal demands for specific programs are mandated by state and federal legislation, the active control and governance function is also increasingly subsumed by the state department of education. This phenomenon will accelerate during the 1990s because of the abovementioned forces and also because natural bureaucratic tendencies normally focus on increased centralization and greater and more rigid control. This is perhaps the strongest and most compelling reason for LEAs to seriously consider a carefully planned move toward SBM.

SUMMARY AND CONCLUSIONS

The instructional support activity has existed for many years and in many ways. The attempt in this chapter was and is to focus on instructional support as a discrete and distinct function of the school system that is moving toward SBM.

The delineation of instructional support activities into a separate function lends credence to the support nature of the various activities.

Because, under SBM principles, the local school building staff has enormous flexibility and autonomy, support staff are *not* in a directing and/or ordering mode. Rather the support staff must adopt a different behavior pattern that indicates the availability of expertise and great program resources for utilization by the building personnel. It might be possible that certain support personnel could become extraneous because their contributions are rejected by building-level patrons and staff. This would happen because of the attitude and demeanor of the particular personnel involved.

It has been the experience of the author that staff behavior adjusts remarkably as realities are brought into focus. As SBM processes become institutionalized, the behavior norms are modified to accommodate the implications of SBM very quickly, support staff generate great demands for their services, and, even more surprisingly, the services are directed at the needs of the clients.

CHAPTER 9

Noninstructional
Support Services

A. INTRODUCTION

As part of the site-based management (SBM) implementation, the provision of the multitude of support services assumes an important priority for the noninstructional staff of the school district. In keeping with earlier discussions about centralization/decentralization dichotomy, the management and delivery of all noninstructional services is recommended to be on a highly centralized basis. The reason for this strong recommendation is that the noninstructional services area does not deal directly with the provision of educational programs to students and, further, that many of the noninstructional tasks are more efficiently and effectively performed on a larger, more massive scale. By establishing these services on a centralized basis, economy of scale is realized. Additionally, the direct management of the noninstructional area by specially trained personnel allows those persons directly involved with the instructional process to devote their full energy and talent to working with the clients to be served.

While treatment of the variety of noninstructional services is neither complete nor comprehensive in this chapter, a number of activities will be briefly introduced and discussed. More complete discussions of what many authors call auxiliary services are available in a number of texts on administration, particularly those dealing primarily with school business administration.

The effort of this chapter is to place the concept of the provision of noninstructional services into an appropriate SBM context. Obviously, each school system entering into SBM will develop its own approach to the provision of support activities. What follows is merely an attempt to establish a model for the reader's consideration.

B. MAINTENANCE SERVICES

The care and maintenance of school facilities and equipment is an important and expensive function. The maintenance services function requires the coordination of a number of highly specialized personnel into an ongoing service for the school district.

Maintenance activities range from routine and preventative to emergency and highly specialized. Such diverse skills as carpentry, electronics, plumbing, masonry, glazing, landscaping, decorating, mechanical, and others are incorporated into the maintenance function.

Many large districts employ maintenance personnel with sufficient expertise to complete projects of rehabilitation and renovation. Such activities, while popular with the skilled craftsmen, often detract from the ongoing maintenance needs of the school system and cannot always be scheduled.

Modern systems of education require facilities and equipment that are most sophisticated and complex. Requirements for heating, cooling, and ventilating are far more demanding than a few decades ago. Additionally, technological developments have placed additional requirements in terms of utilities and other services to the school facility. Standards for construction, lighting, heating, cooling, safety, health, etc., place continuing pressure on the school maintenance department.

Maintenance can be defined as "that function of the school system associated with repairs and replacements which ensure continuous usability of the physical plant, equipment and service facilities. Ensuring availability for continuous use is the key priority in any maintenance program . . ." (Candoli et al. 1984, 231).

The development of work schedules for maintenance personnel must involve attention to three distinct types of maintenance activities. Those activities are as follows:

(1) Those routine preventative maintenance chores that can and should be scheduled on an annual, quarterly, monthly, or weekly basis. Such activities as safety checks, painting, motor repair, filter replacement, and electronic equipment rehabilitation can be regularly scheduled for the school system.

(2) Those maintenance activities that are requested for programmatic reasons. Included here could be such work as wall removal to create

large group spaces, insertion of walls to create seminar spaces, installation of special equipment, and creation of special spaces and utility services. These requests are predicated on program priorities that are established by the various schools and must be considered as vital to the maintenance services.

(3) Those emergency maintenance activities that must be accommodated in order that the system can continue to provide educational services to clients. Included here are such activities as glazing, light fixture replacement, equipment repair, and other unexpected maintenance activities that arise as a result of unforeseen occurrences and activities.

The scheduling of maintenance personnel so that each of the three kinds of needs are provided for is a crucial and difficult task. All too often the maintenance division gets bogged down in the emergency areas and little else is done. Equally serious is the syndrome that suggests all requests for maintenance work are of an emergency nature. The person charged with the scheduling responsibility must develop appropriate guidelines to ensure that fairness and equity will prevail. Requests from buildings must be quickly acknowledged, and early disposition of those requests is important. The placement of the request into the appropriate category with early identification of when a maintenance work order will be issued will ease the concerns of building administrators. The development and following of a work schedule will also assist in building acceptance and credibility.

Those systems that provide the most effective maintenance services have developed a balance between the three major categories. Typically, school systems engaged outside contractors to allow a balance to emerge. As emergencies proliferate, outside contractors are asked to bid on work normally done "in house" to relieve pressures that mount. In this way, the maintenance division can most efficiently and effectively utilize the personnel employed, and the numbers of personnel do not become so large and unwieldy as to be inefficient.

Because maintenance personnel are considered to be skilled tradesmen, the hourly salaries of these people are substantial. It becomes most important to schedule their activities so that the talents of these people are used to the optimum extent. Highly skilled plumbers must be assigned plumbing tasks while finish carpenters must be utilized in their skill area. If this is not carefully scheduled, an inordinate waste of talent occurs, and the maintenance needs of the school system are not addressed to the best and highest potential.

C. CUSTODIAL SERVICES

Custodial support services is another area where school systems run the risk of gross waste and inefficiency. The typical educator knows little about the custodial function and, as a result, deploys those personnel ineffectively. For example, cleaning personnel should perform their tasks at such times when the facility is not in active use. The cleaning task, in order to be most efficient and effective, should be accomplished with a minimum of interference and with no downtime. The sweeping, dusting, and vacuuming of a facility is best done in a time sequence that permits an entire floor or group of rooms to be systematically and totally cleaned at the same time or in the same sequence.

There is substantial and persuasive evidence that suggests that the state of cleanliness and orderliness of a facility strongly influences the treatment accorded it by the users. Students and staff will respect and protect the facility that is routinely and effectively cleaned much more than the facility that is dirty and uncared for. In the long range then, the custodial service can be a major contributor to the efficient operation of the school system.

The planning and coordination of custodial services is a serious and demanding logistics exercise. Because of the importance of the service and because of the need to be highly cost-effective in its provision, the person in charge must be a highly trained and creative administrator. As was mentioned earlier, the most productive return on custodial expenditures is possible if those functions are scheduled during "off" hours or when the facilities are not in heavy use. This means that the bulk of the cleaning activity in schools must be accomplished after the instruction and other activities are concluded. In the typical school that encourages extensive community use of facilities, the bulk of the cleaning activity must take place after 10 P.M.

The scheduling and coordination of custodial activities is an important administrative task. Because of the many varied surfaces and floor treatments, custodial runs must be adjusted in accordance with the traffic patterns, the type of surface, general weather conditions, and the amount and kinds of care equipment available. Custodial schedules must reflect daily, weekly, monthly, semiannual, and annual cleaning tasks. For example, carpeted areas must be vacuumed daily and shampooed periodically according to need. Today there are a variety of both dry as well as wet preparations for carpet care. The size and power of the vacuum is also an important factor in the quantity of area one can adequately clean. In like manner, other floors, i.e., terrazzo, vinyl, asphalt tile, wood, etc., require different equipment and materials and are substantially different in their care requirements.

Chalk boards, shelving, desks, and other areas require regular cleaning by the custodial forces. Special areas, i.e., rest rooms, shower rooms, locker rooms, etc., require regular scrubbing and application of disinfectant to meet safety and health standards. Walls must periodically be scrubbed and spot cleaned while light fixtures must be dusted regularly. Windows and curtain walls must be regularly washed and window shades dusted.

Typically, the average amount of space to be cared for by a custodian ranges from 12,000 to 15,000 square feet. Each facility must be divided into specific custodial runs and a custodial schedule developed for each position. A sample schedule is shown in Figure 9.1.

Custodial schedules, similar to Figure 9.1, must be made available for every person on the custodial staff. Because few persons come to the school district trained as custodians, the staff must develop and implement such a program.

Typically, new custodial personnel are on a three- to six-month probationary period. During this time the training process must take place. Formal class sessions are usually coupled with assignment to experienced personnel for on-the-job instruction.

Pride in the appearance of the building and a genuine commitment to providing an important service for the school system is important. Custodial personnel must feel that there is opportunity for advancement in order to maintain an interest in the job.

10:00–11:00 P.M.	Clean rest rooms. Clean administrative and guidance offices.
11:00–11:30 P.M.	Clean student activity center and corridor around this area.
11:30–MIDNIGHT	Clean dressing room area.
12:00–2:30 A.M.	Clean foyer and lobby and do preventative items noted on list.
2:30–3:00 A.M.	Lunch
3:00–5:00 A.M.	Clean rooms #kindergarten, EMR #1, EMR #2, #4, #5, #6, plus rest rooms in area.
5:00–6:00 A.M.	Clean the gym area.

FIGURE 9.1 Custodial schedule for #_____ run.

Many school districts combine maintenance and custodial services into a single division because of the similarity and compatibility of the two activities. Close coordination between these two services enable optimum return on the source investment. Certain routine maintenance chores can and should be accomplished by custodial personnel as they handle cleaning chores. This frees the more specialized maintenance mechanics to accomplish the highly technical maintenance tasks and results in overall savings to the district. While the custodial services function does not directly impact the instructional program, the wise use of those resources provides additional funds for instructional use.

D. TRANSPORTATION SERVICES

At the present time, roughly half of all public school students are transported to and from school. It is therefore important to recognize that transportation services are an important part of the noninstructional services of a school system. The move toward consolidation of schools coincided with the evolving automotive age and gave a great boost to the development of the comprehensive school systems of the United States. As the U.S. highway system became well developed and as motor vehicles were improved, the sight of the yellow school bus has become common across the United States. One of the original reasons for the rapid expansion of the school transportation systems was the relatively low cost of gasoline. Since the late 1970s and continuing into the 1980s, the dramatic increase in gasoline prices has dramatically altered the rationale originally utilized to justify school bus fleets. If energy costs continue to rise, the now familiar sight of the school bus may become less pronounced and evident.

Because of the versatility and different sizes of vehicles now available, the movement of children from home to school has become a relatively easy task. Statistics show that the issue of student safety is well answered through the provision of transportation services. In addition, school vehicles can be used to provide enrichment opportunities in the form of a variety of field trip experiences for students.

Certain policy issues must be examined when planning the transportation program for the urban school system. Questions to be addressed include:

(1) Is the transportation system to be used only for moving children to and from school?

(2) What are other legitimate uses of the transportation system?

(3) What are the constraints (legal and otherwise) in the transportation system?

(4) What benefits can accrue to the students through expanded use of the transportation system?

(5) What federal, state, and/or local regulations affect the transportation system?

(6) How do children qualify for transportation services? Is distance the only criterion, or are geographic and traffic concerns also important?

(7) What portion of the educational resources is most profitably invested in the transportation system (Candoli et al. 1984, 318)?

Decisions made relative to the above questions will determine the transportation policy and rules for the school system. It goes without saying that periodic review and adjustment of transportation policies and guidelines must be a planned activity.

Another transportation dilemma to be resolved is the issue between contracted transportation services versus district-owned equipment. Without question, there are advantages inherent in each of the options. If, for example, there already exists a well-established and efficient public transportation system in the city, great caution should be exercised in the establishment of a district-owned system, particularly if the existing system has the capacity to handle the student loads. If there exists no efficient public transit system, then the decision is between contract services and district-owned equipment.

Among the advantage private carriers offer are the following:

(1) No large investment is required.

(2) A large administrative management task is eliminated.

(3) The school district is not in competition with private business.

(4) The onerous tasks of maintaining and operating a bus fleet are not the school district's.

(5) Transportation personnel are not added to the complement of school district employees.

(6) Many of the criticisms can be directed to the contractor rather than to the school administration (Candoli et al. 1984, 319).

Conversely, there are advantages inherent in the school district-owned transportation systems. These include the following:

(1) Operating costs are usually less than with private contractors.

(2) Vehicles are available for use for other aspects of the school program.

(3) There is greater control over matters of health, safety, and convenience.

(4) The transportation program can be planned as an integral part of the total educational experience for the learner (as in the use of school buses for field trips).

(5) In many states, state subsidy is available to assist the local district in the capital expenditure.

(6) Transportation personnel can be selected and trained to ensure an appropriate level of both driving and educational competency. (Bus drivers are considered to have instructional roles as they can influence children in areas of citizenship, human relations, good manners, responsibility, cooperation, and so forth.)

(7) There is far greater flexibility inherent in a district-owned and -operated transportation system (Candoli et al. 1984, 319).

Recent data indicate that well over 80 percent of the school transportation systems in the United States are district owned and operated.

Among the important tasks connected with the district-owned transportation system are the following:

(1) Routing and Scheduling. The identification of stops and routes is a difficult yet important task. Care in efficient routing and in minimizing the number of stops requires expertise and can be supported by existing computer software. The effectiveness of the system depends upon the quality of the routing and scheduling.

(2) Inspection and Maintenance of Vehicles. Regular inspection and preventative vehicle maintenance are mandatory for school bus fleets. In addition, capacity must exist for emergency efforts as well. Decisions as to contract maintenance versus district-employed personnel must be made on the basis of cost-effectiveness, services needed, and safety factors.

(3) Staff Supervision and Training. The training of bus drivers is an important and demanding task. In addition to being careful and safe drivers, school vehicle drivers must have the ability to exercise good judgement and exhibit those qualities that make them positive influences on children. These qualities include such attributes as love of children, fairness, firmness, understanding, and a high level of tolerance. The training and supervision task is a continuing and important one with periodic in-service sessions usually provided.

(4) Evaluation of Services. In order to ensure maximum utilization of expensive services, the evaluation of the transportation activity is a must. Cost-effectiveness and variety of services are among the cru-

cial evaluation criteria in addition to the home-school-home concerns of the basic service. Effective evaluation can lead to improved transportation services.

(5) Standards and Specifications. The development of standards and specifications for school vehicles will provide data and opportunity to most efficiently and effectively provide the service. Specifications must be developed around such realities as road conditions, geography, number of children to be transported, climate, and others. In addition, safety and health requirements must also be incorporated.

E. FOOD SERVICES

The growing realization that the hungry child poses serious learning difficulties and that youngsters suffering from nutritional deficiencies will have great difficulty learning has made the food services program one of the more important noninstructional services of the school system. With greatly expanded federal and state assistance, the provision of balanced meals, often both breakfast and lunch, has become an important support activity.

The fact that many urban school systems have a substantial number of students (as high as 60 percent or more) who qualify for reduced or free meals reinforces the crucial nature of the service. Indeed, for many youngsters, the school meal(s) are the only nutritionally balanced meals provided during the day. The dramatic increase in single parent families coupled with the growth in number of working mothers has further emphasized the importance of the school food service program. Increasingly, school districts are using the food service activity as a teaching tool by incorporating nutrition and health instruction as part of the food service delivery program.

As with every other school activity, the promulgation of policies, rules, regulations, and procedures must be accomplished. The following questions must be considered when establishing food service policies:

(1) Is the food service program to be available to all children or just to those who meet certain specified criteria?

(2) Is the school food service program to be a systemwide centralized operation or is it to be a building by building procedure with each building principal, in effect, administering a lunch program?

(3) Is the program to be a hot foods program or a sack lunch?

(4) If the program is systemwide, should an a la carte menu be available, or should all children be expected to participate in "type

A" programs? What provisions are available for children who carry sack lunches?

(5) What provisions are to be made for feeding indigent children?

(6) Is food to be prepared at each building or is central preparation with "hot cart" delivery more desirable?

(7) Shall the school observe "open" or "closed" lunch periods? If closed, what about requests for children living close to the school to be allowed to go home for lunch?

(8) Shall breakfast programs be initiated?

(9) What educational benefits can accrue from the food programs?

(10) What is the line-staff relationship between food service personnel and building principal (Candoli et al. 1984, 327–328)?

In addition to answering the above concerns, the food service policies must deal with the following concerns:

(1) Staffing and Supervision. The type and scope of the program should suggest the kind of staffing and supervision needed. Persons trained in nutrition, dietetics, and mass feeding are needed in supervisory roles while general staff requirements should include the ability to prepare food, compatibility with children, even temperament, and adequate health and personal hygiene standards.

(2) Menus, Prices, and Portion Control. Careful planning of menus and quality and portion control enable the food service department to function at its optimum efficiency. United States Department of Agriculture (USDA) standards are generally the basis for such regulations with minimum requirements for "type A" lunches specified. The intent of food service programs is not to earn a profit but to provide the best food possible at the lowest cost to the student.

(3) Purchasing. Because so much of the materials being used are consumable, purchasing practices can contribute a great deal to the efficiency and quality of the food service program. Knowledgeable purchasing of food stuffs and other items can save a considerable amount of money and provide high-quality foods to the clients of the school system. Quantity buying during peak growing and production seasons will provide food at most reasonable costs. Careful attention to grading variations will further stretch the food dollar.

(4) Food Preparation Systems. Decisions as to central kitchen, individual kitchens, commercial manufacturing kitchens, and satellite kitchens depend on the prevailing philosophy of food service. Each has strengths and weaknesses and the choice will depend on a variety of

factors including space and equipment availability and volume of food to be prepared.

(5) Accounting, Reporting and Cost Analysis. As with every component and service of the school system, ongoing analysis and reporting is merely a good business procedure. Audits performed at regular intervals will reinforce good practices and identify weaknesses. Because the food service operation is usually of such significant volume, careful attention to good business procedures will enhance the total operation.

Finally, as with all noninstitutional support activities, the in-service needs of the staff must be met, and a general understanding of the role of food service in terms of the total educational program should be attempted. Coordination of feeding efforts with educational programs in health, nutrition, and diet is essential to success.

F. DATA PROCESSING SERVICES

The increased complexity and diversity of school systems have led to increased sophistication in handling magnified data needs and to automation efforts through the use of data processing systems. As school systems have grown both in numbers of students as well as in the proliferation of programs, the reporting and information needs of the system have also grown.

The past few decades have seen tremendous development in the data processing area. Each generation of computer brings with it greater capacity, faster operation, and lower cost. The space needs for the high-speed, high-capacity computer have also dramatically reduced. Emerging are a series of desktop models that provide all of the sophistication of previous huge installations at a fraction of the cost. The development of printed circuits and microchips has served to bring data processing to most school systems in the United States.

There is a wide variety of services that can be provided through judicious use of data processing services. In the business sphere, such activities as purchasing, inventory control, payroll, accounting, accounts payable, accounts receivable, personnel records, staff assignments, maintenance records, warehousing, budget development, and control are all enhanced through the mechanical capacity and software potential of the data processing system.

In addition, such noninstructional activities as menu planning and cycling, maintenance scheduling, transportation system scheduling and analysis, personnel activities related to negotiations, and the scheduling of facilities for community use are all greatly assisted by the data processing capacity.

Direct contribution of the data processing service to the instructional program include such diverse applications as student scheduling, which saves principals untold hours, and student grade reporting, which saves teachers much effort and time. Additionally, such activities as computer assisted instruction (CAI), student training in software development, basic skill drills, sequencing of course materials, attendance record keeping, test giving and scoring, and other similar tasks are possible. The data processing system can serve all facets of the educational system and can provide available data in a variety of forms for use by the personnel of the school system.

School system personnel tend to be quite apprehensive about data processing because of the degree of sophistication they feel is needed to communicate with the data processing personnel. Only after considerable exposure and in-service training do most staff recognize the potential for the meaningful contribution to be realized. While hardware costs have been tremendously reduced in the past decade, a complete data processing center represents a sizeable investment in both capital equipment and in operating costs to the school district. The direct costs of hardware and a building to house such equipment is but a portion of the total investment. Technically trained personnel must be engaged or the significant investment in hardware will not be amortized. Key personnel needed include programmers whose basic task is to develop software packages; operators, who produce the multitude of reports, checks, and lists needed; and other similarly trained persons who interpret the system for the users.

There are a number of approaches to becoming involved in data processing for school systems to consider. The first is sole ownership of equipment which gives the school system complete control and freedom to exploit the equipment they buy. A second approach is the concept of time-sharing whereby terminals are used by the local school system and are tied to a large central processor at some remote location. The third option is the use of a service center whereby specific data processing services are provided (payroll, purchasing, grade reporting, etc.) at a per pupil or set fee.

In many areas, groups of school systems enter into a cooperative arrangement in order to generate sufficient resources and uses to justify a sophisticated data processing system. Through such consortium development, sophisticated hardware that is very expensive can be amortized over a far greater number of students at a lower per pupil cost. Additionally, the software development needed is also distributed over a larger clientele with resulting savings to the users.

It would appear that data processing activities are limited only by the creativity and sophistication of the software developers. The hardware is already available to provide an answer to most data processing needs. The development of specific software to provide unique data packages is the key to expanded use of the system. The prognosis is that continued expansion and increased use of data processing systems will occur during the coming decade.

G. SECURITY SERVICES

The typical school district with its thousands of staff and students and its many millions of dollars invested in plant and equipment is most concerned with and conscious of security. The abnormally large incidence of vandalism and increasing concerns about student unrest and disruptions have encouraged the creation of security departments in most urban school systems. Extended use of city police departments is difficult because of other demands on the public safety departments. The stationing of police officers at the school system is not an effective and efficient use of law enforcement personnel and is not a viable option for public school districts. Yet the security needs of the students and staff require a positive response in order that the instructional programs suffer minimal interference and disruption.

The development of school security departments is a relatively recent and emerging reality. While most school systems have arrangements with local police departments so that emergency assistance is readily available on call, the routine and extensive investigative and safety needs of the system must be conducted internally. Activities ranging from investigation of truancies to child abuse and from arson to assault are becoming the purview of school safety decisions. While, in some instances, school safety personnel are deputized and permitted to function as law enforcement officers, the majority of school systems provide that the use of force and the carrying of fire arms are not an appropriate norm for school security personnel. Rather, they are encouraged to notify the police department when the use of law enforcement techniques is required.

School security personnel are extensively utilized to provide patrol services during nonschool hours and during vacation periods. They spot-check school facilities at night and on weekends and rush to the scene of a break-in to provide access for law enforcement officials. Most urban schools have electronic monitoring devices that alert law enforcement agencies in the event of an unauthorized entry or a fire. The use of security personnel to meet law enforcement officials at the scene provides immediate identification of material and equipment as well as access to areas of facility that must be examined.

Security personnel conduct a variety of investigative activities as well as providing counseling support to the guidance personnel. Typically, school security personnel are selected and trained to exploit a natural rapport with hard to reach students. The security staff relates well with students and provides a variety of support to the students. Acts of vandalism and instances of physical attacks on students and staff are quickly addressed by school safety personnel. Routine safety checks and the investigation of wrongdoings by school system employees are also important activities of the security division. Since the typical urban school system employs thousands of persons and serves tens of thousands of students, instances of illegal activities are bound to occur.

Important among the realities under which the school security personnel operate must be an understanding of the legal restrictions under which they must function. An appreciation and some understanding of the law along with a firm grasp of security techniques must be additional attributes to those basic skills of student and community relations that are the foundation of skills needed by the personnel. The capacity to deal with staff and students on an individual basis, as well as in large group confrontations, must be a prime requisite for security department personnel.

Specialized training in human relations, in law enforcement, in guidance and counseling, and in crowd control are important components of the training program provided the security personnel. The support provided by this noninstructional support department often ensures the stability and tranquility needed to allow instructional programs to proceed at their optimum levels.

H. PERSONNEL SERVICES

The personnel division of the modern urban school system has a greatly expanded and complex role. In the district committed to SBM, the personnel services activity is very diverse and important. School systems, because they are largely comprised of people who provide services for other people and because the bulk of the financial expenditures (85 percent) is allocated to paying salaries, must develop and maintain a sophisticated and viable personnel services department. In those systems committed to SBM, the personnel department must serve an expanded role because personnel requirements and disposition becomes so dependent on individual community and particular building needs. Although the personnel department participates in and provides a veritable cornucopia of services, this presentation will include a brief description of a few of those services. Numerous and lengthy books are available for the reader desiring more "in-depth" coverage. The intent of the next sections is to provide an overview of the more important activities.

RECRUITMENT, ASSIGNMENT, AND PLACEMENT OF PERSONNEL

The task of identifying personnel needs is a complex and consuming task for the personnel department. Such variables as enrollment projections, staff stability, contractual arrangements, financial capacity, curriculum priorities, retirements, and other equally hard to predict variables must be accurately assessed in order to determine recruitment strategies. Also affecting the recruitment picture is the somewhat delayed reaction in the supply and demand curve that impacts the numbers of college students who plan to enter the field of education. The wildly fluctuating enrollments at colleges and schools of education compound the already hazardous projection process. The dramatic overproduction of educational personnel that took place in the 1970s has been replaced by a serious drop in undergraduate enrollments in teacher training institutions. This marked decline in enrollments will result in still another teacher shortage, perhaps as early as the mid-1990s, unless immediate efforts are mounted to attract students to the field of education.

Traditionally, the identification of needed personnel was followed by the development of a recruitment plan that included the posting of vacancies with placement offices across the state and nation, the placing of ads in selected professional journals and papers, word of mouth communications with staff and community, and any other measures available to encourage applications from competent persons. Personnel officials scheduled visits to university campuses to interview students expressing an interest in a particular position or system. Most university placement offices provide periodic announcements of vacancies to those persons registered with the office. These persons, usually practicing educators, can arrange to apply for the particular position of interest. Urban school systems, in particular, have traversed the country on a regular basis in order to attract the best possible professional staff. In recent years, the accelerating decline in public school enrollments coupled with the over-production of educational personnel have served to reduce the need for such extensive recruitment efforts. It appears that the next few years will again give rise to such activity.

For the district pursuing SBM with all of its flexibility and autonomy, the recruitment of personnel is even more complex because more people are involved. The staff and principal, working with the community, de-velop the position description with reference to building priority and need. They then request the personnel office to search out a number of candidates for consideration. The final decision is made in concert with the personnel office after the local group has had a chance to examine the top candidates. Under SBM, recruitment is tantamount to assignment and placement since recruitment is with a particular and unique position in mind.

In more traditional settings, the personnel office assumes responsibility for assignment and placement as specific needs unfold. Typically, the office recruits a number of early (preK–2) and later (3–6) elementary teachers, secondary personnel by discipline, and, as vacancies occur, these persons are assigned. In more difficult to fill areas, i.e., math, science, vocational education, and special education, recruitment is by position.

In the SBM district, the recruitment time line is a more extended one because position ability is a prerequisite for offering a contract. Also the active involvement of staff, principal, and community tends to slow the process. On the positive side, however, the potential for employee success is greatly enhanced because the applicant meets with clients, patrons, and staff during the screening stage and major differences are identified early in the process.

EMPLOYEE RELATIONS

Employee relations covers a wide panorama of activities in the personnel services department. With the coming of the age of collective bargaining, the development of the negotiation procedures involving a number of unionized employee groups has been assigned to the personnel department. While many districts employ persons trained in labor relations and/or labor law to direct negotiations, often on a retainer or fee basis, most urban school systems develop their own "at-the-table" capacity by assigning one of the personnel department employees to this task. The personnel services staff member who is the "chief negotiator" must be trained for that role. Many systems actively search for a person trained in the law and/or labor relations to fill the position. Others select the person they feel has the highest potential and provide in-service and seminar training experiences for the person. In most instances, the "chief negotiator" has the consultative services of an experienced labor attorney to advise on contract language, legal ramifications, and other crucial matters.

Contract negotiations is a consuming and wearing task. It involves not only employee relations staff but also other district employees as part of a negotiations team. For example, a team selected to negotiate with teachers would probably include the following persons:

(1) The chief negotiator who acts as spokesman
(2) Another personnel employee who acts as a recorder
(3) An elementary principal to represent elementary interests
(4) A secondary principal or secondary assistant principal
(5) A director from the central office to represent central office concerns
(6) A person from the school business office who knows the financial realities
(7) A curriculum/instructional specialist

These persons are selected to provide expertise in all facets of the educational program and provide a data source for the chief negotiator to draw on.

In like manner, carefully selected teams are assembled to negotiate with every employee group. Since, in many urban centers, the number of public employee unions can exceed ten to twelve units, the task of collective bargaining is most demanding and time-consuming, particularly if contracts are negotiated on an annual basis. Many school systems have gone to multiyear contracts in order to provide continuity of program as well as to save valuable time for the participants.

After a contract has been negotiated and ratified, contract management becomes a prime task for the employee relations personnel. Grievances can and do make inordinate demands on the personnel office because of the many time limitations and schedules that must be followed procedurally. Depending upon the scope and sequence of the grievance clauses, the time and effort expended on such activity can grow to abnormal proportions.

Contract management also involves interpreting the document to middle management and other management personnel. Misinterpretation and misunderstanding of the contract by middle managers can set precedences that render the negotiated items useless. It becomes crucial, therefore, that all persons charged with contract implementation know what the document says and what it means. This is the prime task of the employee relations staff.

Contracts usually deal with hours, wages, and conditions of employment. In each instance, it is the responsibility of the personnel department to adjust discrepancies that arise and to assure that the negotiated conditions are scrupulously followed.

There are, of course, other facets to employee relations. Many of the other activities can be termed staff relations, and they deal with the provision of information about housing, about community affairs, about local mores and attitudes, about adjustment to the city, and about many other such efforts to make staff feel comfortable as a part of the school district. These are important and can serve to introduce new staff to their peers and to the community.

STAFF EVALUATION

An emerging responsibility of the personnel services department is the managing and coordination of staff evaluation. Union contracts are very specific on how such activities can proceed, and the personnel office must adhere to those agreed upon guidelines. In addition, state tenure laws have rigid prescriptive requirements as to time lines and documentation that must be considered.

Typically, the district will have requirements that, before dismissal, an employee must have been permitted an improvement period with specific improvement activities defined. Follow-up evaluations based upon the improvement plan are mandated. Careful documentation and analysis are also important. The personnel office is usually the group that assures compliance in staff evaluation efforts.

Most urban school districts require annual evaluation of probationary teachers and periodic (every three to five years) evaluation of tenured staff. The task of implementation is that of the personnel office. Additionally, administrative evaluations are also required regularly. Generally, administrator evaluations are the responsibility of the immediate superior and include some attention to personal and positional goals and objectives. Because administrators are not ordinarily awarded tenure in position, the evaluation determines the appropriateness of the administrative assignment. Again, the personnel office must monitor and review all of these efforts.

OTHER DUTIES

Included in the myriad of other obligations housed in the personnel services department are such routine yet important tasks as assignment of substitute teachers, maintaining vacation schedules, keeping vacation, sick leave, and personal records, maintaining personnel files, and a variety of other duties that constitute the total personnel functions.

The personnel department also provides a variety of personal support services to the employees of the school district. Included among those activities are such things as assisting persons new to the district in finding housing, introduction to the community of new employees, review and interpretation of school system policies to all employees, notification of special events and of vacation periods to all employees, personal counseling and assistance to employees, and similar activities that promote high employee morale.

In many school systems, the personnel office is also responsible for the management of the various fringe benefits, particularly those that are directly related to the personnel function. These fringes, i.e., vacation and leave benefits, sabbatical and educational leaves, various insurance benefits, and the variety of sick leave and retirement benefits found in school systems require monitoring and a record keeping system that will protect the benefit for those employees earning it. The maintenance of accurate and up-to-date records requires close attention to the use of benefits and to the fair and equitable authorization of the myriad of options available to the employees of the school system.

I. BUSINESS SERVICES

There are, in any large organization, a number of business services without which the organization would flounder and cease to function effectively. The urban school district, as one of the larger organizations both numerically as well as financially, generally provides the most developed and sophisticated business services available. Rather than providing in-depth explanations of the many services, this section will offer an overview of the four services deemed among the most important.

PURCHASING

Any operation as varied and complex as the urban school system requires the purchase of a multitude of goods, materials, services, and equipment in order to function at a level approaching optimum. Items as diverse as books and nails, trucks and paper, cement and microscopes, sugar and tar, and freezers and helmets are among the thousands of items needed in the normal course of school system activity. These items, worth millions of dollars, must be selected on the basis of best return for the public monies expended.

Purchasing departments must determine specific needs, develop specifications for appropriate quality on each item to be purchased, and develop bidding and/or quotation procedures that will ensure the highest acceptable quality at the lowest possible cost to the school district. State regulations and local policy often require specific bidding/quotation procedures and purchasing personnel must understand and follow such regulations.

It is not unusual for the school system to make purchases from several thousand separate vendors and to process several thousand purchase orders monthly. Such a volume requires careful attention to the process and extreme caution and care in assuring that full value is received for the dollars expended. Purchasing is a special and highly developed technical skill, and the persons serving as purchasing agents or buyers have refined their knowledge of the many items for which they assume responsibility and develop expertise for particular sets of items. It is not unusual to have one person responsible for all academic supplies, another for all maintenance equipment and materials, still another for all foods and related equipment, and so on. In this way, the greatest possible knowledge and expertise is made available to the organization.

WAREHOUSING AND DISTRIBUTION

The efficient and effective purchase of the thousands of needed materials is only a part of the total process of supply that must be accomplished in the modern urban school district. In order to receive the best possible unit price and in order to provide materials and equipment at the time they are needed, the purchase of supplies and materials in quantity lots is necessary. This means that these materials must be sorted and distributed at the appropriate time during the academic year, which further means that warehouse space and a distribution system are necessary.

Urban school systems have developed the capacity to anticipate annual needs of thousands of instructional and noninstructional items and are able to order in the quantity needed to guarantee the lowest price. The storage and distribution of these items is a massive logistics problem that is smoothly and efficiently accomplished by the warehousing and distributing personnel.

Computerized inventory listings, catalogs of items available and unit prices charged, regular delivery schedules to users, and the ability to order and deliver special and unique "one-of-a-kind" items are all part of the normal service provided by the warehouse and distribution staff.

After items ranging from furniture and equipment to crayons, chalk, and books to food, coolers, and kettles are ordered for delivery, the warehouse staff becomes involved. They receive shipment, check to make sure the order is fully filled, price the individual units, enter the items into the inventory, and update the catalogue for building and client use. Special areas, bins and/or shelves are identified for each item, and they are stored according to the overall inventory plan. Frozen foods need refrigeration as do such items as produce, meats, fruits, and dairy products. Dry storage also requires special storage capacity as do flammables such as paint, gasoline, and oil.

Typically, deliveries are made daily for perishable and semiweekly or weekly for other materials. A system of ordering to guarantee delivery is developed with certain provisions for emergency orders. The materials delivered to the buildings or departments are then charged to the particular unit upon delivery. Because of this, individual buildings expend funds only for materials actually used and need not carry a large inventory of educational supplies and equipment. The inventory is carried at the warehouse, and with good planning and anticipation, quality materials are provided at lowest possible cost.

PAYROLL

The payroll of the typical school system runs into the millions of dollars annually. Hundreds and thousands of employees must be paid regularly with a minimum of disruption and few mistakes.

Because each employee group is on a different salary basis ranging from hourly to daily to weekly to monthly to annually, the process must accommodate each of these wage procedures. Additionally, persons are at different points on the salary schedules, work shifts that pay premiums, work overtime, and/or receive pay for added responsibility. All of this complicates the payroll process. Fortunately, the development of the data processing capacity to process such tasks as payroll permits rapid response to deviations caused by the aforementioned reasons.

The turnover in personnel also requires a rapid response by the payroll department. Upon termination notification, the payroll department must quickly act to record data and finalize separation pay. Similarly, the initiation of personnel on the payroll requires quick, accurate response. As the hiring office initiates the employment of an individual, payroll personnel are notified of salary, starting date, and the various pieces of data needed to place the person on the payroll. Options such as nine months' versus twelve months' pay for teachers are explained, and the employee's choice is transmitted to the payroll office. As checks are prepared, they are sorted for delivery to the employee at the place where he/she is located. Mistakes and errors are responded to immediately and corrected upon notification. School district employees expect and must be assured of an accurate and timely payroll procedure.

ACCOUNTING AND REPORTING

The keeping of accurate records of all transactions is an important and demanding process. The large urban school system budget is divided into thousands of accounts, each with a specific allocation of funds to support activities for the year. Each transaction is immediately recorded and charged to the appropriate account. As contracts are signed and as purchase orders are initiated, the amounts to pay are reserved (encumbered). As salaries are expended and as charges for particular purchases are due, the checks are written and deductions made from the original appropriations.

Daily posting of purchase orders and periodic posting of payroll expenditures allows instant feedback on the status of particular accounts.

With the present sophistication of data processing systems and software, weekly and/or monthly reports to managers are possible to enable appropriate budget decisions to be made.

Typically, school systems perform quarterly budget revisions to enable current revenue data and emergency needs to be accommodated by the revised budget. The reporting of such information to decision makers and to policy setters becomes an important task of the urban school system. Only with such data available can budget decisions be predicated on optimum use of resources to the best advantage of the students.

J. COMMUNITY SERVICES

Another area of noninstructional support that provides an important service is the area of community services. Included as part of community services are such activities as recreation programs, and cooperative programs with other agencies such as the city, social agencies, scouts, medical and dental groups, and so on. In addition, the opportunity for the community to use school facilities for a variety of purposes ranging from meetings to recreation to food service to instruction falls under the community services rubric.

School districts have become increasingly aware of the need to provide extended use of school facilities in order to justify the enormous capital investment. Increasingly, also, the schools are striving to meet community educational, recreational, and leisure time needs by providing a series of evening and extended day programs and activities. These efforts contribute mightily to the acceptance the school district has in the community and are directly related to the quantity and quality of community support for the school system.

SUMMARY AND CONCLUSIONS

As was indicated at the beginning of this chapter, the provision of noninstructional support services to the school district is of crucial importance. While not directly involved in the instructional process, these services are nonetheless so important that the school system cannot exist without them.

The cursory listing of the services that are customarily included in the noninstructional arena is neither complete nor exhaustive. The intent of this chapter is to provide a general understanding of the types of activities to be included as noninstructional support and not to provide minute explanations of such activities. There are available many texts devoted exclusively to "in-depth" presentations of these activities. It is the hope of the author that the preceding will suffice to convey a general understanding of the scope and importance of the noninstructional services area.

CHAPTER 10

Governance

A. INTRODUCTION

The issue of educational governance is always among the primary topics for consideration. Because the Constitution does not mention education, thereby delegating that responsibility to the various states, Americans have evidenced much confusion when dealing with this issue. The responsibility for education governance is allocated to the state, and, in fact, local board of education members are state officials. Most citizens do not recognize that public schools are state agencies; they prefer to think of schools as local institutions. Within reason, states have historically permitted schools to function as semiautonomous entities and have made few demands other than to insist that certain state laws be followed.

However, as pressure on the educational system has accelerated, and as the state has assumed an increasing proportion of the financial responsibility for the support of schools, state-level demands and expectations have assumed greater importance. Most states are now imposing certain minimum expectations and curricula on local schools.

The notion of autonomous state school systems is unique in the free world because most countries have well-defined national systems of education. Even more unique is the possibility that local school districts, indeed individual schools, can also have a degree of autonomy and flexibility in programmatic decisions. The magnified pressure to more highly centralize the educational function has given birth to a countereffort to decentralize certain portions of the school system to permit diverse and unique individual needs to be recognized and addressed. The democratic philosophy requires that the individual be the basic unit of service and that the capacity to respond to individual differences be inherent in all institutions. With the urbanization of America and the corresponding consolidation of schools into large, complex organizations, the bureaucratic tendency to promulgate rigid rules and regulations has served to minimize the capacity to respond to individual needs.

The ebb and flow of governance edicts and the almost constant struggle for control that typifies the school system is the product of the lack of a definitive focus of the governance activity. More recently, the infusion of the intermediate level of education has served to further complicate the governance issue. States have encouraged and even created the intermediate education bureaucracies to enable more careful and closer monitoring of state mandates. Local education agencies (LEAs), on the other hand, have serious doubts as to the efficacy of such an arrangement.

In the past decade the demand for local participation and governance at the building level has taken issue with emerging state/federal control over education. The notion of site-based management (SBM) and local citizen councils is emerging as a new force in educational governance, and a number of states (California and Florida primarily) and local districts are developing models for such involvement.

This chapter will briefly explore the governance issue from the perspective of the five major levels of education: the federal, state, intermediate, local, and building levels. An attempt will be made to provide SBM rationale for each of these five levels. However, the common theme will be the possibility of providing for SBM while attending to the existing requirements at each level.

B. FEDERAL-LEVEL GOVERNANCE

The historical posture of the federal government toward education has been to become involved only when such involvement is in the national interest under the general welfare clause of the Constitution or when existing actions were in conflict with federal law. Thus, the federal government provided support for education from the very early days of the country via the ordinances of 1785 and 1787 whereby certain sections of every township were allocated toward the support of public education. With passage of the Morrill Act of 1862, each state was allocated 30,000 acres per senator and representative for the support of higher education.

In the twentieth century, federal involvement in the support of vocational/agricultural education began with passage of the Smith-Hughes Act in 1917 and accelerated with the several acts sponsored by Senator George and a number of Senate colleagues. A number of quasi-educational efforts occurred during the 1930s including the establishment of the Civilian Conservation Corps (CCC), the National Youth Administration (NYA), and other related organizations. The CCC provided job and training opportunities for young men, usually at a camp setting in a rural area, while the NYA provided jobs at the educational institution for students in need of assistance.

The first major direct involvement of the federal government in education was the post World War II GI Bill (P.L. 284), which provided financial support for veterans desiring to enroll in educational institutions. This enabled millions of Americans to aspire to and achieve a college education and/or specialized training in a particular arena. This direct subsidy totaling several billions of dollars firmly committed the federal government to support education as an important posture to be ascribed to under the general welfare clause. While still the basic prerogative of the states, education became an important national interest consideration. Examples of this occurred repeatedly in the 1950s, 1960s, and 1970s with the passage of a number of federal laws directed at active support of education. Among the more salient were the following:

(1) P.L. 815 and P.L. 874, which provided federal support for school construction and school operation in federally impacted areas thereby providing millions of dollars annually to school systems serving military bases having large numbers of federal employees as patrons. While efforts to reduce and/or eliminate a portion of these benefits are mounted on an annual basis, the Congress has seen fit to maintain this support.

(2) The National Defense Education Act of 1958 (P.L. 85-865). This was a response to Russian success in space research and provided massive resources to improve programs to meet "critical national needs." Support for science, mathematics, foreign language, and guidance resulted from this act.

(3) The Manpower Development and Training Act of 1962 (P.L. 88-164). This act authorized the U.S. Office of Education to assist in the development of occupational training and retraining programs. It provided for support of adult programs utilizing existing public school facilities and encouraged expansion of existing vocational education programs.

(4) The Vocational Education Act of 1963 (P.L. 88-210) provided for more comprehensive support of vocational education programs. (Amendments in 1968 and in subsequent years dramatically increased the funding for vocational education. Submittal of state plans

with an annual update provides the mechanism for funding of vocational education.)

(5) The Civil Rights Act of 1964 permitted the Commissioner of Education to provide technical assistance, grants, and training institutes to help communities prepare for school desegregation.

(6) The Elementary and Secondary Education Act (ESEA) of 1965 (P.L. 89-10) was an effort to bolster education programs for poor children. Since many concentrations of poor are found in the cities, the ESEA provided extensive resources to the urban school systems of the country. These funds were directed toward the improvement of elementary levels of education to support instruction in the basic skills. Included also were resources to provide support for instruction for those students whose primary language was not English. The bilingual provision provided for basic instruction in the native tongue along with instruction in English as a second language. The ESEA was and is amended by each succeeding Congress to reflect prevailing educational needs and political posture. As might be expected, each effort to amend introduces a variety of politically oriented additions, deletions, and/or advisements. With the passage of Title IX of the Educational Amendments of 1972, equity issues have been finally designated by federal law. Implementation will remain a major issue for the decades of the 1980s and 1990s.

(7) The Education for All Handicapped Children Act of 1975 (P.L. 94-142) is actually part B of an earlier act (P.L. 91-230) establishing the intent to require educational services for all handicapped persons. P.L. 94-142 provides the specific requirements as well as the federal participation pattern in terms of financial support for the programs specified. The law is most specific in requiring that all handicapped children have available to them a "free, appropriate public education . . ." (taken from the text of the Education for All Handicapped Children Act 1975). The act goes on to specify ages of qualifying children (3 through 21) and mandates state plans for serving eligible children. A number of procedural safeguards are also incorporated so that parents are adequately involved and the best interest of the student is protected. Needless to say, the impact of P.L. 94-142 will take decades to assess as rules and regulations (often conflicting) are promulgated by federal and state agencies. Local education agencies find themselves almost in a "Catch 22" situation because interpretations of the intent of the law are changed on a regular basis. The definition of what is meant by mainstreaming alone has consumed volumes as it still is not clear to local officials. What is clear is the

requirement to serve the handicapped, and most local educational agencies are making that effort.

These and other federal acts give direction and substance to federal involvement in education. As one examines the myriad of federal agencies having impact, the following stand out as being most directly significant to governance of education.

THE EDUCATION DEPARTMENT

The 1980s saw the birth of a cabinet-level department of education in the federal government. Passage of legislation creating the Education Department succeeded in 1979 after many years of extensive lobbying on the part of educational organizations, particularly the National Education Association (NEA). The new department was officially in operation in May of 1980 and is the federal agency directed to provide services and to monitor and coordinate all educational activities in the United States.

Educational programs have historically been scattered throughout the federal bureaucracy with many departments having primary jurisdiction over certain programs, i.e., Department of Interior over Indian schools, the Department of Defense over overseas schools, the Department of Labor over manpower training, etc. With the birth of a new cabinet department, efforts to consolidate all education efforts and budget under one rubric are proceeding. Needless to say, progress is slow and painful. Powerful vested interest groups are and will continue to oppose such consolidation. Labor, including the American Federation of Teachers (AFT), opposed the creation of the Education Department because the diffusion of programs through the bureaucracy strengthens labor's power while consolidation strengthens the NEA.

Similarly, the other cabinet offices hesitate to relinquish existing controls. Among the major issues is that concerning which agency shall exercise control over the implementation of the various equity laws, including race, sex, age, etc. These laws are the cornerstone of legitimate federal involvement in educational governance and must be continuously monitored and enforced. Starting with Brown I in 1954 and continuing with the Civil Rights Act of 1964 and the Education Amendments of 1972, the Congress and the courts have exercised great influence over public education in the United States.

The 1990s will see if the Education Department can gain major cabinet-level status to compete with defense, labor, commerce, and health and welfare as major departments of the federal government. The extent to which education can preserve and expand the proportion of the federal budget allocated to education will determine the extent of federal influence on educational governance.

THE CONGRESS

The Congress, by virtue of its legislative role, exercises great influence over educational governance. As noted in Section B of this chapter, a myriad of laws enacted over 200 years ago by the Congress have greatly impacted the governance of education. Additionally, the Congress annually considers hundreds and hundreds of legislative bills that are directly related to educational governance.

There are a growing number of members of the House and Senate who, by virtue of their own interest and/or training, are knowledgeable and committed to the educational process. These legislators provide the avenue for the introduction of most bills and acts directed at education.

Because the national interest is so dependent upon the continued excellence of the public school system, increasing attention from the Congress is predictable.

While both houses of Congress continue to emphasize the primary role of the state in education, they also quickly point out that the general welfare clause and the national interest are sufficient rationale for federal entry into the public school arena. Starting with the sputnik-era legislation of the late 1950s and accelerating into the 1960s, 1970s, and 1980s, the Congress has exhibited a considerable and consistent concern for the progress of the public education system of the United States. Congress has not hesitated to adopt legislation aimed at correcting inadequacies in the public education system by providing resources and mandates impacting school programs and operations.

THE FEDERAL COURT SYSTEM

Entry of the court system into educational governance accelerated rapidly after the *Brown I* decision in 1954. The courts have been almost exclusively concerned with the equity issues, with desegregation cases being, by far, the most numerous and complex. Almost every major school system in the United States has at some point been involved in desegregation litigation. The 1950s and 1960s saw a massive dismantling of the dual systems of education found in the South. Starting in the late 1960s and continuing today is great judicial activity concerning school desegregation in the northern states. In most of these cases the federal court did establish certain governance guidelines to assure that appropriate deseg-regation activities would take place. In many school districts, both south and north, the court appointed persons to implement certain court orders and programs of instruction. The Constitution and the Bill of Rights do take precedence over any and all local and state laws.

Although desegregation activities are seldom popular, particularly in the majority community, the law of the land is and will continue to be en-forced by the federal courts system. Repeated and continuing efforts to change desegregation laws have failed and the integrity of the Constitu-tion has been preserved to date.

In addition to the thousands of desegregation cases involving racial equity, the federal courts have had to become involved in other equity issues. These include sexual equity as well as the age equity issue which were primary issues of the 1980s. During the 1960s and 1970s a number of due process issues were adjudicated with resulting fairness extended to school employees and students. The issue of whether the schools are in loco parentis remains a thorny one although the courts have repeatedly addressed this matter. Another issue that keeps reappearing is the separa-tion of church and state issue with proponents of prayer in the public schools maintaining a barrage in favor of such activity. Each of these issues generate active and loud political support and opposition. The fed-eral court system is repeatedly called upon to reinforce the legal deci-sion(s).

OTHER FEDERAL AGENCIES

As mentioned earlier, many other agencies are involved with educa-tional governance. Some departments like labor, defense, and interior have direct control and jurisdiction over programs and are most resistive toward efforts to consolidate into a Department of Education. Others like the Department of Justice have indirect impact on educational govern-ance but, in the long run, can be even more important to the local school systems. For example, the Justice Department must monitor the multi-tude of equity issues being addressed via federal law. Deviation from compliance places the local and/or state system in jeopardy and brings compliance orders. Penalties for noncompliance can be very severe and can include personal liability for board members and top-level adminis-trators.

Until the establishment of the Education Department, both the Defense Department and the Department of Interior operated school systems while the Labor Department controlled the highest expenditure of training resources of any federal department. The Defense Department with its dependent schools still provides educational services to hundreds of thousands of children scattered around the world. The Department of Interior was charged with the operation of all native American (Indian) schools both on and off the reservation.

THE EXECUTIVE BRANCH

Although every president has had an impact on federal governance of education, the most active president was Lyndon Johnson. Perhaps because of his early history as a school teacher or perhaps because of his commitment to "The Great Society," the Johnson years saw the greatest proliferation of education-oriented legislation emerge from the executive office for congressional approval in the history of the country. The 1960s was truly the decade for federal legislation in education with a manyfold increase in federal support. The executive branch annually proposes levels of expenditures in the form of budget messages, and President Johnson was most active in proeducation efforts.

The executive branch has two primary mechanisms for impacting education. These include the following:

(a) The option to propose legislation to the Congress and to actively lobby for positions in public
(b) The capacity to veto distasteful legislation, particularly those laws in opposition to the executive branch point of view

In addition, the executive branch has informal mechanisms for being either pro or con on a particular issue.

Presidents Nixon and Reagan, for example, exercised pocket vetoes over education programs by not appropriating monies authorized by Congress for programs they did not support.

In summation, while the Constitution does not mention education, thereby extending governance of education to the states, history documents innumerable instances of federal involvement in education. Although federal involvement in SBM seems remote if not impossible, conditions could change. If SBM is the wave of the 1990s (after all, federal legislation requiring parent councils at all Title I schools is in the SBM tradition) and if the Education Department is truly committed to the improvement of educational services for individual students and if the public schools are to survive the many efforts being mounted to destroy them, federal-level support and involvement is crucial. Among the many actions that can be taken to support SBM at the federal level are these:

(1) Adopt micro- as well as macroviews on education.
(2) Provide for federal pass through funds to be directed to the youngsters at the site of attendance.
(3) Allow for and encourage site-based education plans.
(4) Provide flexibility in programming.
(5) Evaluate on the basis of local objectives and needs (based, of course, on federal priorities).
(6) Recognize regional and area differences.
(7) Provide support services that are viable and not make-believe.

It is important to recognize that the success of the SBM approach to education can be immeasurably assisted by the overt support of federal agencies. Permissive rules and regulations, supportive legislation; less restrictive and less rigid program definitions, and increased flexibility are all important to SBM development. As noted earlier, the LEA that commits to SBM will not have the appearance of the highly centralized system.

C. STATE-LEVEL GOVERNANCE

As noted in the previous section, the Constitution, by not including direct reference to education, thereby gives that authority to the various states as one of their primary delegations. Indeed, until the various equity and due process issues were adjudicated in the federal courts, federal involvement in educational governance was minimal and was largely confined to providing financial and technical support for a variety of programs. However, as state education activities began to conflict with individual and group guarantees, as provided under federal law, the federal authorities began to increase pressures for compliance on state and local authorities.

The acceptance by the states of the governance role in education is best reflected by the fact that virtually all state constitutions make direct reference to education and that, by 1900, all states had state superintendents of public instruction. During the same period, state boards of education were also created and, at this writing, only Wisconsin has no lay board to establish educational policy for the state.

The impact and power of the state in educational governance has greatly expanded during the past two decades. Recognition that local board members are really state officials has also given pause for reflection. As the cost of education has accelerated, demands for greater state participation in financing grew. Parallel court decisions, i.e., *Serrano*, etc., required increased state participation in order to meet equity requirements as well. Federal legislation, with its requirements for state-level monitoring and distribution of funds to local education agencies has also increased awareness and power at the state level. With increased state financial support has come increased state-level interest and participation in the governance function.

There are, of course, other compelling reasons for the resurgence of state interest in educational governance. Among these reasons, in addition to those predicated on finance, are as follows:

(1) The public demand for accountability. The National Assessment movement has given birth to a number of state assessment efforts. The establishment of state assessment efforts naturally leads to increased state involvement.

(2) Increased teacher power. Teacher unions have become ever more sophisticated and powerful. They have learned how to function smoothly and effectively in the political arena. The rapid move toward increased teacher bargaining and strengthened teacher unions has forced increased state involvement in the educational governance structure.

(3) Certification requirements. Expanded state rules in educator licensing and certification have served to more directly involve the state in local educational governance. The state determines who enters the profession and can enforce minimal standards.

(4) Statewide equity concerns. The state, as the responsible level by law, must monitor and guarantee that the equity issues are faced. Local educational agencies cannot have the option of ignoring federal and state equity mandates. Compliance in such issues is a state responsibility.

(5) State educational needs. It remains a state responsibility to focus the various educational programs such that the high-priority educational needs are addressed. The citizens of the state have a right to expect services from the public school system and that the services will be consistent with the needs, expectations, and capacities of the clientele.

Because of the dramatic changes that have occurred during the past two decades and because the various states are continuing their momentum toward increased participation in the governance of education, it is im-

portant for school administrators to realize the existing and potential role
of the various state agencies as they are involved with the delivery of
educational services to citizens.

THE STATE EDUCATION AGENCY (SEA)

The state education agency or Department of Public Instruction is the
operating arm for public education in any state. Historically state education agencies performed mostly the monitoring, licensing, and compliance functions mandated by existing laws and regulations. The state
audited enrollment figures for state funding made sure all teachers were
properly certified to teach the particular area, approved curriculum proposals that included mandated topics, i.e., health, government, etc., and
generally served as the compliance agency for education in the state.

This role began to change during the 1950s and accelerated during the
1960s and 1970s until today the state education agency has assumed
greatly expanded governance power over education. It is important to
recognize that the potential for assumption of the governance responsibility has always been available and that the national events of the post
World War II era gave increased state governance a boost.

The many federal education acts also played an important role in encouraging increased state-level participation in education. Many of the
laws require state education plans, i.e., special education, vocational
education, etc., and provide funding for states to develop planning divisions to produce such documents. Additionally, the Elementary and
Secondary Education Act and subsequent amendments provide direct
subsidies for states to expand and improve the number and quality of state
education agency employees. Indeed, the bulk of SEA staff are paid and
their offices are supported by the various federal revenue provisions. In
many instances, federal and state matching funds are utilized to create
and support a particular state-level educational activity. For example, any
state can utilize up to 25 percent of P.L. 94-142 funds (Education of the
Handicapped Act) for state-level activities but must pass through the remaining 75 percent of the resources to the local education agencies. This
and similar provisions provide a significant resource for the state education agency.

As a result of the many social and economic forces, national movements, and laws impacting education, pressure on the SEA from local
and particular interest groups has been steadily increasing. The demand
for technical assistance from local school districts, the increased
sophistication of special interest groups, the concern over quality educa-

tion on the part of parents, the demand for correction of inequities, and the general vulnerability of the local school system have all served to propel the state education agency into a more visible and powerful governance posture.

Such issues as accountability, state-level assessment, competency, textbook selection, student rights, church–state separation, employee bargaining, teacher militancy, desegregation, basic education, sex education, declining enrollments, and other emerging concerns have legitimized increased state participation. The fact is that local school personnel are more at ease when they can point to a state regulation and/or law as a response to a particular demand. It is appropriate to suggest that some of the increase in state influence and power is directly related to a desire on the part of LEA personnel to avoid difficult decisions.

What has occurred as a result of all of the varied pressures is a strong movement toward state-level centralization with all of the attendant dangers and rigidities. State mandates on all educational matters become strict rules to be followed by local districts. Programs planned at the state level are imposed on the many local units with systematic evaluation and monitoring to assure compliance. The 1970s saw the birth of fifty state education systems, each creating massive bureaucracies to ensure implementation of the many and varied mandates. While certain elements of centralization are needed and add to the cost-effectiveness of an operation, blind and total devotion to rigid rules and programs deprives local units of the creativity inherent in any group dealing with educational needs and services. Over-bureaucratization of education at the SEA level has led to serious inadequacies in the delivery of services to local clients.

In the late 1970s and early 1980s, several of the state education agencies became concerned about the relative lack of response to unique and particular student needs that are a result of highly centralized delivery mechanisms. At the same time, several of the federal education acts strongly required building-level parent councils (more importantly, the intent of the legislation was being enforced) so that there was a general reawakening to the importance of local involvement in educational planning and delivery of services. Among the states that led and are leading in this resurgence of site-level participation are California, Florida, Michigan, and Rhode Island. Processes are being established to allow (require) local units (either site or LEA) to submit plans for implementation with state and/or local goals as the parameters for unit plans. Discretion for delivery mechanisms, for budget allocations (within limits), for priority establishment, and for sequencing are the purview of the local unit. It is the opinion of this author that such development will continue to accelerate and will be the mechanism for encouraging the participation of the public in public education. It also will force educators to respond to publicly identified needs and priorities with a certain degree of accountability not presently found.

THE STATE LEGISLATURE

In every state the legislature serves as the final arbiter in matters concerning educational governance. Not only does this body have the power of the purse, it also can control every other dimension of the educational system by the passage of laws directing certain programs and/or behaviors. For example, if the state legislative body wishes to restrict educational services to a particular clientele, it can dictate that no state monies can be expended for that particular purpose. Likewise, it can establish new programs, create new delivery systems, discard existing programs, combine and expand programs, and cause many other behaviors by the passage of laws.

The reality is that legislators are political creatures who constantly work to assure reelection by responding to what they perceive the electorate wants and needs, so that many of the laws and regulations that are promulgated by the state legislative body are the result of a local constituency applying pressure for such a bill. Sometimes the state body overreacts and misinterprets the pressure and finds that the final bill is at odds with what the majority of the voters want. In those instances, the electorate causes the replacement of the legislator. Generally, state legislators do have the pulse of the community and are able to reflect the particular biases of their constituents and pass regulatory legislation that greatly impacts education. As a result of citizen pressure, the accountability movement spread, the state assessment process began, property taxes were adjusted, the "back-to-basics" legislation was instigated, certification requirements were established, competency requirements were introduced, alternative education programs were created, gifted and talented opportunities were provided, and other educational innovations were introduced via the vehicle of state law.

In similar manner, the state legislature reacts to political pressure by passing collective bargaining legislation, restricting state aid to lower taxes, providing categorical aid to assure that certain programs are emphasized, and supporting the SEA to assure compliance with legislative mandates. It is appropriate to emphasize the notion that the state legislature is really a "super board of education" with the final work on governance.

THE EXECUTIVE OFFICE

Every governor of every state has a compelling and continuing interest in the governance of education. As the chief executive of the state, the governor has both legal as well as political responsibility for the well-being of the educational system. Beyond that, most governors recognize the major impact that a well-defined and creditable state school system can have on the economic development of the state. The quality of education in a state often helps determine the location and expansion decisions made by major businesses and industries. Needless to say, such development is a major contributor to the potential for increased tax revenue.

Because the education budget of any state is from one-third to one-half of total state expenditures, fiscal realities demand close executive attention to educational affairs. Much like the federal executive branch, the governor submits annual or biannual budget messages for legislative approval. These budget documents define the state's commitment to the support of education and have great impact on the educational system of the state. Because of the increased sophistication of the many interest groups and because of heightened awareness of the role of the executive and legislative branches in support and governance of education, intensive and continuing lobbying efforts are mounted to influence both bodies. As a result, most governors have initiated an education advisory office within the executive branch. This office acts as a liaison to the SEA and to the legislature as well as performing advising and research tasks related to education.

As with legislative bodies, the executive office does respond to electorate demands and pressures. The office of the governor does and will continue to exercise great impact and influence on educational governance.

OTHER STATE AGENCIES

Similar to the realities found at the federal level, an extensive number of state agencies have great impact on educational governance. While at the federal level a number of agencies actually operate educational systems and schools, at the state level the influence and impact is more subtle and indirect. For example, the fire marshal's office (usually located in the State Police Department) has safety inspection obligations and can close individual schools and/or systems for noncompliance. Similarly the Health Department inspects school cafeterias and determines their mode of operation as well as indicating the expenditure of resources for compliance.

Perhaps the state agency with the greatest impact on the governance of education is the attorney general's department. Most of the equity regulations are developed in that office as are rules governing the myriad of procedures involved in public education. Procedures that are not clearly specified by state law are also verified by the attorney general as well as the multitude of student-related actions taken by local boards. The appropriateness and legality of local board of education policies are also of concern to this department. The attorney general is the legal advisor to all of state government, and, as a part of state government, education and local education agencies fall under that rubric.

Related to the legal concern is the state judiciary. Like the federal court system, the state courts are actively involved in the governance of education. Decisions handed down by the state courts have great impact on governance. For example, the Seranno-type decisions are completely changing the financial structure of education and forcing massive equalization efforts on a state-by-state basis. The state courts provide an important check and balance to the struggle over governance.

A number of other agencies exercise influence over education also. Included are the Office of Management and Budget with its responsibility for budget controls, the Treasury Department in terms of cash flow to the local district, the Labor Department in terms of employment policies, the Highway Department in terms of traffic safety and access to school sites, and the State Civil Rights Commission in terms of equity issues. When an activity like education consumes from 35 to 50 percent of the total resources of the state, there will be great interest and participatory effort on the part of all agencies that enjoy state support and governance.

D. INTERMEDIATE-LEVEL GOVERNANCE

By way of introduction, it is well to recognize that in one state (Hawaii) there exists only one operating school district while, in a number of others (Florida, Virginia, Maryland, and others), the county is the operating school district and therefore serves as the local education agency (LEA) as well. Most of the other states have created intermediate-level educational bureaucracies intended to assist in the provision of support services and monitoring activities to local districts.

INTERMEDIATE EDUCATION AGENCY

In many states the intermediate agency can be the county or a group of counties or a geographically compatible area that is convenient to the local education agencies that it must serve. Duties vary from state to state, but generally the intermediate district provides a variety of support and monitoring activities. Some of the monitoring tasks include the following:

(a) Attendance Audits. State aid is often predicated upon attendance, and intermediate districts are called on to verify local attendance.

(b) Teacher Certification. The intermediate office ensures that all instructional staff of the LEA meet state certification codes.

(c) Student Transportation. Applications for state transportation reimbursement must be verified by the intermediate office.

(d) Inspections and Approvals. Often the intermediate district conducts a variety of inspections (lunch facilities, buses, etc.) and approves the continued operation of particular programs.

(e) Reports and Audits. The intermediate education agency often acts as the collector of the many reports and audits required under state law. The office collects, reviews, and corrects them before they are transmitted to the state.

A more recent and growing phenomenon involving the intermediate education agency is its expanding role as a service agency. Specialists and special services of every persuasion and description are being provided by the intermediate office to its constituent school districts. These include the following:

(a) Data Processing Services. The intermediate education agency provides, for a fee, the multitude of data processing services including financial, payroll, grading, reporting, scheduling, and others to constituent districts. It is much more cost-effective for the intermediate district to purchase or lease and operate equipment.

(b) Instructional Media Centers. The provision of media services, film libraries, books, and other printed materials by the intermediate office is another more cost-effective activity. Particularly helpful to the smaller local education agencies, this service allows for more effective use of equipment and materials.

(c) Consulting Services. The well-staffed intermediate education agency provides specialists of every description as consultive help to local agencies. Personnel ranging from subject matter specialists, i.e., reading, math, science, language, etc., to experts in finance, management, school lunch, and custodial services are available to the local education agencies.

Still more recent in its development is the use of the intermediate educational agency as the direct provider of education programs to clients. In many areas of the country the intermediate education agency delivers such programs as special education, vocational education, and adult education to citizens of the local education agencies. This is usually attempted in order to create a large enough clientele to warrant the scheduling of such programs. For example, highly specialized multiple handicapped programs require very sophisticated staff and equipment and a large enough population base to generate class-sized groups to receive the services. By locating such programs at the intermediate level, the cost is spread over a much broader base and sufficient numbers of students can be identified. Similarly, the delivery of vocational education programs and adult education curricula are enhanced through the intermediate office.

The intermediate education agency is governed by an intermediate board of education, which appoints the chief executive officer. This board is chosen either by popular election or by vote of the constituent member local districts. The intermediate board establishes policies that are consistent with the laws of the particular state and must confine its activities to those duties specified under statute.

COOPERATIVE GOVERNING BOARDS

In many states, local education agencies are permitted and encouraged to work together to provide difficult and expensive services to their clients. With the expanded requirements for the provision of special education services and the increased demands for sophisticated technical programs, many states have encouraged the development of cooperatives to plan, fund, and deliver these highly specialized services to students. Typically, these cooperatives operate under a legally defined organizational statement that specifies the services to be provided, the method for selection of the governing board, staff and student selection procedures, and funding policies. Members of the cooperative can participate in the programs as well as in the governance of the cooperative. The distribution of extremely high-cost activities over a much broader base provides not only a more cost-effective approach to educational delivery but also generates sufficient students with interests and/or needs to justify the establishment of a particular program.

In some areas these cooperatives have limited taxing authority, usually accomplished through an affirmative vote by the electorate. These taxes are not for general operations but to provide services specified in the original tax proposal presented to the voters. Services most often included are instructional programs to meet the needs of the handicapped, vocational/technical offerings, and such services as data processing, instructional media, and film libraries.

While the intermediate education agency could be of valuable assistance to the units involved in SBM, the initiation or elimination of the SBM concept is not overly dependent upon the existence of the intermediate level of education. If SBM were to become a major development in the coming decade, the services and programs provided by the intermediate level would have to be adjusted to accommodate the site-level decisions that address student needs.

E. LOCAL-LEVEL GOVERNANCE

As repeatedly indicated in this book, the basic unit of governance in education has traditionally been the local school district. The emergence of the local school districts in the United States closely paralleled the evolution of the country from an agrarian society to an urban nation. Chapter 1 traces the development of the American system of education from its earliest beginning. The notion of lay governance of education is a uniquely American invention and has served the democratic concept very well.

Recently, emphasis has been placed on the legal description of the local school district, emphasizing the fact that local districts are really state institutions with board of education members being locally elected state officials. The dramatic reduction in the number of school districts as a result of the consolidations that have occurred and the quantum leap in sheer size of many urban districts have served to stress the complexity of the governance task. In addition to the major shifts in size and in number, local school districts have expanded the type and number of program offerings provided so that the typical school district is a very complex, multifaceted organization that strives to meet the diverse and multiple needs of its clientele.

THE LOCAL EDUCATION AGENCY

The local education agency (LEA), or local school district as it is sometimes identified, is the basis for delivery of most educational services in this country. It is charged with the responsibility of meeting all state education requirements, with delivering all state mandated programs, with meeting minimum standards relative to days and hours, with the employment of certificated personnel, and with developing and offering a complete educational program to the students.

Within the parameters established by state and federal law, the LEA has the flexibility to provide the variety of educational services needed and supported by the local community. LEAs typically reflect prevailing community values and mores.

The direct governance responsibility rests with a policy board (the local board of education), which establishes operating policies consistent with state and federal law, and the executive officer or school superintendent whose major task is to implement policy and operate the school system.

The LEA must provide services to accommodate such state mandates as compulsory attendance, health practices, drug and alcohol abuse, state history, government, and physical education. In addition, increasing numbers of states are prescribing basic skills curricula that must be provided through the LEA.

Recent federal mandates concerning education of the handicapped, vocational education, equality of educational opportunity, and similar national concerns are also imposed on the LEA.

As the LEA develops programs to address the various mandates, additional educational concerns that reflect local priorities are addressed. These programs are the result of local priorities and needs and should broaden the curriculum into a comprehensive educational pattern for the students. Beyond the requirement to provide all mandated services, LEAs have historically had greater flexibility as far as their method of operation is concerned. Only in the past decade has there emerged any significant pressure for certain patterns and programs from the state. These pressures show signs of increasing and becoming more restrictive in the coming decade.

THE BOARD OF EDUCATION

As representatives of state government, local boards of education establish all governance structures for the LEA. The already mentioned restrictions are those state and federal requirements associated with education.

Local boards of education vary in size, generally having from five to eleven members (some are larger) with the usual configuration numbering either seven or nine persons. Board members are either elected or appointed; those elected are elected either at large or in single member districts. Those boards that are appointed are usually named by city government (council or mayor) or by the court system. In some sections of the country, LEAs are departments of city government and are called dependent school districts. In these instances, the obvious conflict between the board member as a state official and the board member as a local official can be extreme.

In most school districts, school board members are not paid other than the normal reimbursement for expenses resulting from the performance of the office. In other districts, board membership is a fairly well paid position and is almost a full-time office. By far, the greatest majority of boards are not paid, and most members serve because of their interest in and commitment to education. Others serve because of their interest in political careers and still others for personal reasons related to power or prestige.

Because of the unique structure of American education, the opportunity to make major contributions to the LEA is inherent in the position of board of education member. The reality is that these citizens spend many hours performing tasks that are taken for granted by other citizens for little reward other than the personal satisfaction that comes from public service. Its importance is reflected in the fact that the LEA is generally among the largest employer in a city, its budget is among the largest of any business or agency in the city, and it generally levies the largest tax on property. Urban LEA budgets can total over a billion dollars and generally run into the tens and hundreds of millions. The governance of such a large enterprise is understandably a complex and difficult task yet is a tribute to the American belief that lay governance of education is best suited to the democratic principle.

SBM is possible in an LEA only if the board of education is willing to establish policies that permit its development. In order to provide the greatest support for SBM development, boards should examine educational policies so that most policies are in terms of student outcomes rather than processes. In this way, local units will have the responsibility to provide the processes needed to ensure student growth as requested in the policy.

THE LEA ADMINISTRATION

The administrative structure of the LEA is usually headed by the chief executive officer titled the superintendent. This person is responsible for the day-to-day operations of the LEA and further must interpret board of education policy into administrative rules and regulations.

All programs, staff recommendations, budget preparation, rule promulgation, building care, and all facets of LEA operation are ultimately the responsibility of the superintendent and/or delegated by him/her to others on the staff. The parameters under which the local administration operates are those specified by state and federal law and by board of education policy. The administrative team, headed by the superintendent, has the primary responsibility for the development and delivery of all educational programs provided in the LEA.

For the LEA committed to SBM, the role of the administrative staff becomes a more complex, demanding activity. The central office must accept the notion that their primary function is as a support agency to the various sites. With the development of SBM and its attendant autonomy at the site level, the role of the central staff requires a subtle shift from one of issuing mandates and directives to one of providing a variety of support services mainly in the area of educational planning and evaluation. The shift from top-down to collegial development of appropriate program thrusts is a most difficult transition for many people. It is even more difficult when the teaching staff and the community also become involved in establishing program needs and priorities. Obviously, those administrators who tend toward the autocratic style of leadership will be most adversely affected by a decision to move toward the concept of SBM.

Building administrators, too, need assistance to fully grasp the change implied by a move to SBM. No longer can the building principal have the escape route of laying blame for program inadequacies on the central office, since all programs and methods are now the purview of the local site. This, of course, places another and more restrictive pressure on the local staff: the pressure of achieving those objectives claimed in their own site education plan. The entire SBM concept is predicated on the capacity of a professional staff to develop an educational plan suited to the needs of the clients to be served and then deliver those programs in such a manner that student educational growth objectives are realized. As the site manager, the principal assumes the primary responsibility for the coordination of the many activities that ultimately lead to educational success.

The successful building administrator must learn to utilize the expertise found in every central office to assist in the development of program plans best suited to the needs of the community to be served. This means that the principal must learn the planning process and how to interpret and discover educational needs of the clients. Central staff can provide valuable technical assistance in such activities and can, on request, assist the local staff in gathering and interpreting data, in developing program modules, in conducting evaluation efforts, and in recycling programs to focus on student needs. While local site personnel have ultimate responsibility and autonomy to make program decisions, they are most shortsighted if they don't avail themselves of the expert advice that is a residual part of most districts.

Successful leadership involves the capacity to identify needs, to search out resources, to coordinate the various persons toward a common goal, and to deliver appropriate programs to the clients of the institutions.

NEGOTIATED CONTRACTS

It is important in any discussion of LEA governance to include mention of the impact on governance resulting from negotiated agreements with the various union groups found in most school systems. It is not unusual for the school system to have written employee contracts with the following groups:

(a) Administrators
(b) Teachers
(c) Teacher Aides
(d) Clerical Personnel
(e) Technical Specialists, i.e., librarians, etc.
(f) Custodial and Maintenance Personnel
(g) Cafeteria Personnel
(h) Transportation Personnel
(i) Security Personnel

Because these employee agreements place definitive restrictions on both the employee and the organization, SBM development could cause some dissonance with certain groups. With increased capacity to allocate resources and make decisions concentrated at the building level, there is a danger that the SBM concept will be viewed as an effort to circumvent the negotiated union contract. Strict adherence to a union contract that specifies teacher/pupil ratios, hours of work, materials to be utilized, cocurricular obligations, and other specifics does not provide the flexibility needed to implement a site-based, decision-making model that is predicated upon evolving decisions based on local needs and local data with little concern for systemwide operational patterns.

It becomes important, therefore, to proceed carefully with the various staff groups in order that they can assist in correcting the restrictive covenants found in existing union contracts.

Assuming concurrence between the local board of education and the state and federal bureaucracies in terms of permitting the implementation of SBM, the development of a local site governance structure becomes a very high priority.

F. BUILDING-LEVEL GOVERNANCE

Educational governance at the site is traditionally highly controlled at the local board of education and central administration level with state and federal laws and board policies being interpreted into operating rules and procedures for every building to follow. Minute curriculum guides, line–item budget allocations, and procedures of every description for every occasion are prepared for the individual building and, indeed, for the classroom teacher. Flexibility is the exception rather than the rule, and program deviance is the result of individual teachers and buildings being willing to risk censure for not following prescribed procedures.

In more recent times, the requirement for local site advisory committees has forced some adaptability, but the change has been largely cosmetic and superficial. In those locals where SBM has been mandated, the implications are for massive and continuing change with the local community and the building staff working together on the problems they face. How, then, can a local school site accommodate the governance issue in the LEA that has committed itself to SBM?

BOARD OF EDUCATION POLICY

The local board of education must, by policy statement, provide the mechanism for the development of a strong SBM organization. It does this by specifically stating the intent to decentralize to the building level and indicates, in policy, the responsibilities to be housed at the site level.

The board must provide the basic philosophy to govern at the site level and must also protect its integrity by specifying the support nature of the central staff. In its role of policymaker, the board of education has the ability to delineate the type of organization the school system shall have. It alone decides on the issue of centralization versus decentralization and, even more important, what is to be centralized and what is to be decentralized. Of greatest importance is the decision of who shall be the chief executive officer. This selection will largely determine the success and/or failure of the SBM effort. If the chief executive believes in SBM and the board of education supports SBM with policy statements, successful implementation is probable. If, however, the superintendent is not committed to SBM, all of the policy statements in the world will not guarantee success.

BOARD OF EDUCATION PRIORITIES

As the board of education of the local school district adopts goals and objectives, the mechanism for supporting SBM is available in the kinds of objective statements that are adopted. If, for example, one of the board priorities is that of student growth in reading, an objective should be stated in terms of product expectation, i.e., "every student in the school system shall evidence month-for-month growth in reading during the school year." This type of product objective (identifying student outcome rather than process) allows the local unit to develop the delivery system best suited to the needs of the students and the strength of the staff.

Similarly, the adoption of student outcome objectives rather than process objectives in every curricular area provides the needed flexibility to allow individual sites to function most effectively.

As the board examines and reviews policy for its periodic revision, it is important that the board establish a series of priorities that become the product expectations to which all buildings must address themselves. In this way, the board of education does determine the curriculum of the school district and incorporates state and federal mandates while providing the process flexibility needed for local sites to respond to individual student needs. The process of education is and should be the professional responsibility of trained educators and should not be dictated centrally because individual student needs and teacher strengths have great impact on process.

The priorities, as established by the board of education, determine the parameters within which local units can exercise "responsible autonomy."

THE COMMUNITY INVOLVEMENT COMMITTEE

In the SBM development, extensive community involvement is important. The Community Involvement Committee (CIC) is conceived as the prime vehicle for linkage and participation between the building and the local community. It functions as a liaison between the school organization and the public. Information must flow both ways. The CIC will be a starting place where people can learn about the school system, ask questions, express opinions, and begin to think about the future. The CIC should help to prepare recommendations and provide community reaction to the site-based planning and development process.

The CIC is an organization widely representative of the immediate attendance area served by the individual school. Its function is to provide parents, teachers, students, and community an opportunity to participate in the development of educational priorities, assessment of a school's needs, and identification of local resources. As an organization, it relates exclusively to its service area and is composed of all persons interested in serving the educational planning process.

Membership in the CIC is open to all parents and citizens residing in the attendance area of the school. Principals and staffs of each building should vigorously promote the CIC and actively recruit persons from all ethnic groups to participate toward assuring broad representation in each school area. Meetings should occur as often as is necessary to involve the community and staff in planning for the use of resources available to the building.

The CIC is the local governance unit but must recognize its role as largely advisory. The board of education is the legal body in charge of the educational processes for the LEA. However, by its active participation, the CIC provides valuable and constant influence on the decisions that are made.

LOCAL PLANS

With the assistance of the CIC, the staff and principal develop a series of short- and long-range educational plans to serve the needs of the clientele of the building. These plans become the vehicle for the delivery of educational services to students and impact governance at the building level by setting allocation priorities, program specifications, and other student services for that site.

The implementation of the SBM concept is the delivery of the educational programs developed on-site to meet student needs at that site. Local building governance is accomplished by the principal in causing the cooperatively developed programs to be delivered. Local plans are the result of a student needs assessment and careful planning by staff, community, and planning specialists to establish priorities and programs to be provided at the site.

The principal, as the instructional leader, must assume the major responsibility for coordination of the various components and groups into a cohesive plan and organization. SBM demands outstanding leadership at the site level.

The principal *is* the chief executive at the site level. He/she must provide leadership to staff and community, must exercise decision-making power, and must provide the operational setting and planning expertise to enable the delivery of programs that will impact student growth. The principal is the key element in SBM and must be provided the support and autonomy needed to function as the building leader.

SUMMARY

This book is an effort to propose a number of operational changes that will encourage and support the development of a site-based management SBM system of educational program delivery. Suggestions for institutional change are many and varied throughout this publication.

In the opinion of the author, the SBM vehicle may be the one remaining mechanism to permit citizen participation in the educational decisions that impact their children. It is one of the very few ways in which the extreme pressures for centralization can be mitigated. Site-based management (SBM) also provides for the identification and movement toward goals and objectives developed at every level: federal, state, intermediate, local, and site. The recognition of educational objectives at every level provides the parameters within which site-level processes are developed and delivered. It also allows for the recognition of a difference in learning styles, in priorities, and in local needs.

Implicit throughout this book is the notion that no two sites are alike, that no two school districts are alike, and that the finite educational plans for implementation are the product of the educational planning process experienced in every system entering a SBM operational concept. There will be differences between and among LEAs as there will be differences between and among sites. What has been attempted in this book is a broad definition of what SBM could be, how it could function, and what it portends for its participants.

Obviously, the LEA staff would have to undergo an in-service process leading to a redefinition of roles and expectations. The local site principals, staff, and community would also have to undergo a learning process to enable the SBM concept to be implemented.

Finally, the key skill to be nurtured and developed is the planning skill. At every level—federal, state, intermediate, local, and site—the capacity to plan for the delivery of educational programs to meet local needs and mandated objectives will remain the avenue to success. If SBM is to be successful, the LEA (with the assistance of the state) must provide the planning expertise and support needed at each site in order that the planning process can become a part of the normal activity of the building. In many instances, the site staff and principal already have planning skills, and such support is unneeded. In other sites, however, a complete and constant support system will be crucial to success.

It is the hope of the author that a number of models will soon emerge so that educational leaders who are searching for mechanisms to address student needs can have a variety of alternatives at their disposal and can proceed with refinements and fine-tuning rather than reinventing the basic concept. Continuing efforts to address student learning needs are the cornerstone of American public education, and any departure from that basic premise will be to the detriment of the American school system.

References

ARGYRIS, C. *Personality and Organization: The Conflict Between the System and the Individual*. New York:Harper and Row (1957).

ARGYRIS, C. *Interpersonal Competence and Organizational Effectiveness*. Homewood, IL:The Dorsey Press, Inc. (1962).

BAKKE, V. Board of Regents of the University of California Medical School 98S. Ct. 2733 (1978).

BERLO, D. K. *The Process of Communication*. New York:Holt, Rinehart and Winston (1960).

Brown v. Board of Education of Topeka, 347 U.S. 483 (1954).

Brown v. Board of Education of Topeka, 349 U.S. 294 (1955).

CAMPBELL, R., L. L. Cunningham, R. W. McPhee, and R. O. Nystrand. *The Organization and Control of American Schools*. Columbus:Charles E. Merrill Publishing Co. (1970).

CAMPBELL, R. F., L. Cunningham, R. Nystrand, and M. Usdan. *The Organization and Control of American Schools, Third Edition*. Columbus, OH:Charles E. Merrill Publishing Co. (1975).

CANDOLI, I. C., W. G. Hack, J. R. Ray, and D. H. Stollar. *School Business Administration: A Planning Approach*. Boston, MA:Allyn and Bacon Inc. (3rd Edition) (1984).

CIPP (Content, Input, Process, Product) Model — Decision Model Developed by the PHI Delta Kappa Committee on Evaluation chaired by Daniel L. Stufflebeam.

CUBBERLY, E. P. *The History of Education*. Boston:Houghton Mifflin (1920).

DOWLING, W. ed. *Effective Management and the Behavioral Sciences*. New York:AMACOM (1978).

Education for All Handicapped Children Act of 1975 (P.L. 94-142).

Elementary and Secondary Education Act (ESEA) of 1965 signed into law by President Lyndon B. Johnson on April 11, 1965.

FANTINI, M. "The What, Why, and Where of the Alternatives Movement," *Education U.S.A.*, p. 55 (May 6, 1974).

Farrington v. Tokushige, 273 U.S. 284, 47 Sup. Ct. 406 (1927).

GETZELS, J. W. and E. G. Guba. "Social Behavior and the Administrative Process," *School Review*, 65:423–441 (Winter 1957).

LEVINE, D. U. and R. J. Havighurst. *The Future of Big City Schools*. Berkeley, CA:McCutchan Publishing Co. (1977).

LIKERT, R. and J. Gibson Likert. *New Ways of Managing Conflict*. New York:McGraw-Hill Book Company (1976).

Pierce v. Society of Sisters of the Holy Name of Jesus and Mary, 268 U.S. 510, 45 Sup. Ct. 571 (1925).

RELLER, T. L. *The Development of the City Superintendency of Schools in the United States*. Philadelphia, published by the author (1935).

Rodriguez v. San Antonio, 337 F. Supp. 2801 (1971).

Serrano v. Priest, 5 Cal. 3d 584, 96 Cal. Rptr., 601, 487p 2d 1241 (1971).

Singleton v. Jackson, Mississippi Board of Education, 419 F 2d 1211, 1218 (1970).

Stainback vs. MoHock Lok Po, 336 U.S. 368, 69 Sup. Ct. 606 (1949).

Stuart v. School District No. 1 of Village of Kalamazoo, 30 Michigan 69 (1874).

STUFFLEBEAM, D. L., et al. *Evaluation and Decision Making*. Itasca, IL:F.E. Pecock Educational Publishers, Inc. (1971).

Index